Collins

Cambridge IGCSE™

Biology

REVISION GUIDE

Mark Levesley, John Beeby,
Amanda Graham, Anne Pilling, Mike Smith

About this Revision book

REVISE

These pages provide a recap of everything you need to know for each topic and include key points to focus on and **key terms** to be learned (full definitions are given in the Glossary). Supplementary content, for the Extended papers, is clearly marked with **S**.

You should read through all the information before taking the Quick Test at the end. This will test whether you can recall the key facts.

> **Quick Test**
> 1. What name is given to reactions that occur in cells?
> 2. Give the name of the part of an enzyme that changes a substrate into products.
> 3. a Look at the graph above. What is the optimum pH of trypsin?
> **S** b) Explain the activity of the enzyme at this pH.
> 4. The amylase experiment is repeated using amylase that has been boiled. Explain the results you would expect.

PRACTISE

These topic-based exam-style questions appear at the end of a revision section and will test whether you have understood the topic. If you get any of the questions wrong, make sure you read the correct answer carefully.

For selected questions, Show Me features give you guidance on how to structure your answer.

> **Show me**
>
> A control is when the .... variable is not applied, so you can tell if this variable is having
>
> the effect. A suitable control would be ....

MIXED QUESTIONS

These pages feature a mix of exam-style questions for all the different topics, just like you would get in an exam. They will make sure you can recall the relevant information to answer a question without being told which topic it relates to.

PRACTICE PAPERS

These pages provide a full set of exam-style practice papers: Paper 1 Multiple Choice (Core)/Paper 2 Multiple Choice (Extended), Paper 3 Theory (Core)/Paper 4 Theory (Extended) and Paper 6 Alternative to Practical. Practise your exam technique in preparation for the Cambridge IGCSE™.

ebook

To access the ebook visit
collins.co.uk/ebooks
and follow the step-by-step instructions.

CONTENTS

	Revise	Practise

Section 18: Variation and selection

Section 19: Organisms and their environment

Section 20: Human influences on ecosystems

Section 21: Biotechnology and genetic modification

Classifying living organisms

Learning aims:

- Describe seven life processes
- Describe how organisms are classified
- Classify organisms, including the main groups of animals **S** and plants
- **S** Explain why classification is useful

Syllabus links:

1.1.1, 1.2.1–1.2.4,
1.3.1–1.3.3,
S 1.2.5–1.2.7,
1.3.4–1.3.7

Life processes

Living organisms show *all* seven **life processes: movement, respiration, sensitivity, growth, reproduction, excretion, nutrition.**

> **S** **Virus** particles are simple structures, made of of **genetic material** (**DNA** or **RNA**) surrounded by a **protein coat**. They do not show any life processes, and so are not living organisms.

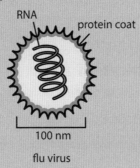

RNA

protein coat

100 nm

flu virus

> **Key Point**
>
> The first letters of the life processes spell MRS GREN. Make sure you understand all the meanings, especially 'excretion' and 'nutrition'.

Classification

In **classification**, organisms with shared features are in the same group. The biggest groups are **kingdoms**:

- **plant** kingdom … are **multicellular** organisms … make their own food … cellulose cell walls
- **animal** kingdom … multicellular organisms … eat other organisms … do not have cell walls

> **S** • **fungus** kingdom … multicellular … use **saprophytic nutrition** (release enzymes to feed on dead organisms) … cell walls contain chitin
> - **protoctist** kingdom … usually **unicellular** … and some have chloroplasts
> - **prokaryote** kingdom … unicellular … do not have nuclei or mitochondria

Each kingdom is divided into smaller and smaller groups. As the groups get smaller, their organisms become more similar. For example, animals can be **vertebrates** (with backbones) or **invertebrates**. The vertebrates are divided into:

- **mammals** (hair, lungs, produce milk, have live young)
- **reptiles** (dry scales, lungs, lay leathery eggs)
- **fish** (slimy scales, gills, lay jelly-coated eggs)
- **amphibians** (thin moist skin, gills and then lungs when adult, lay jelly-coated eggs)
- **birds** (feathers, lungs, beaks, lay hard-shelled eggs).

> **Key Point**
>
> MR FAB will help you remember the different types of vertebrates.

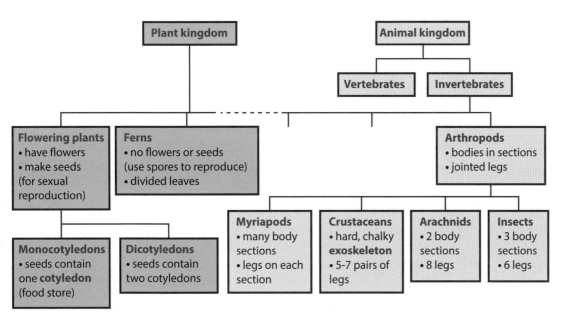

Binomial system

A **species** is a group of organisms that can have offspring that can also reproduce (are 'fertile').

The names of the last two classification groups (**genus** and species) form a species' binomial (scientific) name. Lions have the binomial name *Panthera* (genus) *leo* (species).

Keys

A **dichotomous** (branching) **key** is used to identify organisms.

S Evolutionary relationships

Evolution is when the features of a group of organisms of the same species change over time. The feature changes are due to changes in the sequence of **bases** in **DNA** molecules.

As different groups of the same species evolve, the DNA base sequences become more and more different between the groups. The greater the differences, the less closely related the organisms. Eventually, they can become new species.

Classification makes use of DNA. For example, two species with similar DNA base sequences may be put in the same genus. So, classification systems show **evolutionary relationships** between species.

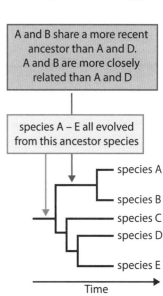

> **Quick Test**

1. Organism X has cells with cellulose cell walls. State its kingdom.
2. A small organism has six legs. Give as many of its classification groups as you can.
3. Arctic roses are *Rosa acicularis*. Give the genus of these plants.
   S 4. Look at species D in the evolutionary relationships diagram. Identify which of the other species it is most closely related to.

Cells, tissues, organs, organisms

Learning aims:

- Describe the functions of the structures in plant, animal and bacterial cells
- Describe production and organisation of cells in multicellular organisms
- Describe how some cells are specialised
- Calculate magnifications **S** and convert between μm and mm

Syllabus links:
2.1.1–2.1.7, 2.2.1–2.2.2,
S 2.2.3

Different types of cells

Plant cells have similarities and differences compared to animal cells.

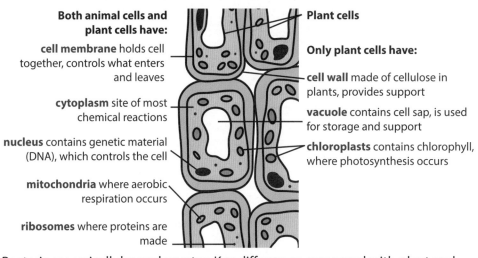

Both animal cells and plant cells have:

cell membrane holds cell together, controls what enters and leaves

cytoplasm site of most chemical reactions

nucleus contains genetic material (DNA), which controls the cell

mitochondria where aerobic respiration occurs

ribosomes where proteins are made

Plant cells

Only plant cells have:

cell wall made of cellulose in plants, provides support

vacuole contains cell sap, is used for storage and support

chloroplasts contains chlorophyll, where photosynthesis occurs

> **Key Point**
>
> In 'compare' questions, you identify similarities and differences between things, such as cells.

bacterial cell

plasmid

cytoplasm

ribosomes

large circular chromosome

cell membrane

cell wall

Bacteria are unicellular prokaryotes. Key differences compared with plant and animal cells:

- no nucleus or mitochondria (respiration occurs in the cytoplasm)
- genetic material (DNA) is in a large circular **chromosome** and smaller **plasmids**
- cell walls do not contain cellulose.

Specialised cells

Multicellular organisms (for example, plants, animals) have **specialised cells** that are adapted for their functions. Ciliated epithelial cells and neurones are examples.

Cell name	Adaptation	Function
ciliated epithelial cell	cilia that wave	sweep mucus in trachea and bronchi
neurone	often long, many branches	quickly carry electrical impulses and connect with many other neurones
red blood cell	large surface area, haemoglobin	absorb and carry oxygen
egg cell	store food in cytoplasm	provides nutrients for cell division
sperm cell	acrosome, flagellum with mitochondria	digest egg cell jelly coat and propulsion towards egg cell

palisade mesophyll cell	many chloroplasts	photosynthesis
root hair cell	large surface area	absorb water (and mineral ions)

Multicellular organism organisation

Multicellular organisms produce new cells by **cell division**, in which an existing cell becomes two new cells.

Groups of the same cells form a **tissue** (for example, muscle cells form muscle tissue). Different tissues form an **organ** (for example, muscle tissue and nerve tissue in the heart). Organs work together in an **organ system** (for example, heart and blood vessels in the circulatory system). Organisms contain many organ systems.

Observing cells and tissues

Cells and tissues are observed using a **microscope**, which **magnifies** the **specimen**.

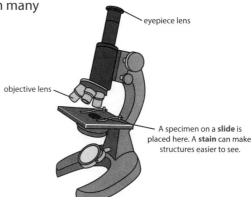

eyepiece lens

objective lens

A specimen on a **slide** is placed here. A **stain** can make structures easier to see.

$$\text{total \textbf{magnification} of a microscope} = \text{eyepiece lens magnification} \times \text{objective lens magnification}$$

The magnification is how many times bigger the microscope image is than the actual object.

$$\text{magnification} = \frac{\text{image size}}{\text{actual size}} \qquad \text{actual size} = \frac{\text{image size}}{\text{magnification}}$$

> **S** Cell sizes are often measured in μm (**micrometres**). There are 1000 μm in 1 mm. To convert μm to mm, divide by 1000. To convert mm to μm, multiply by 1000.

> **Key Point**
>
> Make sure you can rearrange the formula to calculate magnifications or actual sizes.

> **Practical skills**
>
> To draw cells seen under a microscope:
>
> - use a sharp pencil to draw single lines (not sketched or broken lines)
> - do not use shading or colours
> - draw label lines with a ruler so that they touch a feature and do not overlap one another

> **Quick Test**
>
> 1. **a)** In which part of a plant cell does aerobic respiration occur?
>   **b)** In which part of a bacterial cell does respiration occur?
> 2. Name the specialised cells that sweep mucus out of the tubes in the lungs.
> 3. Explain how root hair cells are adapted for their function.
> 4. **a)** A palisade cell is 2 mm long at a magnification of ×50. Calculate its actual length.
>   **S b)** Give the cell's length in micrometres.

Diffusion and active transport

Learning aims:

Syllabus links:
3.1.1–3.1.5, 3.3.1,
S 3.3.2–3.3.3

- Explain how particles diffuse
- Explain the effect of different factors on the rate of diffusion
- Describe the importance of diffusion for organisms
- Describe active transport, **S** its importance and the involvement of carrier proteins

Diffusion

Particles are more **concentrated** when there are more in a certain volume. There is a **concentration gradient** if there is a change in concentration between two places. As you go down a concentration gradient, the concentration of the particles gets less.

going *down* the concentration gradient

higher concentration   lower concentration

diffusion

All particles have **kinetic energy**, and so are constantly moving in random directions. In the diagram, some particles are moving from lower to higher concentration. However, there are more particles at the higher concentration so more particles move from higher to lower concentration. This net (overall) movement of particles down a concentration gradient is **diffusion**.

> **Key Point**
>
> Diffusion stops when there is no concentration gradient (and equal numbers of particles move in all directions).

Importance of diffusion

Very small molecules diffuse into and out of cells through tiny gaps in the cell membrane. Cells obtain some molecules (e.g. oxygen) and get rid of others (e.g. carbon dioxide) in this way.

Factors affecting diffusion

Cubes of agar jelly made with alkali and phenolphthalein are used to measure the **rate** (speed) of diffusion. Phenolphthalein is pink above pH9 and colourless below this pH.

> **Practical skills**
>
> 1. Put identical agar cubes into a tube or beaker.
> 2. Add dilute hydrochloric acid (it will diffuse into the agar).
> 3. Time how long the cubes take to go completely colourless.

We can investigate the effects of different **independent variables** on diffusion:

- distance (compare cubes of different widths and volumes)
- temperature
- concentration gradient (change the acid concentration)
- **surface area** (e.g. cut up cubes to increase surface area).

Increasing the ...	Effect on diffusion	Reason
... distance ↑	↓	particles take longer to move between points that are further apart
... temperature ↑	↑	particles have more kinetic energy at higher temperatures and so move faster
... concentration gradient ↑	↑	diffusion is faster when the difference between two concentrations is greater
... surface area ↑	↑	there is more space through which particles can pass

Exchange surfaces

The lungs and small intestine have exchange surfaces (surfaces through which particles move). To increase the rate of diffusion, exchange surfaces have:

- large surface areas
- good blood supplies (to maintain concentration gradients)
- thin walls (so that substances do not need to travel far).

Active transport

A cell does not use energy for diffusion, which is a **passive** process. Its energy comes from the kinetic energy of the random movement of the particles. A cell can move particles against the concentration gradient using **active transport**, which requires energy from the cell.

S For example, a root hair cell takes in mineral ions from the soil. The ions are more concentrated in a cell than in soil; they are pumped against their concentration gradient.

Mineral ions stick to special carrier proteins in the cell membrane. Energy from respiration is used to make a **carrier protein** change shape, moving the ion into the cell.

Concentration gradient

① carrier protein

particle

membrane

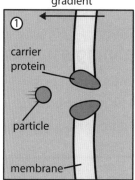

②

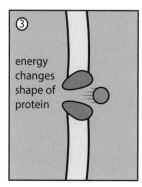

③ energy changes shape of protein

> ## Quick Test

1. What is diffusion?
2. State the effect of the following on diffusion:
   a) increase in surface area   b) decrease in temperature
   c) decrease in distance   d) decrease in concentration gradient.
3. State where the energy for diffusion comes from.
4. a) Name the process that cells use to move particles against a concentration gradient.
   S b) Give an example of a plant cell that uses this process.

Osmosis

Learning aims:

- Describe the roles of water in organisms
- Describe how water moves by osmosis **S** and explain how this occurs
- Describe the effects of osmosis on plant tissues **S** and explain them
- **S** Explain the importance of water potential in cells

Syllabus links:
3.2.1–3.2.6,
S 3.2.7–3.2.9

Importance of water

Water is a **solvent**.

- Food molecules are **digested** into small *soluble* particles for **absorption**.
- Blood **plasma** dissolves substances (e.g. glucose, amino acids) for transport around the body.
- Many wastes (e.g. urea) are dissolved in water to remove them in **urine**.

The cytoplasm and vacuole in plant cells push the cell membrane against the cell wall. This makes the cells rigid, so they support the plant. With too little water, there is less 'pushing' and plants **wilt**.

S The pushing force against the cell membrane is **turgor pressure** and occurs in **turgid** cells.

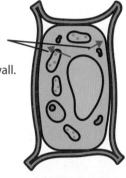

Pressure from the cytoplasm and vacuole pushes the cell membrane against the cell wall.

Defining osmosis

Osmosis is a special type of diffusion. It is a net movement:

- of solvent particles (usually water)
- through a **partially permeable membrane** (only allows some molecules to pass)
- from higher to lower concentration (of *solvent* particles).

> **Key Point**
>
> Do not confuse **solute** concentration and water particle (solvent) concentration. A dilute solution has a low solute concentration and a high water particle concentration The opposite is true for a concentrated solution.

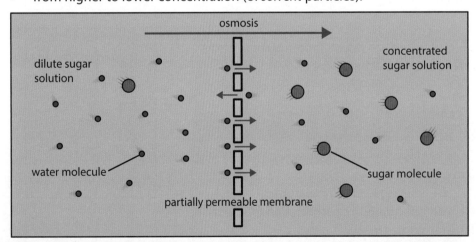

Cell membranes are partially permeable, so water flows into and out of cells by osmosis.

S **Water potential** is how freely water molecules can move. The molecules in pure water are totally free. Solute particles stop water molecules being so free. So, as solute concentration increases, water potential decreases. In osmosis, water moves from higher to lower water potential.

Investigating osmosis

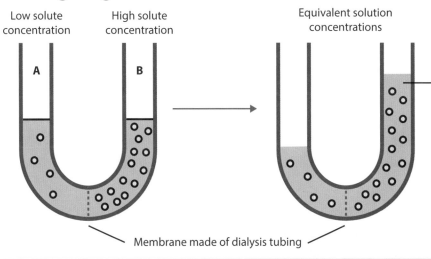

Low solute concentration

High solute concentration

Equivalent solution concentrations

A

B

The higher the solute concentration on side B the more water moves into it and the higher the final level of liquid

The net flow of water stops when the solute concentrations are equal

Membrane made of dialysis tubing

Practical skills

Plant tissue experiments

1. Make six potato cores of equal diameter and length.
2. Blot them dry and measure the mass of each.
3. Put each core in a different concentration of sucrose solution (0%, 20%, 40%, 60%, 80%, 100%).
4. Leave for 15 minutes.
5. Remove the cores, blot them dry and measure the masses.
6. Calculate the percentage change in mass for each.

$$\text{percentage change in mass} = \frac{\text{final mass} - \text{starting mass}}{\text{starting mass}} \times 100$$

> ### Key Point
>
> 0% sucrose is pure water. It is the **control**, in which the independent variable is not applied. A control lets you check that the independent variable has an effect.

If the solute concentration in the cells is less than the sucrose concentration, water flows out of the cells, and there is a loss in mass (negative change). The opposite is true if the cell solute concentration is greater than the sucrose concentration. There is no net water flow if the concentrations are the same.

S Turgid and flaccid cells

Water enters and leaves a cell when there is a difference in water potential between its cytoplasm and its surroundings. This can cause cells to burst or shrivel up. In plants, if a turgid cell loses water, its turgor pressure drops and the cell becomes **flaccid** (floppy). If more water is lost, the cell membrane pulls off the cell wall (a process called **plasmolysis**).

turgid

> ### Key Point
>
> The starting mass of each core is slightly different. To make accurate comparisons, we calculate the percentage change in mass (change in mass for 100 g of tissue).

flaccid

Quick Test

1. Osmosis describes the movement of what type of particle?
2. List two control variables needed in the potato core experiment.
3. S 10% sucrose solution causes no change in the mass of some plant tissue. Describe what this tells you about the water potentials of the cells and the sucrose solution.

plasmolysed

Important molecules in living things

Syllabus links:
4.1.1–4.1.3,
S 4.1.4

Learning aims:

- Describe the chemical structures of carbohydrates, fats and proteins
- S Describe the structure of DNA
- Describe how to carry out tests for different food substances

Carbohydrates, proteins and fats

Molecules in living things (**biological molecules**) are often large molecules made from smaller ones.

Carbohydrates:

- contain the elements carbon, hydrogen and oxygen
- can be small, soluble **sugars** (e.g. **glucose, maltose, sucrose**) or large insoluble chains of sugars.

Starch (an energy storage molecule in plants), **glycogen** (an energy storage molecule in animals) and **cellulose** (found in plant cell walls) are all made of many glucose molecules joined into long chains.

starch (a large carbohydrate)

glucose molecule

Proteins:

- are chains of different types of **amino acids**
- contain carbon, hydrogen, oxygen, nitrogen and sometimes sulfur.

sucrose, maltose (a small, soluble sugar)

protein

amino acid

Fats and **oils:**

- are long **fatty acid** chains attached to a molecule of glycerol
- are **lipids**
- contain carbon, hydrogen and oxygen.

fat

glycerol

fatty acids

S DNA

DNA is an organism's **genetic material** (carries the 'instructions' for making an organism that can be passed from generation to generation). The molecule has two coiled strands that form a **double helix**. The strands are held together by **bonds** between pairs of **bases** (A and T, C and G).

> ### Key Point
>
> S A only pairs with T, and G with C. The similar shapes of C and G act as a memory aid for the rule.

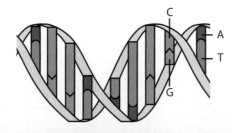

Small section of DNA

Food tests

> ### Practical skills
>
> Prepare solid food samples to test. Liquid foods do not need preparation.
> ....
>
> 1. Grind up the food.
> 2. Add 1 cm^3 of the food to a tube.
> 3. Add 1 cm^3 of water (or 1 cm^3 of **ethanol** for the fats test since fats do not dissolve in water).
> 4. Mix well.

Starch test

- add 1 cm^3 of **iodine solution**
- positive result: orange/brown → blue–black

Protein test

- add 1 cm^3 of **biuret solution**
- leave for 5 minutes
- positive result: pale blue → purple

Reducing sugars test

- add 1 cm^3 of **Benedict's reagent**/solution and mix
- leave in an 80 °C water bath for 2 minutes
- positive result: pale blue → green, yellow, orange, red or brown (increasing amounts)
- glucose is a reducing sugar (sucrose is not)

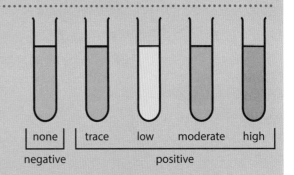

| none | trace | low | moderate | high |
| negative | positive | | | |

Try a mnemonic to help remember the order. For example: Bob Gave You Orange Roses.

Fats and oils test

- add 1 cm^3 of ethanol and mix
- leave to settle for 5 minutes
- pour some of the liquid from the tube into 1 cm^3 of distilled water
- positive result: clear, colourless → milky emulsion

Vitamin C test

- add 1 cm^3 of **DCPIP** and mix
- positive result: dark blue → colourless

1. Give the name of the small molecules used to make the substance in plant cell walls.
2. Milk contains a lot of a protein called casein.
   a) Give the name of the reagent used to detect casein.
   b) Describe the expected colour change when milk is tested with this reagent.
3. List the elements you would find in a glucose molecule.
S 4. Six bases on one DNA strand are shown below. Write out the bases, and underneath each one, write in the correct letter of the other base it pairs with.
   ATG GGC

Enzymes and how they work

Learning aims:

Syllabus links:
5.1.1–5.1.5,
S 5.1.6–5.1.9

- Describe the importance of enzymes
- Describe how enzymes work
- S Explain enzyme action and specificity
- Describe the effects of pH and temperature on enzymes S and explain those effects

Biological catalysts

A **catalyst** is a substance that:

- increases the rate of a chemical reaction
- is not changed by the reaction.

Enzymes are proteins that are biological catalysts. They catalyse all **metabolic reactions** (reactions in cells). Without enzymes, metabolic reactions would be too slow to support life. Enzymes are very specific and so only catalyse useful reactions.

Enzyme action

A **substrate** is a molecule that is changed by an enzyme's **active site**. The shapes of the substrate and the active site are **complementary** – they fit together.

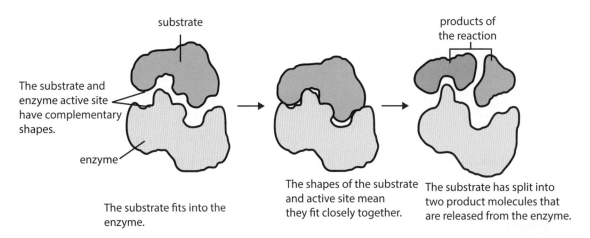

substrate

products of the reaction

The substrate and enzyme active site have complementary shapes.

enzyme

The substrate fits into the enzyme.

The shapes of the substrate and active site mean they fit closely together.

The substrate has split into two product molecules that are released from the enzyme.

S Enzymes are specific because only substrates with the correct shapes fit in the active sites. When fitted together, they form an **enzyme–substrate complex**.

As the complex forms, the enzyme changes shape slightly, which breaks or makes bonds in the substrate to form the products. The **products** no longer fit in the active site, and so are released.

> ### Key Point
>
> Saying that the active site and substrate 'match' or 'are the same shape' is a common mistake. They fit together or are complementary (and not complimentary).

Temperature and pH

Amylase (a digestive enzyme that breaks down starch) is often used in investigations on the effects of pH and temperature on enzyme activity.

1. Leave tubes of amylase and starch suspension in a water bath (so they are the same temperature).
2. Place a drop of iodine solution into each well of a dimple tile.
3. Add starch, then amylase to a new tube in the water bath.
4. Every 10 seconds, use a pipette to take a small quantity of liquid and add one drop to a tile well.
5. If there is a colour change to blue-black, starch is present.
6. Repeat steps 4 and 5 until there is no colour change and calculate the time taken. The shorter the time, the greater the rate of reaction.

To test the effects of temperature and pH:

- use water baths at different temperatures
- add 'buffer solutions' at set pHs to tubes containing starch in step 3. Then add amylase.

An enzyme's rate of reaction is greatest at its **optimum temperature** and **optimum pH**.

Above and below its optimum temperature and pH, an enzyme works less well. High temperatures can change the shape of an enzyme permanently, so that it stops working. This is called **denaturation**.

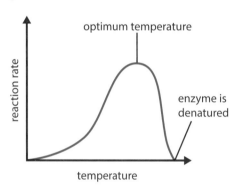

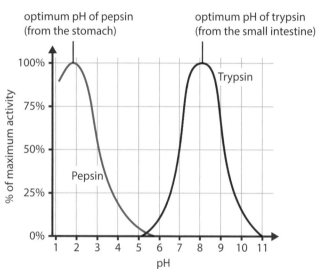

S An enzyme's active site changes shape above and below its optimum pH, so it works less effectively. A pH that is far from the optimum can permanently damage an enzyme and denature it.

Temperature also changes the shape of the active site but has other effects. At higher temperatures, particles have more kinetic energy and so move faster. Collisions are more frequent, and a substrate is more likely to collide with an enzyme's active site.

Faster-moving particles also collide with more force. The greater the collision force, the more likely an enzyme-substrate complex will be formed. A collision in which an enzyme-substrate complex forms is an 'effective collision'. So, increasing the temperature increases the frequency of effective collisions.

1. What name is given to reactions that occur in cells?
2. Give the name of the part of an enzyme that changes a substrate into products.
3. **a)** Look at the graph above. What is the optimum pH of trypsin?
    S b) Explain the activity of the enzyme at this pH.
4. The amylase experiment is repeated using amylase that has been boiled. Explain the results you would expect.

Classifying living organisms

1 One life process shown by plants is growth. State the life process needed for growth to occur. [1]

2 The elimination of undigested food from the digestive system (**faeces**) is not an example of excretion. Which of these statements best explains why?

   A. Excretion is storing waste products inside the body before they are released.

   B. Excretion is the removal of liquid wastes from the body.

   C. Excretion is the removal of substances that the body cannot use.

   D. Excretion is the removal of waste substances made by chemical reactions inside cells. [1]

3 *Hyla savignyi* is an endangered species that lives in the Middle East and Arabian peninsula. The adult females breathe using lungs and lay jelly-coated eggs.

a State the group of vertebrates in which this species is found. [1]

b Which genus is this organism in? [1]

   A. animal   **B.** *Hyla*   **C.** *savignyi*   **D.** vertebrate

   [Total marks 2]

S **4** The virus SARS-CoV-2 spread around the world between 2020 and 2022, killing millions of people. As it spread, its protein coat proteins changed, forming different strains of the original virus.

Parts of the genetic material from four different strains are shown below.

Strain A   GAG GGC CAC GCG   Strain C   GAG GCC CAC GCG

Strain B   GCG AAC GCC ACG   Strain D   GAG CCG CGG ACG

a State the reason the coat proteins changed. [1]

b Explain which of the other strains is most closely related to strain A. [2]

> **Show me**
>
> The one that is most closely related to strain A is strain ....
>
> You can tell this because ....

   [Total marks 3]

Cells, tissues, organs, organisms

1 The photo shows a layer of tissue from an onion which has been stained with a purple dye.

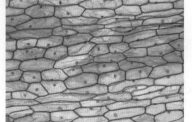

a State how you know that the photo shows a tissue. [1]

b Give the reason why the tissue has been stained. [1]

c Draw one of the cells and label the parts that you can see. [3]

d State one common part of a plant cell that is not found in onions. [1]

e i) Give the name of two parts that are in these cells but cannot be seen. [2]

ii) State the function of each part in your answer to part i). [2]

(f) When viewed under the microscope, one of the cells appears 2.4 mm long. Its actual length is 0.06 mm. Calculate the magnification of the microscope. [1]

> **Show me**
>
> First, write out the equation. It may help to write it out as a fraction rather than to use ÷.
>
> $$\text{magnification} = \frac{\text{image size}}{\text{actual size}}$$
>
> Next, do the calculation and do not forget to include the units in your answer.

(g) The actual width of the cell is 0.01 mm. Calculate the width of the image under the microscope. [1]

(h) State the actual length and width of the cell in micrometres. [2]

[Total marks 14]

2 Compare the genetic material in bacterial cells and animal cells. [2]

> In a **compare** question, look at the number of marks. There are two here, which means that you need to find two similarities and/or differences.

3 Identify and state the purpose of the process shown in this diagram. [2]

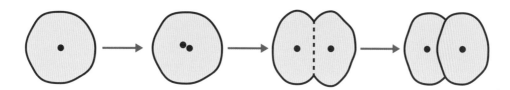

4 Explain how a red blood cell is adapted to its function. [2]

Diffusion and active transport

1 Sugar solution is at different concentrations in different regions of a beaker.

Region	Concentration of salt (g/dm³)
P	4.1
Q	1.2
R	5.3
S	3.0
T	0.2

Explain between which two concentrations the rate of diffusion will be slowest. [2]

> For an **explain** question, state what happens and then give a reason why it happens.

> **Show me**
>
> The rate of diffusion will be slowest between region .... and region ....
>
> This is because ....

2 Explain the effect of the following on diffusion:

a decrease in distance [2]

b decrease in concentration gradient. [4]

[Total marks 6]

3 Oxygen diffuses from the air inside the lungs and into the blood.

a Give the reason that diffusion occurs in this direction. [1]

b Explain why a fast flow of blood in the lungs helps to maintain a good rate of diffusion. [2]

[Total marks 3]

4 Some students made agar jelly containing alkali and phenolphthalein (an indicator that is pink in solutions above pH9, and colourless below this pH). The students cut three cubes out of the jelly. Each cube was a different size. One had sides of 1 cm. The other two had sides of 1.5 cm and 2 cm.

They put the three cubes in different tubes and added hydrochloric acid to the tubes. They then timed how long each cube took to go completely colourless.

a Explain one safety precaution you would take when doing this experiment. [2]

b State:

i) the independent variable   **ii)** the dependent variable   **iii)** a control variable. [3]

c The table shows the results.

Side of cube (cm)	Surface area of cube (cm^2)	Time taken for cube to change colour completely (min)
1		4
2	24	10
3	54	15

i) Calculate the missing surface area. [1]

ii) Make a conclusion from the results. [1]

iii) State the reason why this happens. [1]

[Total marks 8]

5 **a** Compare the processes of diffusion and active transport. [2]

S **b** Give the name of the structures in the membrane that move substances in active transport. [1]

[Total marks 3]

Osmosis

1 Complete the definition of osmosis below. Use words from the list. Each word can only be used once or not at all.

diffusion   impermeable   permeable   pumping   solute   solvent

Osmosis is a type of .... in which .... particles diffuse through a partially .... membrane. [3]

2 Explain **one** way in which water is important for removing wastes from the human body. [2]

3 The diagram shows an inverted 'thistle funnel' with dialysis tubing covering one end. Dialysis tubing allows osmosis.

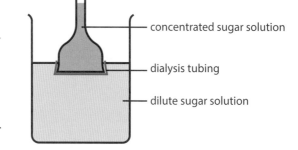

- funnel
- concentrated sugar solution
- dialysis tubing
- dilute sugar solution

a Which sentence best describes the movement of water particles in this experiment?

   A. All the water molecules move from a higher concentration of water molecules to a lower one.

   B. There is a net flow of water molecules against their concentration gradient.

   C. There is a net flow of water molecules down their concentration gradient.

   D. There is no overall flow of water molecules. [1]

b Give the name of the solute shown in the diagram. [1]

c State what will happen (if anything) to the level of the liquid in the funnel. [1]

d Explain your answer to part (**c**). [2]

e The concentration of the solution in the funnel is increased. State the effect this has on the water potential of the solution. [1]

f Explain the effect of increasing the concentration of the solution inside the funnel. [2]

[**Total marks 8**]

4 Some students made four potato cores and cut them into 5 cm lengths. They measured the masses of the cores and put each into a different concentration of a solute solution. After 20 minutes, they dried the excess solution from the outsides of the cores and measured their masses again. The table shows their results.

Concentration of solute in solution (%)	Initial mass of potato core (g)	Final mass of potato core (g)	Percentage change in mass (%)
10	9	13.5	
20	10	12.5	
30	10	7	
40	9	6	

a Calculate the percentage change in mass for each cylinder. Give each value to two significant figures and present your answer in a table, with the independent variable in the left-hand column. [2]

Show me

Start by writing out the equation you need.

$$\text{percentage change in mass} = \frac{\text{final mass} - \text{starting mass}}{\text{starting mass}} \times 100$$

b Give the reason why percentage changes are used (rather than comparing the changes in mass). [1]

c The teacher tells the students that it would have been better to use a control experiment. Suggest a suitable control experiment for this investigation. [1]

d State why it would be better to use more than one potato cylinder in each concentration. [1]

e Suggest two control variables for this investigation. [2]

A control or control experiment is different from control variables.

[Total marks 7]

5 a Explain why a plant cell is rigid, and so can help to support the plant. [2]

S b If the cell become plasmolysed, it can no longer help to support the plant. Explain what happens during plasmolysis. [2]

[Total marks 4]

6 Suggest an explanation for what happens when human red blood cells are placed in pure water. [3]

Important molecules in living things

1 Which of the following is an example of a sugar?

    A. glucose   **B.** glycerol   **C.** glycogen   **D.** starch   [1]

2 Which of these elements do only some proteins contain?

    A. boron   **B.** carbon   **C.** nitrogen   **D.** sulfur   [1]

3 A student did food tests on four different foods. The results are shown in the table on page 25.

Reagent used	Colour at end of experiment			
	Food A	Food B	Food C	Food D
DCPIP	colourless	blue	blue	blue
Benedict's solution	brown	light blue	orange	light blue
biuret solution	light blue	light blue	purple	purple
iodine solution	blue–black	blue–black	orange	orange

a Give the name of the food substance that DCPIP is used to test for. [1]

b Explain which food was pure starch. [2]

c The teacher says the investigation would be better if there were a control. Identify a suitable substance to use in the control experiment and state how this will improve the experiment. [2]

Show me

A control is when the .... variable is not applied, so you can tell if this variable is having

the effect. A suitable control would be ....

[Total marks 5]

4 Compare the chemical structure of insoluble carbohydrates and proteins. [3]

Only small carbohydrates (sugars) are soluble.

5 A student carried out tests for reducing sugars on four different sugar solutions, made with either glucose or sucrose. The results are shown in the table.

Colour after testing for reducing sugars			
Solution W	Solution X	Solution Y	Solution Z
green	red	yellow	light blue

a Identify the solution that only contained sucrose. [1]

b Identify the solution that contained the highest concentration of glucose. [1]

[Total marks 2]

6 Fats test instructions tell you to add 1 cm^3 of solvent to a food, stopper the tube and shake it. After leaving the tube for 5 minutes, you pour some of its liquid into 1 cm^3 of distilled water.

a Give the name of a suitable solvent to use. [1]

b Describe a positive result for fats. [1]

[Total marks 2]

7 **a** State the shape of a DNA molecule. [1]

b Describe how the two strands in a molecule of DNA are held together. [2]

[Total marks 3]

Enzymes and how they work

1 Which of the following is the best definition of a catalyst? [1]

   A. a protein that increases the rate of a chemical reaction

   B. a substance that gets used up as it increases the rate of a reaction

   C. a substance that increases the rate of a chemical reaction but is not changed itself

   D. a substance that speeds up metabolic reactions

2 Identify the enzyme, A–D, responsible for catalysing the reaction shown. [1]

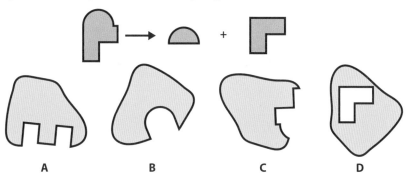

3 **a** State the name given to molecules that enzymes change into products. [1]

S **b** Describe the steps by which a molecule is changed by an enzyme. [3]

When answering a question in which you need to show stages, make sure you put them in order and use linking words and phrases such as 'next', 'after this', 'then'.

[Total marks 4]

4 **a** Give the reason that organisms need biological catalysts (**enzymes**). [1]

b State two metabolic reactions in which enzymes are involved. [2]

[Total marks 3]

5 Explain why enzymes are specific. [2]

6 In an investigation, a tube containing 10 g of starch mixed in water and a tube of amylase were placed in a water bath at 20 °C. Similar sets of tubes were left in water baths at other temperatures.

After 10 minutes, the amylase was poured into the starch and samples were taken every 20 seconds and tested for the presence of starch using iodine solution. Readings were stopped after 10 minutes.

The results are shown in the table.

Temperature (°C)	Time taken for starch to be used up (s)	Rate of reaction (g/s)
20	360	
30	220	
40	120	
50	160	
60	300	
70	580	
80	>600	0.000

a Describe how the iodine solution shows the presence of starch. [1]

b Calculate the rate of reaction for each temperature, in grams of starch broken down each second. Give your answers to two significant figures. [3]

Show me

Rate of reaction = grams of starch used per second (g/s)

$$= \frac{\text{grams of starch at the start of the reaction}}{\text{time taken}}$$

$$= \frac{............}{............}$$

= .... g/s (2 significant figures)

c   Plot your rates of reaction on a line graph.   [5]

> On a line graph, the independent variable (the variable you change) goes on the *x*-axis.
> Your graph should try to take up as much of the graph paper as possible.

d   Suggest an estimate for the optimum temperature.   [1]

e   **i)**   State the word used to describe the enzyme at 80 °C.   [1]

    ii)   State what happens to the enzyme at this temperature.   [1]

f   Between 20 °C and 40 °C, the reaction is getting faster. Explain how the kinetic energy of the particles helps to increase the rate of reaction by increasing the number of effective collisions.   [2]

[Total marks 14]

7   The table shows the results from an investigation when an enzyme was added to glucose solution. A small sample was taken from the mixture regularly and added to iodine solution.

Time since enzyme and glucose solution were mixed (min)	0	5	10	15	20
Colour of mixture when added to iodine	orange	orange	blue	blue–black	blue–black

a   Use the evidence from the table to suggest which of the following enzymes was the most likely to have been used in this investigation.   [1]

    amylase   glucose oxidase   maltase   protease   starch synthase

b   Explain the effect that using warmed enzyme and glucose solutions would have on the results.   [3]

[Total marks 4]

Photosynthesis

Syllabus links:
6.1.1–6.1.9, 6.1.10,
6.1.11

Learning aims:

- Describe the process of photosynthesis and identify its products, **S** state its chemical equation
- Outline the function of chlorophyll in chloroplasts
- Explain the importance of nitrate ions and magnesium ions
- Outline the use and storage of the products of photosynthesis
- Investigate the need for chlorophyll, light and carbon dioxide
- Investigate the effects of varying light intensity in an aquatic plant
- **S** Identify rate-limiting factors of photosynthesis

Photosynthesis

- Plants absorb water and carbon dioxide to produce carbohydrates for nutrition.
- During **photosynthesis**, a green pigment (**chlorophyll**) in **chloroplasts** uses energy from light (energy transferred by light) for photosynthesis.
- Energy from light is converted into chemical energy to form **glucose** and **oxygen** from **carbon dioxide** and **water**.

A word equation summarises photosynthesis:

$$\text{carbon dioxide + water} \xrightarrow[\text{light}]{\text{chlorophyll}} \text{glucose + oxygen}$$

S Or a chemical equation:

$$6CO_2 + 6H_2O \xrightarrow[\text{light}]{\text{chlorophyll}} C_6H_{12}O_6 + 6O_2$$

Products of photosynthesis

Glucose is used for respiration and to make other **carbohydrates**.

The table summarises the use and storage of carbohydrates made by photosynthesis.

Carbohydrate	Use
starch	energy store
cellulose	to build cell walls
sucrose	soluble sucrose is transported in phloem around the plant
nectar	for pollination by insects

Mineral requirements

Ion	Needed to make
nitrate	**amino acids** (for **proteins**)
magnesium	chlorophyll

Investigations into photosynthesis

1. The need for light and chlorophyll.
- Leave a variegated plant in the dark for 24 hours to de-starch it.
- Cover part of one leaf with black card. Leave the plant in sunlight.

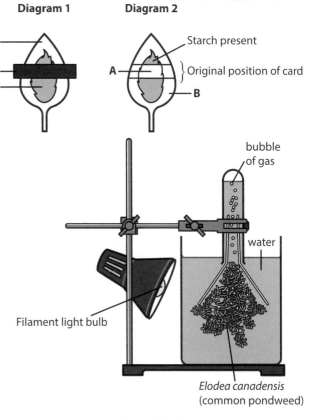

Diagram 1 — White part of leaf, Black card, Green part of leaf

Diagram 2 — Starch present, A, B, Original position of card

2. The effect of light intensity on the rate of photosynthesis.
- Using the apparatus shown right, the rate of photosynthesis by an aquatic plant can be measured by counting the number of bubbles produced over time.

3. The effect of light or dark.
- Set up experiment 2, but add hydrogencarbonate indicator to the water. The indicator makes the water red.
- Leave some plants in the dark and others at a fixed light intensity.
- In the dark, respiration produces carbon dioxide, which lowers the pH and the indicator turns yellow.
- In the light, the rate of photosynthesis is faster than respiration, so carbon dioxide is used up and the pH increases, which turns the indicator purple.

4. The effect of carbon dioxide concentration
- Set up experiment 2 but add different masses of sodium hydrogen carbonate (which adds carbon dioxide to the water).
- Increasing the carbon dioxide concentration increases the rate of photosynthesis.

5. The effect of temperature.
- Set up as experiment 2 but vary the temperature of the water surrounding the pond weed.
- Measure the number of bubbles at 5 °C increments up to 45 °C.

bubble of gas

water

Filament light bulb

Elodea canadensis (common pondweed)

The effect of light intensity on the rate of photosynthesis can be found by varying the distance of the light source from the plant.

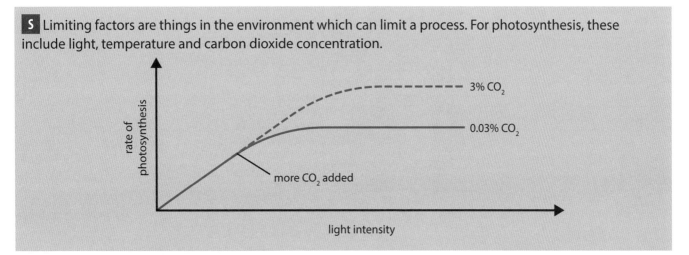

S Limiting factors are things in the environment which can limit a process. For photosynthesis, these include light, temperature and carbon dioxide concentration.

rate of photosynthesis

3% CO_2

0.03% CO_2

more CO_2 added

light intensity

> **Quick Test**

1. Give two examples of stored products of photosynthesis and their uses.
2. Identify the pigment in chloroplasts which uses energy from light to make glucose.
3. Predict the results for experiment 1.
S 4. Describe three limiting factors of photosynthesis.

Leaf structure

Syllabus links:
6.2.1–6.2.3

Learning aims:

- Explain how large, thin leaves in plants are adapted for photosynthesis
- Identify leaf structures in a dicotyledonous plant
- Explain how these structures are adapted for photosynthesis

Leaf adaptations

Photosynthesis mainly takes place in leaves, which are adapted for photosynthesis and gas exchange, and the transport of substances throughout the plant, shown in the diagram.

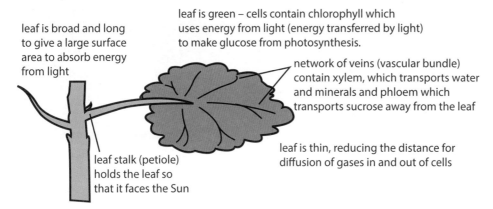

leaf is broad and long to give a large surface area to absorb energy from light

leaf is green – cells contain chlorophyll which uses energy from light (energy transferred by light) to make glucose from photosynthesis.

network of veins (vascular bundle) contain xylem, which transports water and minerals and phloem which transports sucrose away from the leaf

leaf stalk (petiole) holds the leaf so that it faces the Sun

leaf is thin, reducing the distance for diffusion of gases in and out of cells

Leaf tissues and cells adaptation for photosythesis

The diagram below shows cells in a section of leaf tissue from a **dicotyledonous plant**, which has broad flat leaves. Each tissue is adapted for photosynthesis and the diagram shows the exchange of oxygen and carbon dioxide.

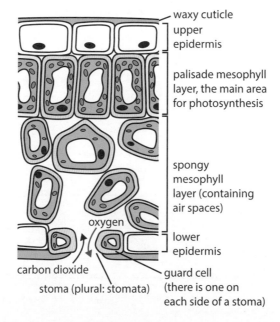

waxy cuticle
upper epidermis

palisade mesophyll layer, the main area for photosynthesis

spongy mesophyll layer (containing air spaces)

oxygen

lower epidermis

carbon dioxide

guard cell (there is one on each side of a stoma)

stoma (plural: stomata)

Stoma are adapted for photosynthesis by having **guard cells** on each side of the stoma open in daylight to allow gas exchange for photosynthesis. The stoma closes at night to retain water when photosynthesis stops.

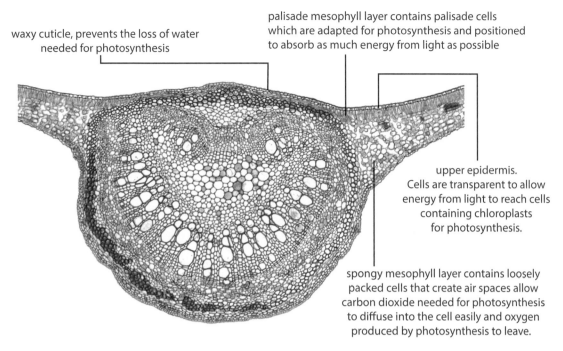

waxy cuticle, prevents the loss of water needed for photosynthesis

palisade mesophyll layer contains palisade cells which are adapted for photosynthesis and positioned to absorb as much energy from light as possible

upper epidermis. Cells are transparent to allow energy from light to reach cells containing chloroplasts for photosynthesis.

spongy mesophyll layer contains loosely packed cells that create air spaces allow carbon dioxide needed for photosynthesis to diffuse into the cell easily and oxygen produced by photosynthesis to leave.

The diagram (right) shows a palisade cell from the **palisade mesophyll layer** which is adapted for photosynthesis.

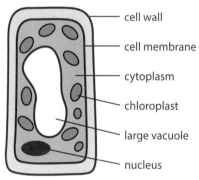

cell wall
cell membrane
cytoplasm
chloroplast
large vacuole
nucleus

- **Palisade cells** contain a large number of **chloroplasts** which contain **chlorophyll** needed for photosynthesis.

Vascular bundles, phloem and xylem

- **Vascular bundles** have central **xylem** surrounded by **phloem**.
- Phloem transports sucrose, formed from glucose produced by photosynthesis. Sucrose is transported away from the leaf to growing parts of the plant to make new plant cells and is also converted into other carbohydrates.
- Xylem tissues transport minerals and water from the soil to the stem and leaves where they are needed for photosynthesis

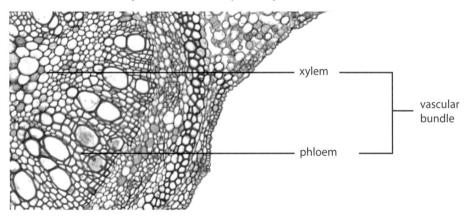

xylem

vascular bundle

phloem

> **Quick Test**

1. Identify the cells in the leaf tissue in which most photosynthesis takes place and explain how these cells are adapted for photosynthesis.
2. Describe the spongy mesophyll layer and explain how this tissue is adapted for gas exchange.
3. Explain the function of stoma (plural stomata).
4. Explain why many plants have large thin leaves and the importance of a large surface area inside leaves.

Diet and the digestive system

Syllabus links:
7.1.1–7.1.3,
7.2.1–7.2.2

Learning aims:

- Describe a balanced diet
- Identify essential nutrients, their sources and explain their importance
- Identify and describe the functions of the main organs of the digestive system
- Describe deficiency diseases

Balanced diet

- A **balanced diet** contains the amounts of nutrients needed to stay healthy, in the right proportions.

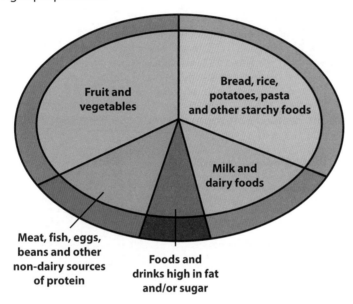

Essential nutrients

Nutrient	Function	Food source (examples)
carbohydrates	broken down into simple sugars, such as glucose used to provide energy from respiration	bread, pasta, potatoes, yams
fats and oils	some helps maintain body temperature, also acts as a store of energy for respiration if carbohydrates are unavailable	meat, oils, milk products, oily fish, nuts, avocados
fibre	also called '**roughage**', made up of indigestible plant cell walls. Adds bulk to food to move it through the **digestive system**, preventing constipation and protecting against bowel cancer.	green leafy vegetables, brown rice, wholegrain wheat
proteins	broken down into amino acids to form other proteins including enzymes	eggs, milk, meat, fish, legumes, nuts and seeds
Vitamin C	needed for healthy gums, teeth, skin and blood vessels	green vegetables, potatoes, citrus fruit. lack of vitamin C causes scurvy (**deficiency** disease)

Nutrient	Function	Food source (examples)
Vitamin D	needed for strong bones and teeth	eggs, fish, cheese, liver, milk lack of vitamin D causes rickets (deficiency disease)
Mineral ions (calcium and iron)	Calcium is needed for strong bones and teeth and for blood clotting Iron is needed to make haemoglobin in red blood cells	milk and eggs, some dried fruits, leafy green vegetables red meat, kidney, liver, green leafy vegetables, soybeans
water	Makes up most of the body, needed for all cell processes Excretion and sweating lose water which has to be replaced to maintain life	drinking water, liquid foods and drinks

The digestive system

- The **alimentary canal** is another term for the digestive system, from the mouth to the anus.

Oesophagus – pushes food down to stomach by rhytmic contractions to the anus (peristalsis)

Liver cells make urea from amino acids not used to make protein. Urea is transported to the kidney where it is excreted. Liver cells store excess glucose as **glycogen**. Liver cells also make **bile**.

Mouth

Liver

Gall bladder

The **gall bladder** stores bile, releasing it into the **duodenum** through the bile duct and into the small intestine where the bile helps break down fat.

Stomach
Pancreas
Large intestine
Small intestine

Rectum
Anus

Faeces are removed by **egestion**

Ingestion takes food into the body. The mouth contains **salivary glands** whichsecrete digestive enzymes that begin starch digestion in alkaline conditions. **Teeth** break down food intosmaller peieces which are moistened creating a **bolus** which can be swallowed. Muscular walls of the stomach churn food up forming liquid food (chyme) which increases the surface area for digestive enzymes to work.

Gastric juice secreted by cells lining the stomach creates an acidic pH for optimal digestion of protein by digestive enzymes and kills harmful microorgansims.

The **pancreas** secretes digetsive enzymes into the duodenum in an alkaline solution.

absorbtion of water and nutrients from the **small intestines**, part of the **ileum**, into the blood. The **colon** and **rectum** in the **large intestine** absorb water, and produce **faeces** from undigested food.

assimilation. Cells uptake and use nutrients

Quick Test

1. State which vitamins cause scurvy and rickets when not supplied in the diet.
2. a) Identify **two** essential mineral ions needed in the diet.
   - i) Explain their functions.
   - ii) Provide an example of a food source for each.
3. Explain why eating fibre is beneficial.
4. Explain what happens to food in the mouth.
5. Describe what happens to food in the small intestine.

Enzymes and digestion

Syllabus links:
7.4.1–7.4.5,
S 7.4.6–7.4.8

Learning aims:

- Describe chemical digestion to produce soluble food molecules
- Describe the functions of amylase, proteases and lipase. State where they are secreted and act.
  S Describe the action of amylases, maltase and trypsin in the small intestine and pepsin in the stomach
- Describe the function of gastric juice S and explain how digested food from the stomach is neutralised by bile
- Investigate the effects of pH on a protease

Digestive enzymes

- **Digestive enzymes** are secreted by the cells lining different parts of the digestive system, where they break down insoluble **carbohydrates**, **fats and oils** and **proteins**.
- Small soluble food molecules are produced, which are absorbed into the blood. They diffuse from blood into cells to provide energy for respiration, growth and repair.
- **Chemical digestion** uses additional substances such as hydrochloric acid in gastric juice.

There are several types of digestive enzyme. Each type catalyses the breakdown of a specific type of food (**substrate**) shown in the table.

Digestive enzyme	Site of production	Site of action	Substrate	Products
amylase	**pancreas/ salivary glands**	**small intestine, mouth**	**starch** (a carbohydrate)	**simple reducing sugars**
S **maltase**	small intestine	membranes of epithelial cells lining the small intestine	**maltose** (two glucose molecules joined)	**glucose**
lipases	pancreas	small intestine	fats and oils	**fatty acids** and **glycerol**
proteases	stomach lining (hydrochloric acid in **gastric juice** secreted by the stomach provides an acidic **pH** needed for optimum enzyme activity to kill bacteria) pancreas small intestine	**stomach** small intestine cells lining the small intestine	proteins	**amino acids** (from the action of several proteases in different sites of action)
S **pepsin**	stomach	works in acidic conditions in the stomach	proteins	small chains of amino acids
S **trypsin**	pancreas	small intestine–needs alkaline pH to work which is produced by bile secreted into duodenum which neutralises gastric juice from the stomach	small chains of amino acids	amino acids

Practical skills

Investigating the effect of pH on trypsin

- Trypsin is a protease. It catalyses the breakdown of insoluble amino acid chains into soluble single amino acids in alkaline conditions.
- **Casein** in milk contains insoluble amino acid chains. Trypsin breaks these down into soluble amino acids, observed when the milk solution in the investigation turns from cloudy to clear.

Universal indicator is used in this investigation. It changes colour depending on the solution it is added to.

pH4: orange   pH7: green   pH8–9: blue

Litmus paper changes colour roughly the same as universal indicator.

Method:

- Set up four large test tubes as shown in the diagram and follow the method given.
- Add 5 ml of milk and four drops of **universal indicator** to each large test tube.
- Then add buffer as follows.

Tube 1	Tube 2	Tube 3	Tube 4
Add 5 ml acidic pH4 buffer	Add 5 ml neutral pH7 buffer	Add 5 ml alkaline pH8.5 buffer	Add 5 ml alkaline pH8.5 buffer

Check the pH of each test tube using **litmus paper**.

Place the test tubes in a water bath at 37 °C.

Add 5 ml of 2 per cent trypsin solution to Tubes 1–3, and the same amount of trypsin to Tube 4.

Leave for 5 minutes.

Observe the contents of the tubes. Recheck the pH of the contents with litmus paper.

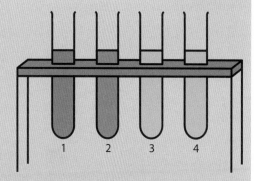

Results:

Tube	pH	Expected appearance of milk solution after 5 minutes at 37°C
1	4	cloudy
2	7	semi-cloudy
3	8.5	transparent
4	8.5	cloudy

Quick Test

1. Explain why the pH of the tubes was checked with litmus paper at the start and end of the investigation.
S 2. Explain why Tube 4 contained boiled trypsin.
S 3. State where trypsin acts in the digestive system.
4. In another experiment, the effect of temperature on amylase was investigated using potato (starch), at 4 °C, 37 °C and 50 °C. Predict and explain the results.
S 5. An investigation at 37 °C tested pepsin activity at pH 4, 7 and 8.5. Predict and explain the results after 5 minutes.

Physical digestion and absorption

Syllabus links:
7.3.1–7.3.6,
S 7.3.7,
7.5.1–7.5.2,
S 7.5.3–7.5.5

Learning aims:

- Describe physical digestion as the breakdown of food into smaller pieces, increasing the surface area for digestion
- Identify and describe the structure and function of human teeth in physical digestion
- Describe the role of the stomach **S** and bile in physical digestion

Physical digestion

- **Physical digestion** does not cause chemical changes in food.
- Physical digestion helps the **chemical digestion** of food by **digestive enzymes**.
- Chewing by **teeth** increases the surface area of food for digestive enzymes to act.

Human teeth

Incisors have cutting edges for biting through food.

Canines are pointed to hold food.

Premolars grind and cut food on a small surface.

Molars chew food and have large surfaces for grinding.

The diagram shows the structure of a human molar and the function of each part.

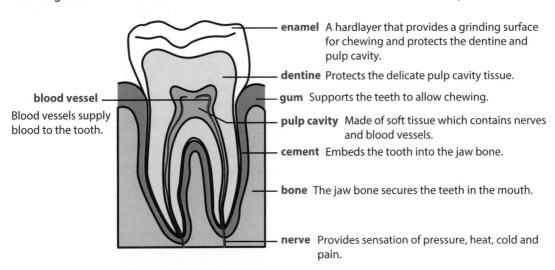

blood vessel — Blood vessels supply blood to the tooth.

enamel A hardlayer that provides a grinding surface for chewing and protects the dentine and pulp cavity.

dentine Protects the delicate pulp cavity tissue.

gum Supports the teeth to allow chewing.

pulp cavity Made of soft tissue which contains nerves and blood vessels.

cement Embeds the tooth into the jaw bone.

bone The jaw bone secures the teeth in the mouth.

nerve Provides sensation of pressure, heat, cold and pain.

Physical digestion in the **stomach**

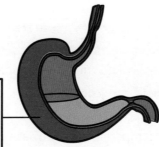

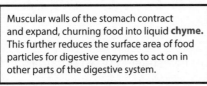

Muscular walls of the stomach contract and expand, churning food into liquid **chyme**. This further reduces the surface area of food particles for digestive enzymes to act on in other parts of the digestive system.

S Bile in physical digestion

- **Fats and oils** do not dissolve in water in the digestive system.
- **Bile** emulsifies fats and oils in the small intestine, forming small droplets.
- This increases the surface area for **lipase** enzymes to act and speeds up fat digestion.

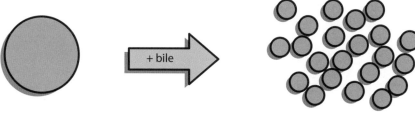

large fat or oil droplet

+ bile

small fat or oil droplets

Absorption

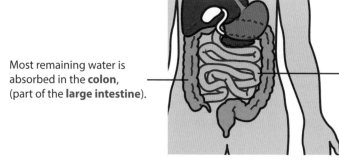

Most remaining water is absorbed in the **colon**, (part of the **large intestine**).

Most water, digested food molecules such as glucose and amino acids, are absorbed along the length of the **ileum** (**small intestine**). The length of the small intestine provides a large surface area and time for digested nutrients to be absorbed into the boodstream.

Villi and microvilli

A single **villus**:

- The surface area available for absorption in the small intestine is increased by villi. Each has a thin outer layer of cells that contain **microvilli**, which further increase the surface area for absorption.
- Fats and oils do not dissolve in blood. The **lacteal** is part of the lymphatic system, and transports fats and oils to the body outside of the bloodstream.
- The close proximity of **blood capillaries** allows nutrients to diffuse into the bloodstream down a concentration gradient, over a short distance.

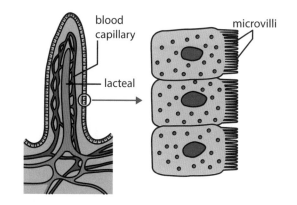

blood capillary

microvilli

lacteal

> **Quick Test**

1. Describe the pulp cavity in a tooth.
2. Explain the role of the stomach in physical digestion.
3. State where nutrients are absorbed in the digestive system.
S 4. Explain the role of villi and microvilli in absorption.
S 5. Explain the function of blood capillaries and the lacteal in a villus.

Tissues for transport in plants

Syllabus links:
8.1–8.1.2,
[S] 8.1.3,
8.2.1–8.2.2

Learning aims:

- State the functions of xylem and phloem and identify their positions in plant sections
- [S] Explain how the structure of xylem (thick walls, no cell content) is related to its function
- Identify root hairs and state their functions giving reasons for their large surface area

Xylem and Phloem

Xylem and **phloem** are part of a plant's transport system. They have different structures and functions, summarised in the table.

Structure	Xylem	Phloem
	Contains long tubes (**xylem vessels**) of dead cells which have strong walls to support the plant **Strengthening cells**, not part of xylem, give added support to **leaves** and **stems**	contains living phloem cells linked together in columns
Function	Xylem vessels carry **water** and **dissolved minerals ions** from the **roots** to all parts of the plant Water supplied to leaves is needed for **photosynthesis**. [S] Xylem vessels have no cell content and are arranged in columns with no walls between them, forming continuous tubes [S] Xylem cell walls contain **lignin** which thickens and strengthens xylem tissues	contains living phloem cells linked together transports dissolved nutrients including **amino acids** and **sucrose** formed in leaves, to the rest of the plant

The arrangement of xylem and phloem

The diagram shows a cross-section of a root, where xylem and phloem are separated.

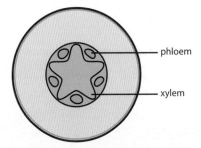

- In the leaves and stem, xylem and phloem are grouped together in tissues called **vascular bundles**, or in leaves, as leaf **veins**.
- When xylem vessels in vascular bundles in stems, or leaf veins, are full of water they are more rigid, and provide support to these parts of the plant.

Stem cross-section

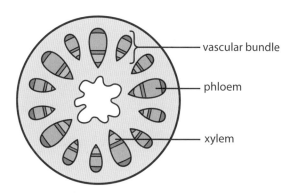

vascular bundle

phloem

xylem

Leaf cross-section

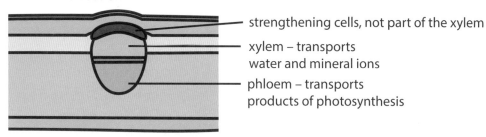

strengthening cells, not part of the xylem

xylem – transports
water and mineral ions

phloem – transports
products of photosynthesis

Root hairs

- **Root hairs** are fine protrusions which extend into the soil.
- Root hairs are located just behind **root tips**. They increase the surface area for the absorption of water and mineral ions from the **soil**.
- Water enters the root hair cell and passes through **root cortex cells** and **passage cells** to xylem.

The diagram shows the passage of water from the soil, into the root hair and to the xylem vessel.

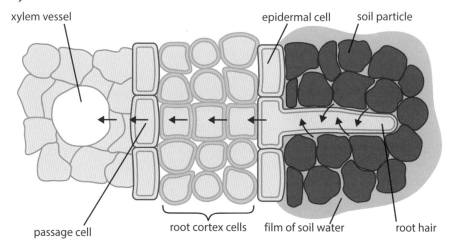

xylem vessel

epidermal cell   soil particle

passage cell

root cortex cells   film of soil water   root hair

> **Quick Test**

1. Describe **two** main functions of xylem.
2. Describe **one** main function of phloem.
3. Name two plant tissues where xylem and phloem are located together.
4. Describe the structure and functions of root hair cells.
S 5. Describe the structure and function of xylem.

Transpiration and translocation

Syllabus links:

8.3.1–8.3.3,

S 8.3.4–8.3.7,

8.4.1–8.4.3

Learning aims:

- Describe transpiration and the leaf tissues involved
- S Explain the mechanism of water vapour loss and its relationship to large surface area and explain wilting
- Investigate and describe factors affecting wind and temperature on transpiration rate S and explain the effects of humidity

Transpiration

- **Transpiration** is the process of water loss from **leaves** of a plant.
- Loss of **water vapour** is associated with the size and number of **stomata** and the large internal surface area provided by the **spongy mesophyll layer**.
- Transpiration is summarised by the diagram.

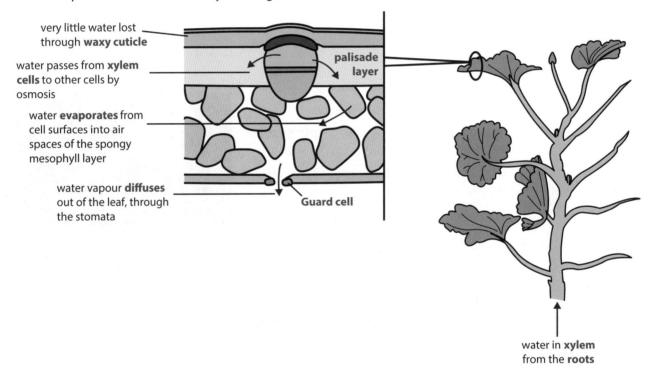

very little water lost through **waxy cuticle**

water passes from **xylem cells** to other cells by osmosis

water **evaporates** from cell surfaces into air spaces of the spongy mesophyll layer

water vapour **diffuses** out of the leaf, through the stomata

palisade layer

Guard cell

water in **xylem** from the **roots**

S Transpiration pull

- **Transpiration pull** describes a column of water being 'pulled' from xylem to **vascular bundle** in the leaf **vein**.
- Loss of water from spongy mesophyll cells lowers the cell's water potential causing water to leave by **osmosis**.
- The resulting water gradient leads to water moving out of xylem into surrounding tissues by osmosis.
- This creates a 'pull' due to **tension** between water molecules, caused by forces of attraction between them.
- Water is pulled as a column up xylem to the leaf.
- The resulting continued water potential gradient pulls water out of the root hair cells in the soil.

S Factors affecting the transpiration rate

- Increased **temperature** causes faster movement of water particles into air spaces in the leaf and out through the stomata.
- Increased wind speed increases transpiration by reducing water vapour around the leaf. This increases the water concentration gradient to the outside of the leaf.
- **S** **Wilting** occurs when more water is lost by transpiration than replaced. The reduced water pressure inside plant cells causes them to become less rigid and droopy.
- **S** **Humidity**, when air is damp, increases water vapour around the leaf, and reduces the water concentration gradient and the transpiration rate.

Investigating transpiration rate

A **potometer** measures the rate of transpiration.

Set up the experiment and method as shown.

Method:

Measure the time in seconds for the water bubble to move 5 cm under different conditions:

- no wind, cool temperature
- wind, warm temperature.

Use a lamp to provide heat and a fan to provide windy conditions.

Keep the brightness of the lamp and the leaf used the same to make the investigation a fair test.

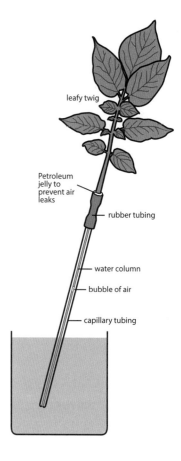

leafy twig

Petroleum jelly to prevent air leaks

rubber tubing

water column

bubble of air

capillary tubing

S Translocation

- Sucrose and amino acids are moved by **translocation** from **sources** to **sinks**.
- Sinks use or store these nutrients; sources release them.
- Sources and sinks may be used at different times of year, summarised in the table.

Sources and/or use	Sinks
Spring/Summer:	Autumn/ Winter:
Starch converted into glucose for respiration, growth, flower and seed production	**Sucrose** converted into starch in storage organs such as **tubers**
Amino acids used to produce enzymes and proteins for growth	Amino acids stored in leaves, stems, roots and **fruits**

> **Quick Test**

1. Define transpiration.
2. Describe and explain **two** probable results of the practical: investigating transpiration rate.
   S 3. Explain how water moves upwards in xylem.
   S 4. Define translocation.
   S 5. Give **one** example of the use of a source and a plant tissue which acts as a sink.

Circulatory systems and hearts

Learning aims:

Syllabus links:
9.1.1,
S 9.1.2–9.1.4,
9.2.1–9.2.6,
S 9.2.7–9.2.11

- Describe the role and parts of the heart **S** and explain how it pumps blood in one direction
- **S** Compare single and double circulatory systems
- Describe the effect of exercise on the heart **S** and explain this
- Describe risk factors in coronary heart disease.

Heart structure

- The **heart** is an **organ** that pumps blood through the **circulatory system**.

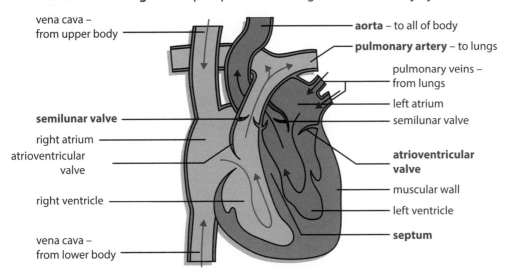

vena cava – from upper body

aorta – to all of body

pulmonary artery – to lungs

pulmonary veins – from lungs

left atrium

semilunar valve

semilunar valve

right atrium

atrioventricular valve

atrioventricular valve

right ventricle

muscular wall

left ventricle

vena cava – from lower body

septum

- The heart has four muscular chambers: two **atria** and two **ventricles**.
- One-way **valves** stop backflow of **blood**.
- The walls of the heart are made of thick elastic muscle tissue, which allows it to withstand high blood pressures as it pumps.
- **Coronary arteries** supply blood to heart muscle.
- Blood is pumped out of the heart in arteries and back to the heart in veins.

S Blood from the body is forced from the atria to the ventricles by contraction of the atria walls. Contraction of the ventricle walls forces blood out of the heart.

If a hole in the septum causes deoxygenated blood to dilute oxygenated blood, cells receive insufficient oxygen for **respiration** leading to tiredness and shortness of breath.

- Atria have thin walls compared to ventricles because they pump blood short distances into the ventricles.
- The left ventricle has thicker walls than the right ventricle because it has to pump blood to the body.

Disease

Coronary heart disease develops when cholesterol blocks the coronary arteries, limiting oxygen and glucose supply to heart muscle. Risk factors:

- high saturated fat diets
- lack of exercise
- genetic tendency
- age
- smoking
- stress
- sex

Heart rate

Heart rate in beats per minute can be measured by taking a **pulse** at the wrist.

- Alternatively, heart rate can be measured by listening to the heart and counting a 'lub dub' sound when valves open and close for each beat.
- Heart rate and activity can be observed by taking an **electrocardiogram**, or ECG.

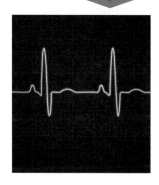

Single and double circulatory systems

The **double circulatory system** is shown in the diagram.

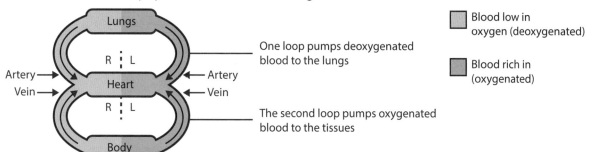

One loop pumps deoxygenated blood to the lungs

The second loop pumps oxygenated blood to the tissues

☐ Blood low in oxygen (deoxygenated)

☐ Blood rich in (oxygenated)

Fish have a **single circulatory system**. Blood passes through the heart once.

- Oxygen from water enters the blood and enters the fish tissues.
- Deoxygenated blood and carbon dioxide pass back to the heart, then the gills. Carbon dioxide diffuses back into the water.

Advantages of double compared to single circulation:

- Blood reaches the lungs at low pressure, preventing damage to capillaries and lung tissues.
- A double system allows blood to be pumped faster, so oxygen is supplied to cells at a greater rate.

Exercise

S Heart rate increases when exercising to meet the demand for oxygen and glucose in the tissues caused by increased respiration, and to remove the waste products.

> **Practical skills**

Investigating the effect of exercise on heart rate

Method:

1. Measure the pulse rate at rest. (Count the pulse beats in 15 seconds and multiply by four to get beats per minute.)
2. Do two minutes of exercise, then measure the pulse rate again.
3. Repeat the measurements, changing the intensity of exercise. Leave a five-minute rest period between each trial.

> **Quick Test**

1. i) Explain why students recorded the pulse at the start of the practical.
   S ii) Predict and explain the students' results.
2. Explain how the thickness and elasticity of heart muscle tissues relate to their function.
   S 3. Predict the effects of a hole in the heart septum.
   S 4. Explain the advantages of a double circulation compared to a single circulation.

Blood vessels and blood

Learning aims:

- Describe different blood vessels  and explain how they are adapted for their functions
- Identify the main blood vessels to and from organs in the body
- State the functions of the components of blood
- [S] Identify how white blood cells and platelets are adapted for their functions

Syllabus links:
9.3.1–9.3.3,
[S] 9.3.4–9.3.6,
9.4.1–9.4.4,
[S] 9.4.5–9.4.7

The human circulatory system

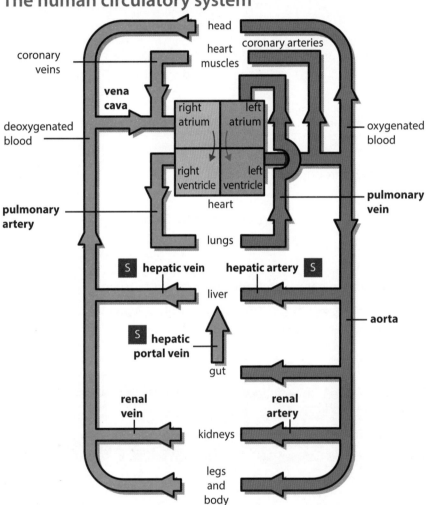

> **Key Point**
>
> In this diagram of the human circulatory system, terms shown in bold are ones you may need to identify in your exams.

Blood vessels

Vessel	Function and structure
Arteries	Transport blood away from the heart. Arteries have a narrow central cavity (**lumen**) and thick elastic muscular walls [S] to transport blood at high pressure. The vessel walls recoil after each heartbeat to maintain blood pressure at an even level.
Veins	Transport blood back to the heart. Veins have **valves**, to prevent blood flowing away from the heart (backflow). They have thinner, non-elastic walls and wider lumens than arteries, [S] so bloods flow easily and under lower pressure than in arteries.
Capillaries	Narrow blood vessels that connect arteries to veins, and form a network around tissues to supply cells with substances and remove wastes. They have very thin walls [S] to increase the rate of diffusion of substances. A capillary network in the lungs enables efficient gas exchange of oxygen and carbon dioxide.

Blood

Blood transports many substances around the body.

Substance	Carried from	Carried to
glucose, amino acids, fatty acids and ions from digestion	small intestine	all parts of the body
water	intestines	all parts of the body
oxygen	lungs	all parts of the body
carbon dioxide	all parts of the body	lungs
urea (waste) from	liver	kidneys
hormones	glands	specific target organs and tissues

Blood contains liquid plasma, red blood cells, white blood cells and platelets.

- **Plasma** contains water, products of digestion such as amino acids and ions, urea from amino acid breakdown, hormones and dissolved carbon dioxide.
- **White blood cells** are involved in **antibody** production and **phagocytosis**.
- **Red blood cells** have no nucleus to provide more space for haemoglobin. Their biconcave shape helps red blood cells pass through small blood vessels and provides a large surface area for gas exchange.
- Platelets are involved in blood clotting.

S The sequence of events in **blood clotting** is shown to the to the right:

Lymphocytes and phagocytes

- Phagocytosis describes the process when a **phagocyte** engulfs a bacteria, fungi or protoctist parasite.

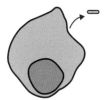

1 A phagocyte moves towards a bacterium

2 The phagocyte pushes a sleeve of cytoplasm outwards to surround the bacterium

3 The bacterium is now enclosed in a vacuole inside the cell; it is then killed and digested by enzymes

S **Lymphocytes** have a large nucleus and produce **antibodies**.

The liver makes **fibrinogen**, a protein which is transported in blood plasma

↓

The **platelets** in the blood respond to the damaged blood vessel by releasing an enzyme

↓

The enzyme changes soluble fibrinogen in the plasma into insoluble **fibrin** strands

↓

Fibrin strands form a mesh, trapping red blood cells and creating a clot when exposed to the air; the clot dries and forms a scab

> **Quick Test**

1. Briefly describe the structures of arteries and veins.
2. Give four examples of substances transported in blood.
   S 3. Summarise how the structure arteries, veins and capillaries is related to their function.
   S 4. Identify two types of white blood cell.
   S 5. Describe the change in fibrinogen as part of blood clotting.

Diseases

Syllabus links:
10.1.1–10.1.5,
S 10.1.6–10.1.17

Learning aims:

- Describe a pathogen and their role in transmissible diseases
- State how pathogens are transmitted
- Explain the importance of measures used to control the spread of disease
- **S** Describe cholera as a disease caused by a bacterium and the effects of its toxin
- Describe how the body defends itself against pathogens

Pathogens and disease

A **pathogen** is an organism that causes disease. Diseases caused by pathogens are **transmissible**.

Pathogens can be transmitted by direct contact or indirectly:

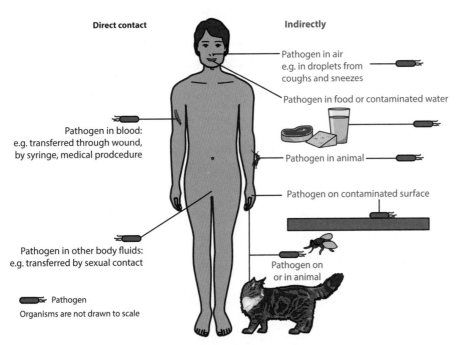

Direct contact

Indirectly

Pathogen in air
e.g. in droplets from
coughs and sneezes

Pathogen in food or contaminated water

Pathogen in blood:
e.g. transferred through wound,
by syringe, medical prodcedure

Pathogen in animal

Pathogen on contaminated surface

Pathogen in other body fluids:
e.g. transferred by sexual contact

Pathogen on
or in animal

Pathogen
Organisms are not drawn to scale

> **Key Point**
>
> Transmissible diseases are transferred from one **host** to another. The hosts may be of the same **species** or from different species.

> **Key Point**
>
> Make sure you understand the difference between explaining the importance of controlling the spread of disease and the measures we take to do this. In each case, controlling the spread of disease will involve reducing or preventing the spread of pathogens.

Controlling the spread of disease

Measure	Importance
Clean water supply	Needs to be free from pathogens for: drinking, cooking, washing, cleaning
Hygienic food preparation	Reduces or prevents spread of pathogens that cause food poisoning. These may: • be present in uncooked food • be transferred by poor hygiene, organisms, kitchen utensils.
Good personal hygiene	Reduces the number or presence of pathogens on the surface of the body that could be transferred to food or drink or to other people.
Waste disposal	Wastes: • may contain pathogens • can be food sources for insects and rodents that spread pathogens.
Sewage treatment	Needs treatment to eliminate pathogens – water can then be safely released into the environment or recycled.

S Cholera

Cholera is a disease caused by a bacterium. The bacterium is transmitted in contaminated water.

The bacterium produces a **toxin** that causes secretion of chloride ions into the small intestine.

Chloride ions cause the movement of water into the small intestine by **osmosis**. The excess water results in diarrhoea and loss of ions from the blood, and the dehydration produced can lead to death.

Defence

The body's defences provide barriers to the entry of pathogens:

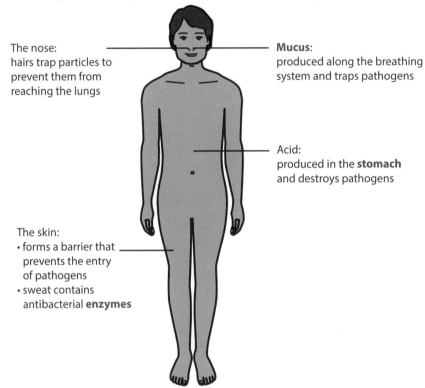

The nose:
hairs trap particles to
prevent them from
reaching the lungs

Mucus:
produced along the breathing
system and traps pathogens

Acid:
produced in the **stomach**
and destroys pathogens

The skin:
• forms a barrier that
  prevents the entry
  of pathogens
• sweat contains
  antibacterial **enzymes**

Internal defences are required if a pathogen passes through these barriers. Types of **white blood cell** called **phagocytes** are involved in defending the body against pathogens. The pathogen is destroyed by the process of **phagocytosis**. (see page 47)

Lymphocytes are also involved in defence and **immunity**. One type of lymphocyte produces **antibodies**.

> **Key Point**
>
> Be able to identify phagocytes and lymphocytes in micrographs and diagrams.

> **Quick Test**
>
> 1. Describe the term pathogen.
> 2. State **two** ways in which pathogens can be transmitted by **direct** contact.
> 3. Describe how the skin contributes to the body's defences.
> 4. Name the types of white blood cell involved in the body's defence against pathogens.

S Immunity

Syllabus links:
S 10.1.6–10.1.15

Learning aims:

- S State that a pathogen has specific antigens and antibodies have complementary shapes to these antigens
- S Describe antibodies and their role in destroying pathogens
- S Describe and explain how active immunity is obtained through infection or vaccination and outline how vaccination is used to control the spread of disease
- S Explain how passive immunity is obtained and its importance

Antibodies

Antibodies are proteins involved in the body's defence. Antibodies bind to **antigens** of **pathogens**, leading to the destruction of the pathogen.

Each type of pathogen has its own, specific antigen.

Different types of pathogen

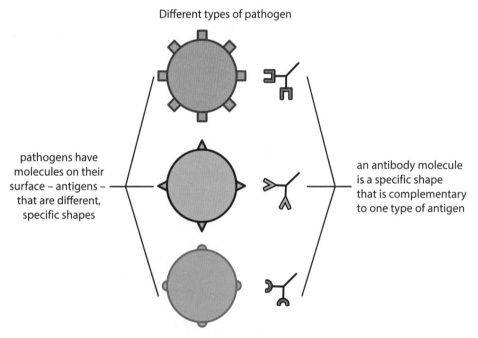

pathogens have molecules on their surface – antigens – that are different, specific shapes

an antibody molecule is a specific shape that is complementary to one type of antigen

> **Key Point**
>
> Antigens do not just occur on the surface of pathogens and other microorganisms. Other particles that are not part of the body can act as antigens and produce a response by the immune system. Pollen grains are one example.

When a particular type of pathogen invades the body, **lymphocytes** produce antibodies. Antibodies destroy the pathogens:

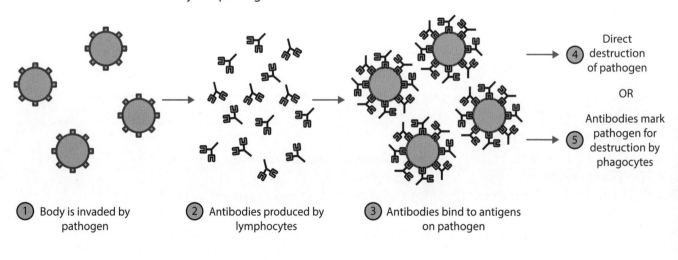

1. Body is invaded by pathogen
2. Antibodies produced by lymphocytes
3. Antibodies bind to antigens on pathogen
4. Direct destruction of pathogen

OR

5. Antibodies mark pathogen for destruction by phagocytes

Active immunity

Active immunity is when **immunity** is achieved by the production of antibodies.

It occurs when:

- the body is infected by a pathogen, or
- by **vaccination**. The pathogen, which has been weakened, is introduced into the body. Vaccinations are given by injection or through the mouth or nose.

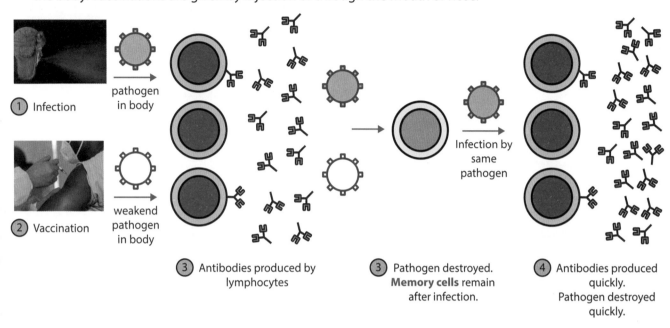

1. Infection

2. Vaccination

pathogen in body

weakend pathogen in body

3. Antibodies produced by lymphocytes

3. Pathogen destroyed. **Memory cells** remain after infection.

Infection by same pathogen

4. Antibodies produced quickly. Pathogen destroyed quickly.

Memory cells produced after infection or vaccination give long-term immunity. The immune system responds rapidly if exposed to the pathogen again.

Vaccination is very effective in controlling the spread of disease:

- If exposed to the pathogen, a vaccinated person will have a mild infection or not become infected.
- If a large proportion of a population is vaccinated against a disease, it will be difficult for someone to become infected. Cases of the infection will disappear.

Passive immunity

Passive immunity is achieved by antibodies being given to an individual. One example is the transfer of a mother's antibodies to her baby. This occurs:

- across the **placenta** during pregnancy
- in breast milk.

Breastfeeding therefore gives the baby some immunity before their own immune system develops fully.

> ## Key Point
>
> In passive immunity, antibodies are not produced in the normal way by lymphocytes. Therefore, no memory cells are produced to fight future infections. The immunity is short-term.

> ## Key Point
>
> Ready-made antibodies, given as medication, must be given in life-threatening infections. The person may die from the infection before the body can produce its own antibodies.

> ## Quick Test
>
> **S 1.** Define the term antibody.
>
> **S 2.** Compare active immunity and passive immunity.
>
> **S 3.** Outline the importance of memory cells.
>
> **S 4.** Explain the importance of breastfeeding.

Photosynthesis

1 Which of these statements about photosynthesis is correct?

    A. Photosynthesis uses oxygen and glucose to form carbon dioxide and water.

    B. Photosynthesis is not affected by carbon dioxide concentration.

    C. Photosynthesis will continue in the dark.

    D. Photosynthesis uses carbon dioxide and water to produce glucose and oxygen. [1]

2 **a** (Circle) the main carbohydrates produced by photosynthesis.

    starch   nectar   amino acids   cellulose   protein sucrose glucose [4]

    b **i)** Copy and complete the word equation for photosynthesis.

$$\text{carbon dioxide + water} \xrightarrow[\text{light}]{\text{chlorophyll}} \underline{\hspace{2cm}} [1] + \underline{\hspace{2cm}} [1]$$

        [2]

    ii) State the name of the pigment required for photosynthesis and where it is located. [2]

    [Total marks 8]

S 3 Write a balanced equation for photosynthesis and circle one main limiting factor. [5]

S 4 Describe how to use the apparatus in the diagram to investigate the effect of temperature on the rate of photosynthesis. [2]

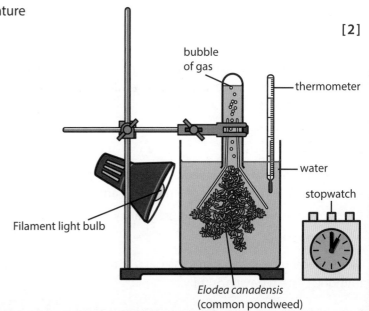

bubble of gas

thermometer

Filament light bulb

water

stopwatch

Elodea canadensis (common pondweed)

> **Show me**

I would change the .... of the water and measure the ....

5 The graph shows the effect of light on photosynthesis by an aquatic plant.

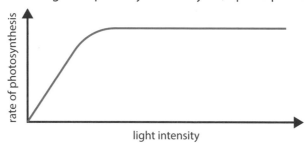

a Explain the shape of the curve. [3]

b State three factors that limit the rate of photosynthesis. [3]

[Total marks 6]

Leaf structure

1 This question is about palisade cells in dicotyledonous plants.

a Describe one adaptation of palisade cells that makes them efficient for photosynthesis. [1]

b Explain why it is important for palisade cells to be located close to the surface of the leaf. [2]

[Total marks 3]

Describe means to recall facts to give information about what something does, its position and/or its appearance.

Cross section of leaf tissue

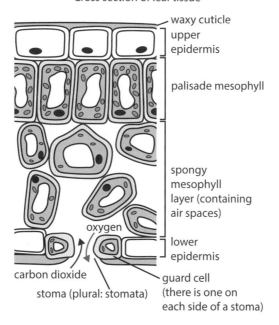

2 This question is about leaf tissues in dicotyledonous plants, shown in the diagram.

a Explain two adaptations of the spongy mesophyll layer in leaves that are important for photosynthesis. [2]

b Describe the function of the waxy cuticle. [1]

c Explain why stomata are open during the day and closed at night. [2]

d State the feature of the upper and lower epidermis and explain how this enables photosynthesis. [2]

[Total marks 7]

3 ▸ The diagram shows a yucca plant.

The yucca is adapted to live in conditions where there is very little water and plenty of sunlight.

Explain how each of these features mean that the yucca is adapted for survival.

> **Show me**

a. deep roots:
allows the plant to access .... and ....

b. Long spiky leaves with a thick waxy coating rather than flat thin leaves: ....

....

c. Yucca plants close their stomata during the day when it is hot and open them at night for carbon dioxide to enter, which is stored for photosynthesis during daylight

Stomata close during the day to: ....

The number of marks in an exam question tells you how many points you have to make.

[5]

Diet and the digestive system

1 ▸ **a** The boxes on the right contain some true and some false statements about a balanced diet.

Draw lines to identify **three** correct statements.

food and drink high in fat and sugar should make up half of all food eaten
fruit and vegetables and starchy foods should both be eaten in equal amounts

Balanced diet

water is not needed
must supply essential nutrients
does not include grains
should include fibre

[3]

b State **two** essential vitamins that must be included as part of a balanced diet and maintain health.

[2]
[Total marks 5]

2 The diagram shows parts of the human digestive system.

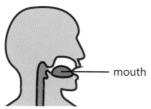

mouth

a **i)** Describe how food is broken into smaller pieces in the mouth creating a bolus before swallowing. [2]

ii) State which glands in the mouth secrete saliva. [1]

iii) Explain the importance of chewing food for digestion by digestive enzymes. [2]

When there are **two** marks for a question you need to make **two** points.

b The diagram shows parts of the human digestive system.

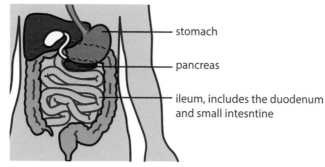

stomach

pancreas

ileum, includes the duodenum and small intesntine

i) Describe **two** things that happen to food in the stomach. [2]

ii) Describe **one** thing that happens to digested food in the small intestine. [1]

iii) The pancreas secretes digestive enzymes in an alkaline fluid which is transported into the small intestine.

Explain why the fluid needs to be alkaline. [1]

[Total marks 9]

3 **a** Copy and complete the table showing food types by writing one example of a source. [5]

b Describe absorption and assimilation [2]

Show me

Fats and oils	
Protein	
Starch (carbohydrate)	
Calcium	
Iron	

Absorption is the process where nutrients from food are taken up into the ....

.... incorporates nutrients into cells where they are used in various functions.

[Total marks 7]

4 The diagram shows part of the human digestive system.

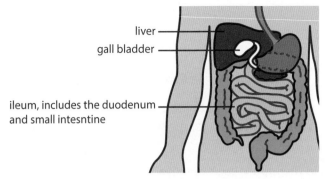

liver

gall bladder

ileum, includes the duodenum and small intesntine

a State **two** functions of the liver in digestion. [2]

b State **one** function of the gall bladder. [1]

[Total marks 3]

5 This question is about the effects of essential vitamin and mineral deficiency.

a Read the paragraph about sailors on long voyages between the 15th and 18th centuries:

'On long journeys the sailors had a diet containing only grains. They developed bleeding gums, skin problems, tooth loss and bruising.'

Identify which essential vitamin deficiency the sailors were suffering from. [1]

b Identify which essential mineral deficiency could reduce red blood cell production. [1]

c Read this sentence about poor childhood nutrition:

'In the period from 1914–1918, the effects of war led to food shortages and diets which lacked essential nutrients. Many children experienced softening and weakening of their bones.'

Identify which essential vitamin deficiency the children were suffering from. [1]

[Total marks 3]

Enzymes and digestion

1 Draw **three** lines from the box containing the word 'proteases' to match their correct description.

| digest starch into simple reducing sugars |

| some work best at acidic pH |

| all work best at alkaline pH in the small inestine. |

proteases

| work best at 37 °C |

| digest proteins into amino acids |

| digest fat and oils into fatty acids and glycerol |

[3]

2 This question is about lipases.

a State the location of lipase production in the digestive system and where lipase acts. [2]

b Describe the function of lipase. [2]

[Total marks 4]

3 Amylase is an enzyme which digests carbohydrates, such as starch into glucose. Starch turns black when tested with iodine. Glucose does not turn black with iodine. Look at the apparatus in the table. Describe how you would use this to investigate the optimal temperature for amylase activity.

test tubes and rack numbered 1–6	iodine solution
amylase solution	stopwatch
starch solution	spotting tile
2, 5 cm^3 syringes or pipettes	disposable gloves
water bath range 30-40 °C, temperature controlled in 2 °C increments	eye protection

[5]

> **Show me**

I would change the .... of the water bath and use the stopwatch to record

the .... when the iodine tests showed that there was no ....

present in the tubes.

I would write down the number of the tube where there was .... reaction with iodine

first and the temperature of the solution in that tube. This would tell me the ....

temperature for amylase in the investigation.

4 A pH4 solution was made using hydrochloric acid and pepsin to represent gastric juice secreted by the stomach. The pH was checked using universal indicator. Ground beef was added to the solution placed in a water bath at 37 °C . After two hours the cloudy mixture at the start became a transparent solution. Before concluding that pepsin had digested the beef, suggest which of these controls you could carry out.

   A. Boil the gastric juice solution before adding the meat.

   B. Repeat the experiment at a different temperature.

   C. Repeat the experiment using a sample from fish.

   D. Use a different pH indicator.

5 Some people are 'gluten intolerant'. They are unable to digest gluten, a protein found in foods containing wheat, barley and rye.

a Suggest which group of digestive enzymes are unable to break down gluten proteins, in gluten intolerant people. [1]

b State two locations where the group of enzymes in part i) work in the digestive system. [2]

c Suggest which small soluble food molecule may be deficient in gluten intolerant people. [1]

Suggest means to apply what you already know to offer a solution.

[Total marks 4]

Physical digestion and absorption

1 The diagram shows the structure of a human molar tooth.

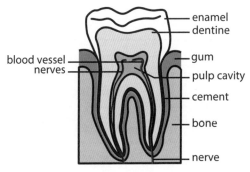

a **i)** Identify and explain the function of each part of the pulp cavity. [4]

ii) State **two** reasons why teeth have a hard covering of enamel. [2]

b This question is about tooth decay.

Tooth decay occurs when eating sugary food and drinks increases bacteria in the mouth producing acid. The acid gradually breaks down tooth enamel causing tooth decay and cavities to form.

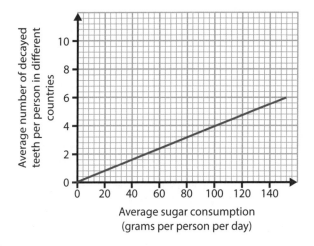

i) Look at the graph.

Describe the relationship between average sugar consumption per day and the number of decayed teeth. [2]

ii) A fizzy drink can contain 50 g of sugar.

Looking at the graph, what is the average number of decayed teeth caused by drinking **two** cans of the fizzy drink per day? Give your answer to the nearest whole number. [2]

[Total marks 10]

2 The diagram shows the small intestine.

a   (Circle) **two** substances which are absorbed in the small intestine.   [2]

   water   protein   starch   nutrients   enzymes

b   The small intestine is 6m long. How is this beneficial for food absorption?   [3]

[Total marks 5]

3 The table shoes some true and false descriptions of physical and chemical digestion.

Which **one** row matches **two** true descriptions of physical and chemical digestions?   [1]

	Physical digestion	Chemical digestion
A	Only takes place in the mouth	Only takes place in the colon
B	Only takes place in the colon	Only takes place in the mouth
C	Breaks down food into smaller pieces in the mouth and the stomach	Uses digestive enzymes and can also use hydrochloric acid to break down food
D	Uses digestive enzymes and can also use hydrochloric acid to break down food	Breaks down food into smaller pieces in the mouth and the stomach

4 Describe the role of bile in physical digestion.   [4]

Show me

Fat globules are insoluble in water. Fats need to be emulsified in order to be digested.

Bile emulsifies large .... droplets producing smaller ....

droplets which .... the surface area for lipase enzymes to digest fats and oils.

This makes the rate of fat digestion much ....

S **5** The diagram shows two villi which line the small intestine.

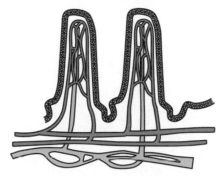

a State **two** structures in a villus. [2]

b Explain **three** adaptations of villi which are beneficial for absorption of digested food molecules into the body. [3]

[**Total marks 5**]

Explain means to give reasons for a process occurring or the role of a specific feature.

Tissues for transport in plants

1 Which statement about phloem vessels is correct?

A. are only found in the stems of plants

B. have one main function

C. help provide support to stems and leaves

D. transport mineral ions [1]

2 Look at the diagram which shows the cross-section of a stem from a flowering plant.

Tick the box for the line which makes a correct sentence about xylem.

		Tick one of these boxes	Tick one of these boxes
A	Xylem contains dead xylem vessels	which transport sucrose	
B	Xylem vessels are living cells	which transport water and minerals	
C	Xylem contains dead xylem vessels	which transport water and minerals	
D	Xylem vessels	are only located in the roots	

[1]

3 Look at the image of a baobab tree.

Baobab trees grow mainly in dry regions such as Africa and Australia. The tree's transport system is adapted to enable it to survive when there is very little rainfall.

Suggest a difference in the structure of xylem vessels in the baobab tree's trunk compared to trees in wetter climates. Explain your answer. [3]

Show me

The baobab trunk has more ... 1.... xylem vessels.

This adaptation means that xylem can function as a ....2... store under drought conditions which

trees in wetter climates do ......3..... need.

Suggest means to apply what you already know to offer a possible solution or an answer.

4 Look at the image of root hairs.

What **two** adaptations of root hairs adapts them for their function? [2]

Transpiration and translocation

1 The diagram shows a cross-section of a leaf. The blue arrows indicate the movement of water.

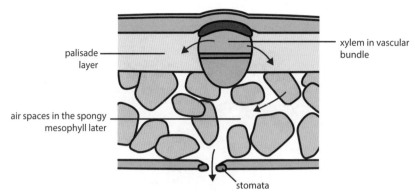

palisade layer

xylem in vascular bundle

air spaces in the spongy mesophyll later

stomata

a Name the process of water vapour loss from leaves. [1]

b Describe, in detail, the movement of water through the leaf tissue, shown in the diagram. [3]

[Total marks 4]

2 Look at the apparatus in the diagram, which uses a potometer to investigate the effect of wind and temperature on the rate of transpiration.

You want to investigate the effect of wind and temperature on the rate of transpiration.

Describe the method you would use.

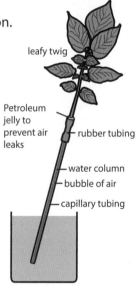

leafy twig

Petroleum jelly to prevent air leaks

rubber tubing

water column

bubble of air

capillary tubing

[7]

> **Show me**

I would time how many seconds it took for the air bubble to move 5 cm. The bubble moves as

water is taken up and lost from for the leaf by ....

I would vary the conditions so that the leaves were in warm and windy conditions and ....

the investigation with .... conditions and .... wind.

I would keep the amount of .... and the .... the same to make the

investigation a .... test.

3 ▷ Describe and explain 'transpiration pull' in detail. [7]

> 7 marks is the number of points you need to provide to give a detailed answer.
> Always read the question carefully.
> **Describe** means to outline the characteristics of something.
> **Explain** means to give reasons or a purpose.

4 ▷ When plants wilt, their stems and leaves become soft and flaccid.

Describe the cause and effect on the rate of transpiration, leading to wilting. [4]

5 ▷ Which statement describes translocation?

A. The movement of amino acids from the roots to the rest of the plant in in xylem

B. The movement of sucrose and amino acids in phloem from sources to sinks

C. The movement of starch from sink tissues to source tissues

D. The movement of water and mineral ions from the roots to the rest of the plant in xylem [1]

Circulatory systems and hearts

1 ▷ The diagram shows a cross-section of a human heart.

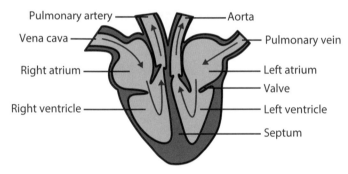

Pulmonary artery — — Aorta
Vena cava — — Pulmonary vein
Right atrium — — Left atrium
— Valve
Right ventricle — — Left ventricle
— Septum

a Describe the function of the septum which divides the left and right sides of the heart. [1]

b Explain why the left ventricle has a thicker muscular wall than the right ventricle. [3]

> Diagrams of the heart generally use an 'anatomical view'. So, when the left side of the heart is on the right, as shown in the diagram, it is shown as if you were looking directly at someone's heart. Think about when you are facing a person. Your right is their left and your left is their right.

[Total marks 4]

2 Describe the function of heart valves. [4]

> **Show me**

Valves in the heart are located between the .... and the ....

When the valves .... they prevent blood flowing in the

.... direction.

S 3 **a** Explain what is meant by the 'double circulatory system' in mammals. [3]

b Compare the speed of oxygen delivery between single circulatory systems in fish and double circulatory systems in mammals. [3]

Compare means to describe how things are similar or different, to write about both things not just one of them.

[Total marks 6]

S 4 Coronary heart disease is caused by the build-up of cholesterol on the lining of the coronary arteries. Smoking, stress, high fat diets, sedentary lifestyle, age over 50 and sex have been associated with the risk of cardiovascular disease.

Look at the bar chart which shows the relationship between coronary heart disease and exercise based on scientific studies.

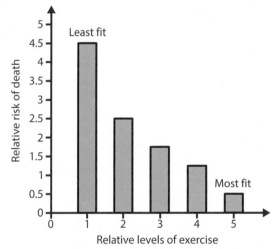

a Calculate the difference between the relative risk of dying from cardiovascular disease for least fit people compared to most fit. [1]

b Explain how heart muscle cells are affected by blockage to coronary arteries and why this causes risk of death. [3]

Remember: the number of marks awarded means you need to make that number of points in your answer.

S c The diagram shows a cross-section of the human heart. Valves are shown as pale brown flap-like structures at the base of blood vessels and between the atria and ventricles. Valves close to prevent the backflow of blood in the wrong direction.

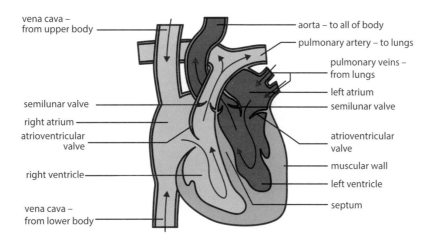

i) Explain what would happen to blood flow in the heart if the atrioventricular valve between the right atrium and ventricle failed and suggest what effect this could have on the ventricle muscle. [2]

ii) Predict what would happen to blood flow in the heart if the semilunar valve at the base of pulmonary artery, travelling to the lungs became leaky. [2]

[Total marks 8]

Blood vessels and blood

1 State the functions of white blood cells and platelets. [3]

2 Look at the photomicrograph of human blood.

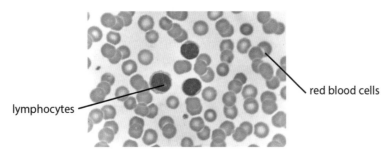

a i) What feature of red blood cells helps you identify them from the other cells in the photomicrograph? [1]

S ii) Explain why lymphocytes have a different structure compared to red blood cells. [2]

[Total marks 3]

S **3** The illustration shows a blood clot formed by red blood cells trapped in a mesh of fibrin.

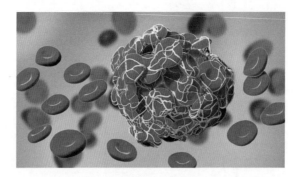

Describe the sequence of blood clot formation. [4]

> **Show me**

| The liver makes a(n) .... protein (fibrinogen) | → | Platelets in .... are transported to a damaged blood vessel | → | An enzyme from platelets changes fibrinogen into .... fibrin | → | Fibrin mesh traps .... blood cells forming a clot |

To **describe** something, you provide information about what it is. Examples include details such as appearance or structure, function, location, age, or what it is made of.

4 At high altitude (**height**) there is less oxygen in the air than at sea level. The heart has to work harder to supply oxygenated blood from the lungs to the tissues.

Scientists studied 20 climbers on a mountain expedition to investigate the effects of reduced oxygen on red blood cell production.

The top graph shows the climbers' red blood cell numbers. The graph below shows the climbers' altitude where the blood samples were taken.

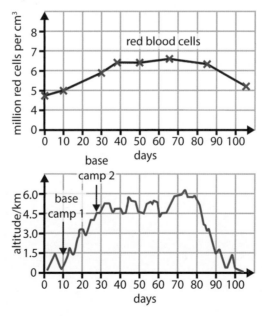

a Look at both graphs. Describe the effect of increasing altitude on the number of red blood cells in the climbers' blood. [1]

b Look at the graph showing the climbers' average red blood cell count. Between which days did the climbers' red blood cell count increase most rapidly? [1]

c Explain why the climbers' average red blood cell count increased between the periods you observed. [3]

[Total marks 5]

Diseases

1 Which statements about pathogens are correct?

1. All serious human diseases are transmissible.

2. Cholera is a disease caused by a pathogen.

3. HIV is a disease caused by a pathogen.

4. Pathogens are organisms that cause disease.

A. 1 and 3

B. 1 and 4

C. 2 and 3

D. 2 and 4 [1]

2 Humans take measures to control the spread of disease.

a Explain why hygienic food preparation is important. [1]

b Suggest **two** ways in which pathogens can be transferred by unhygienic food preparation. [2]

c List **three** other measures used to control disease. [3]

[Total marks 6]

3 Cholera is a disease transmitted in contaminated water.

a Suggest how water can be contaminated. [1]

b Explain how sufferers of cholera produce very watery faeces. [9]

You need to refer to work on osmosis to produce a full answer to the question. At Supplement level, be careful to use the correct terminology when describing osmosis. Refer to water potential, for instance, and not the concentration of water.

c Suggest what types of drugs can be used to treat cholera. Explain your answer. [2]

[Total marks 12]

4 Which of the following types of acid kills pathogens in the stomach?

A. Amino acid

B. Fatty acid

C. Hydrochloric acid

D. Lactic acid [1]

s Immunity

1 Which statements about immunity are correct?

1. Humans are not born with a fully developed immune system.

2. Immunity is achieved by antigen production by lymphocytes.

3. Immunity is the ability to resist infection by a pathogen.

4. Once immune to a disease, the immunity lasts for life.

A. 1 and 3

B. 1 and 4

C. 2 and 3

D. 2 and 4 [1]

2 Rabies is a caused by a virus spread by the bite of an infected mammal. It is a very serious illness that is almost always 100 per cent fatal in people that are unvaccinated. A person is usually only expected to live for seven days after the symptoms appear.

A person is bitten by an infected dog while on holiday.

a State why antibiotics are **not** suitable for treating rabies. [2]

b The person is given an injection of antibodies against rabies called HRIG.

Explain why the person is **not** given a normal vaccination. [2]

c HRIG is given as a dose of 20 units/kg of body mass.

The solution of HRIG available contains 300 units/cm^3.

The person's body mass is 64 kg.

Calculate the volume of HRIG the person should be given, in cm^3.

Remember that the dose given must be sufficient to control the infection. [3]

> **Show me**

The dose is 20 units/kg of body mass, and the person's body mass is 64 kg.

Therefore, the dose required = 20 × 64 = 1280 units

The concentration of HRIG in the solution is 300 units/cm^3

The volume of HRIG required = $\frac{1200}{300}$ cm^3 = ...cm 3

Set out your calculation clearly on the exam paper, even if it can be done quickly on your calculator. You may pick up marks when you show your working, even if the final answer is incorrect, and it is easier to see any errors if you do the calculation in stages.

[Total marks 7]

3 Explain how vaccines can be used to control the spread of disease. [2]

4 The graph below shows the response of a patient when receiving a vaccination against cholera.

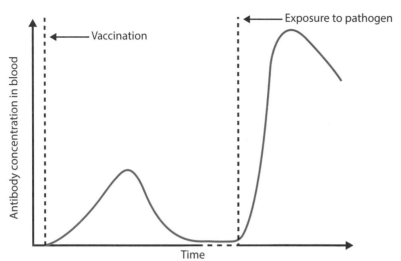

a Describe how the concentration of antibody in the blood changes as a result of vaccination and exposure to the cholera pathogen. [8]

> **Show me**

To describe changes, first comment on the antibody concentration before vaccination.

Before vaccination, the concentration of antibodies against cholera is ....

When describing the trend shown in the graph, look for the rate of change in the antibody concentrations, and the final concentrations, following vaccination and after exposure to the cholera pathogen.

Following vaccination, the concentration increases .... ,

reaches a .... ,

then falls to ....

After exposure to the cholera pathogen, the antibody concentration ....

.... and to a

.... concentration than following vaccination.

After reaching a peak, the antibody concentration then falls ....

When asked to **outline** a process in a question, you only need to set out the main points.

b Long-term protection against cholera requires a follow-up, or booster, vaccination.

Suggest two reasons why a booster is required.

[2]

[Total marks 10]

Gas exchange

Learning aims:

Syllabus links:
11.1.1–11.1.5,
S 11.1.6–11.1.11

- Identify the parts of the breathing system **S** and explain how they allow ventilation
- Describe and investigate gas exchange **S** and explain changes in air composition
- Investigate how exercise affects breathing **S** and explain how this is controlled
- **S** Explain how the breathing system is protected

The human breathing system

- The human breathing system carries and exchanges gases between the lungs and the blood.

> **Key Point**
>
> Make sure you can trace the path that air takes into and out of the lungs.

air inhaled – **inspired air** (contains oxygen for the blood)

air exhaled – **expired air** (contains carbon dioxide from the blood)

larynx – closes off the trachea when swallowing and used to make sounds

trachea – C-shaped rings of cartilage strengthen its walls and prevent collapse

bronchiole (air in and out)

blood to alveoli

blood away from alveoli

alveolus

blood capillary

rib

intercostal muscle

SUPPLEMENT **internal intercostal muscle**

SUPPLEMENT **external intercostal muscle**

group of **alveoli** at the tip of each **bronchiole**

lung

bronchus – bronchi divide into smaller branches

bronchiole (very narrow air tube)

rib

diaphragm

S The trachea

- The **epithelium** lining the **trachea** protects the breathing system
- **goblet cells** – produce **mucus** that traps pathogens, dust and pollen
- cells with **cilia** that beat and sweep the mucus to the top of the trachea, where it is swallowed or removed by coughing.

> **Key Point**
>
> The four key features of gas exchange surfaces are:
> - large surface area
> - thin surface
> - good blood supply
> - good **ventilation**.

The gas exchange surfaces

Gas exchange takes place between the **alveoli** of the **lungs** and blood **capillaries**.

S Ventilation

- **Ventilation** in humans is the movement of air into and out of the lungs.
- The **intercostal muscles** and **diaphragm** are muscular structures involved in these changes.

> **Key Point**
>
> Don't confuse breathing (musculoskeletal movements to change pressure in the thorax) and respiration (chemical process to release energy from food) with ventilation.

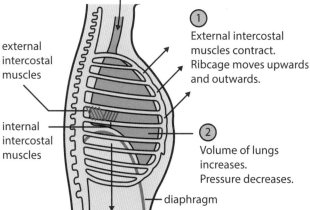

③ Pressure in lungs is lower than air. Air moves into the lungs.

① External intercostal muscles contract. Ribcage moves upwards and outwards.

external intercostal muscles

internal intercostal muscles

② Volume of lungs increases. Pressure decreases.

diaphragm

① Diaphragm contacts and moves downwards.

Inhalation

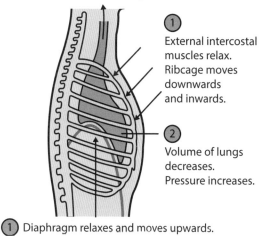

③ Pressure in lungs is higher than air. Air moves out of the lungs.

① External intercostal muscles relax. Ribcage moves downwards and inwards.

② Volume of lungs decreases. Pressure increases.

① Diaphragm relaxes and moves upwards.

Exhalation

Differences between inspired and expired air

	Proportion in (%)	
	Inspired air	Expired air
oxygen	21	16
carbon dioxide	0.04	4.5
water	variable	high

> **Key Point**
>
> The proportion of gases changes in expired air:
> - oxygen is lower as it some has been used for aerobic respiration
> - carbon dioxide is higher as it has been produced by aerobic respiration

> **Practical skills**

Investigate inspired and expired air
- limewater is turned milky by carbon dioxide
- inspired air: draw air through a boiling tube of limewater
- expired air: breathe through a tube into limewater.

Investigate breathing

Breathing rate: count the number of breaths over and period of time and convert to breaths per minute.

Depth of breathing: measure by exhaling into an upturned, water-filled container or a **spirometer**.

Investigate the effects of physical activity on the rate and depth of breathing

S Physical activity and changes to breathing
- The increased rate of respiration during exercise increases the carbon dioxide produced.
- Carbon dioxide enters the blood and the brain detects increased levels.
- Nerve impulses sent to the muscles of the **thorax** increase the rate and depth of breathing.

> **Quick Test**

1. Explain why the thickness of much of the gas exchange surface is less than 0.5 μm.

S 2. Explain how pressure changes in the thorax lead to the inspiration of air.

Aerobic and anaerobic respiration

Learning aims:

- State how organisms use energy
- Investigate and describe the respiration of yeast
- Describe aerobic and anaerobic respiration and write word and **S** symbol equations for the processes
- **S** Describe oxygen debt and outline how it is removed

Syllabus links:
12.1.1–12.1.2,
12.2.1–12.2.2,
12.3.1–12.3.4,
S 12.2.3,
12.3.5–12.3.7

Respiration

Respiration involves the breakdown of food molecules to release the energy organisms need to live.

> **Key Point**
>
> Be careful not to confuse respiration with ventilation and breathing. Types of respiration are chemical processes organisms use to release energy from food. Use the term ventilation when referring to breathing.

S Energy is needed for:

• protein synthesis	• the passage of a nerve impulse
• growth	• muscle contraction
• cell division	• maintaining a constant body temperature
• active transport	

> **Practical skills**

The effect of temperature on the respiration of yeast.

One method used to investigate respiration:

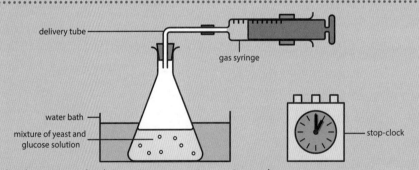

- Use a water bath to provide the temperature investigated.
- Methods to measure respiration rate include:

Method	Measurement
Connect the delivery tube to a:	
gas syringe	measure the volume of carbon dioxide over time period
boiling tube containing water	count the bubbles of carbon dioxide over time period
boiling tube containing an acid–base indicator (carbon dioxide is acidic)	measure the time for colour change

Calculate the respiration rate from the data collected.

Aerobic respiration

Aerobic respiration uses oxygen to break down glucose to release energy.

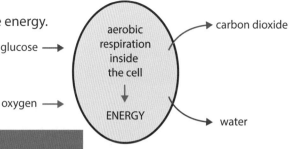

> **S** The balanced chemical equation for aerobic respiration is:

$$C_6H_{12}O_6 + 6O_2 \rightarrow 6CO_2 + 6H_2O$$

> **Key Point**
>
> The word equation for aerobic respiration and **S** the symbol equation:
> $$C_6H_{12}O_6 + 6O_2 \rightarrow 6CO_2 + 6H_2O$$
> glucose   oxygen   carbon dioxide   water

Anaerobic respiration

In **anaerobic respiration**, glucose is broken down to release energy in the absence of oxygen.

Certain organisms and tissues can respire anaerobically.

- Anaerobic energy releases much less energy than aerobic respiration.

> **Key Point**
>
> Here is a comparison of aerobic respiration and anaerobic respiration in yeast and muscle.
>
> The cells are not drawn to scale

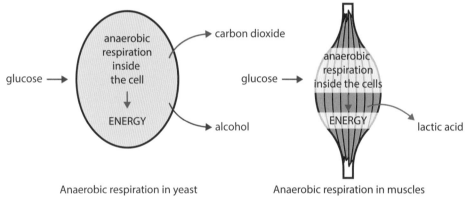

Anaerobic respiration in yeast - occurs when the oxygen runs out.

Anaerobic respiration in muscles - occurs when oxygen runs out during vigorous exercise

> **S** The balanced chemical equation for anaerobic respiration in yeast is:
>
> $$C_6H_{12}O_6 \rightarrow 2C_2H_5OH + 2CO_2$$

S Oxygen debt

Lactic acid produced by anaerobic respiration of muscle is toxic and must be removed. It is processed by the liver.

Oxygen debt is the oxygen needed to remove the lactic acid built-up. The oxygen is needed for the aerobic respiration of lactic acid.

Changes in breathing and heart rate during exercise are maintained. The increased depth and rate of breathing provides the oxygen required. Increased heart rate is continued to transport lactic acid to liver.

> **Quick Test**
>
> 1. State three reasons why organisms need energy.
> 2. State the word equations for anaerobic respiration in yeast and muscle.
> **S** 3. State the chemical (symbol) equation for anaerobic respiration in yeast.
> **S** 4. Describe how lactic acid is removed from the body after a period of exercise.

Getting rid of metabolic wastes

Syllabus links:
13.1.1–13.1.3,
S 13.1.4–13.1.9

Learning aims:

- Identify the lungs and kidneys as main organs of excretion and identify the wastes they excrete
- **S** Describe the metabolism of amino acids
- Identify the kidneys, ureters, bladder and urethra
- **S** Outline the structure and function of the kidney and nephron

Excretion

Excretion is the getting rid of waste produced by an organism's **metabolism** and substances in the body in excess of requirements.

Carbon dioxide is excreted by the **lungs**. The **kidneys** excrete **urea** and eliminate excess water and ions as urine.

> **Key Point**
>
> Do not confuse excretion with **egestion**. Egestion is the elimination of undigested food.

S Amino acid metabolism

Amino acids are:

- the product of protein **digestion**
- transported to the liver in blood following absorption
- used to synthesise most of body's proteins in the liver.

Excess amino acids cannot be stored. The nitrogen-containing part is removed by **deamination** to form urea. Urea is toxic and transported to the kidneys for removal from the body.

The excretory system in humans

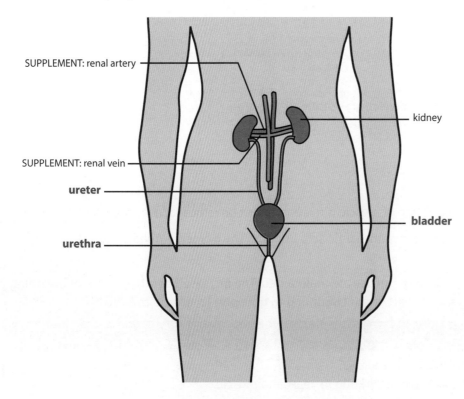

SUPPLEMENT: renal artery

kidney

SUPPLEMENT: renal vein

ureter

bladder

urethra

S The structure and function of the kidney

The structure of the kidney:

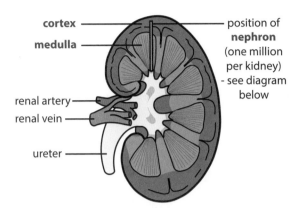

cortex
medulla
renal artery
renal vein
ureter

position of **nephron** (one million per kidney) - see diagram below

The formation and excretion of urine by the kidneys involves two processes:

- **filtration** of substances from blood in the **glomerulus** into the nephron
- **reabsorption** of useful substances back into the blood as the **filtrate** passes along the nephron.

Glucose reabsorption involves **active transport**.

Water reabsorption involves **osmosis**.

Ions are reabsorbed according to levels in the body/the body's requirements.

> **Key Point**
>
> Large molecules such as proteins, and blood cells, are not forced through the capillary walls into the nephron. They are too large to pass through. They remain in the blood.

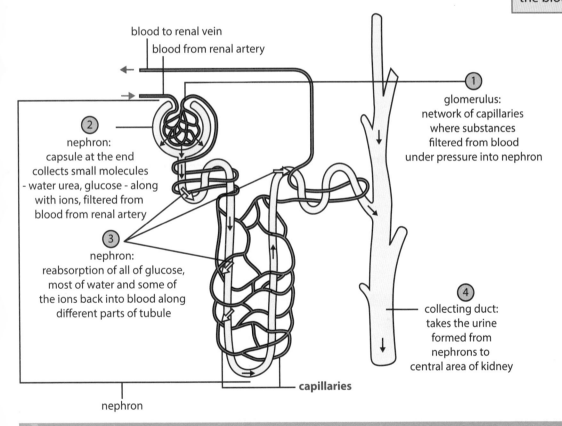

blood to renal vein
blood from renal artery

1 glomerulus: network of capillaries where substances filtered from blood under pressure into nephron

2 nephron: capsule at the end collects small molecules - water urea, glucose - along with ions, filtered from blood from renal artery

3 nephron: reabsorption of all of glucose, most of water and some of the ions back into blood along different parts of tubule

4 collecting duct: takes the urine formed from nephrons to central area of kidney

capillaries

nephron

> **Quick Test**
>
> 1. Define the term excretion.
> 2. State **two** excretory products.
> **S** 3. State **two** molecules that enter the nephron from the glomerulus.
> **S** 4. Describe the function of the liver in protein metabolism.

The nervous system

Learning aims:

Syllabus links:
14.1.1–14.1.7,
S 14.1.8–14.1.10

- Describe the structure and function of the nervous system
- State that in neurones, signals travel as electrical impulses
- Identify types of neurone
- Describe a synapse and **S** the events at a synapse as a nerve impulse is transmitted across it
- Describe the function of reflex actions and the pathway taken by nerve impulses

The nervous system

In mammals, this is made up of the **central nervous system (CNS)** and **peripheral nervous system (PNS)**.

> **Key Point**
>
> Be prepared to calculate the speed of transmission of a nerve impulse using the equation: distance = speed × time.

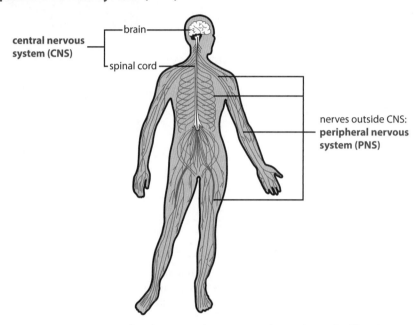

central nervous system (CNS) — brain — spinal cord

nerves outside CNS: **peripheral nervous system (PNS)**

The nervous system is involved in coordination and regulation of body activities and functions. Signals in the nervous system travel along nerve cells or **neurones** as electrical impulses.

Types of neurones:

> **Key Point**
>
> You need to recognise features to identify different types of neurone.
> Sensory neurones:
> - long dendrons
> - short axons
> - cell body between dendron and axon.
>
> Motor neurones:
> - cell body is at the start of the neurone
> - axon is long.

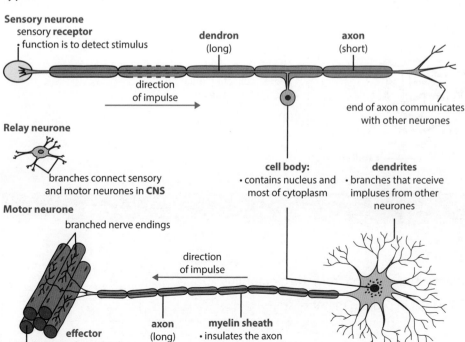

Sensory neurone
sensory **receptor**
• function is to detect stimulus

dendron (long)

axon (short)

direction of impulse

end of axon communicates with other neurones

Relay neurone
branches connect sensory and motor neurones in **CNS**

cell body:
• contains nucleus and most of cytoplasm

dendrites
• branches that receive impulses from other neurones

Motor neurone
branched nerve endings

direction of impulse

effector
• muscle or gland

axon (long)

myelin sheath
• insulates the axon

Synapses

At the junction of two or more neurones, there is a gap called a **synapse**.

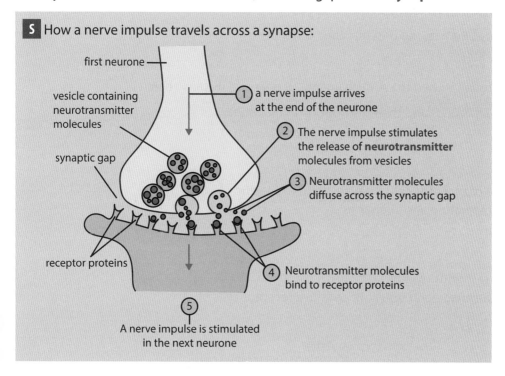

S How a nerve impulse travels across a synapse:

first neurone

vesicle containing neurotransmitter molecules

synaptic gap

receptor proteins

① a nerve impulse arrives at the end of the neurone

② The nerve impulse stimulates the release of **neurotransmitter** molecules from vesicles

③ Neurotransmitter molecules diffuse across the synaptic gap

④ Neurotransmitter molecules bind to receptor proteins

⑤ A nerve impulse is stimulated in the next neurone

> **Key Point**
>
> There is no physical contact between neurones. The lack of contact means that many neurones can communicate with each other across a synapse.

> **Key Point**
>
> Synapses ensure that nerve impulses can travel in one direction only.

Reflex actions

A **reflex action** is a rapid, automatic response to a stimulus that protects the body from damage. The pathway taken by nerve impulses during a reflex action is called a **reflex arc**.

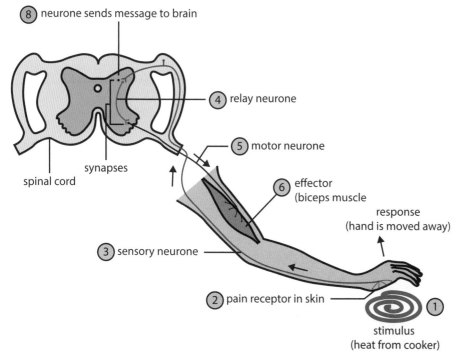

⑧ neurone sends message to brain

④ relay neurone

⑤ motor neurone

⑥ effector (biceps muscle)

synapses

spinal cord

③ sensory neurone

② pain receptor in skin

①

response (hand is moved away)

stimulus (heat from cooker)

> **Key Point**
>
> Be able to identify the components of reflex arcs not familiar to you. You may be required to suggest how the reflex action helps to prevent a person from harm or helps with their survival.

> **Key Point**
>
> **S** Be able to summarise the pathway, for instance, in a flow chart.

> **Quick Test**
>
> 1. Describe the two parts of the nervous system.
> 2. Suggest why many neurones have a myelin sheath.
> 3. Draw a flow chart to describe a reflex arc.
> **S** 4. Describe in detail the structure of a synapse.

Sense organs

Syllabus links:
14.2.1–14.2.4,
S **14.2.5–14.2.9**

Learning aims:

- Describe sense organs and the stimuli to which they respond
- Identify the main structures of the eye and describe their functions
- Explain the pupil reflex and S how it is produced
- S Explain how accommodation is used to produce images of near and distant objects
- S Explain the role of rods and cones and their distribution in the retina

Sense organs

Sense organs consist of groups of **receptor** cells. They respond to specific stimuli – light, sound, touch, temperature and chemicals.

The eye

The eye is the sense organ that responds to light.
The structures of the eye focus an image onto the light-sensitive receptor cells of the **retina**.

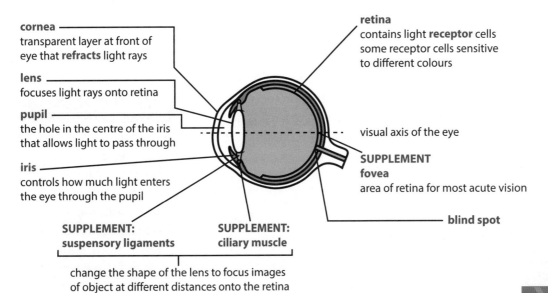

cornea
transparent layer at front of eye that **refracts** light rays

lens
focuses light rays onto retina

pupil
the hole in the centre of the iris that allows light to pass through

iris
controls how much light enters the eye through the pupil

**SUPPLEMENT:
suspensory ligaments**

**SUPPLEMENT:
ciliary muscle**

change the shape of the lens to focus images of object at different distances onto the retina

retina
contains light **receptor** cells some receptor cells sensitive to different colours

visual axis of the eye

**SUPPLEMENT
fovea**
area of retina for most acute vision

blind spot

The pupil reflex

In different light intensities, the pupil diameter can be changed to let the optimum amount of light into the eyes to produce a good image.

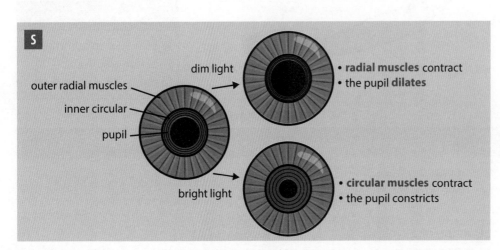

S

dim light
outer radial muscles
inner circular
pupil

- **radial muscles** contract
- the pupil **dilates**

bright light

- **circular muscles** contract
- the pupil constricts

> **Key Point**
>
> S Muscles - including those of the iris - work in pairs called antagonistic pairs.
> Contraction of one produces movement in one direction; contraction of the other produces movement in the opposite direction.

S Accommodation

A healthy eye can produce an image of distant and near objects by **accommodation**. Accommodation involves the change in shape of the lens.

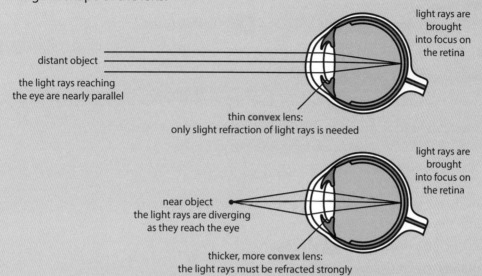

Accommodation is brought about by changes to the ciliary muscle and suspensory ligaments.

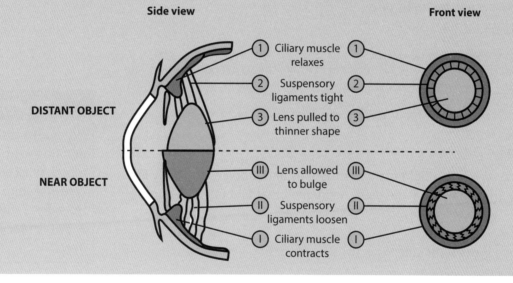

S Rods and cones

- The types of receptor cell are called **rods** and **cones**.
- Rods have greater sensitivity to light. They are responsible for night vision and concentrated away from the visual axis of the eye.
- Cones are responsible for colour vision. There are three types, sensitive to different colours. Cones are most concentrated on the visual axis of the eye and absent from the periphery.

> **Key Point**
>
> You need to be able to describe the distribution of rods and cones in the retina.

> **Quick Test**

1. Describe the term 'sense organ'.
2. State the part of the eye that has receptor cells sensitive to light.
S 3. Describe the shape of the lens when viewing a ship on the horizon.
S 4. Explain why:
   a) in a darkened room, objects can be seen best from the corner of our eyes
   b) human peripheral (at the edges) vision is in black and white.

Hormones and homeostasis

Learning aims:

Syllabus links:
14.3.1–14.3.4,
S 14.3.5–14.3.6,
14.4.1–14.4.2,
S 14.4.3–14.4.8

- Describe the term hormone and identify the endocrine glands that produce them
- Describe the effects of adrenaline on the body and **S** its metabolism
- State and **S** describe how blood glucose concentration is controlled by insulin and glucagon **S**
- **S** Outline the treatment of type 1 diabetes
- Describe the term homeostasis and **S** explain how negative feedback is involved
- **S** Describe methods used to maintain a constant internal body temperature.

Hormones

- **Hormones** are chemical substances produced by **endocrine glands**. They are secreted into the blood.
- the **pancreas** – secretes **insulin** and **S** **glucagon**
- the **adrenal glands** – secrete **adrenaline**
- the **ovaries** – secrete **oestrogen**
- the **testes** – secrete **testosterone**.
- location of endocrine glands.

S The endocrine and nervous systems are both involved in coordination and control. Effects of hormones are usually slower and last over a longer period of time.

Adrenaline

- Adrenaline secreted in 'fight or flight situations' and prepares the body for rapid, emergency action. It increases heart and breathing rate and pupil diameter – the pupil dilates

S Adrenaline increases metabolic activity by increasing:

- blood glucose concentration
- heart rate, to transport glucose and oxygen to muscles.

> **Key Point**
>
> Hormones are carried around the body in the blood, so all organs will be exposed to them. Hormones affect the activity of **target organs** only.

Homeostasis

Homeostasis: the maintenance of a constant environment in the body.

S Conditions are maintained at a required level or range. This is called the **set point**. The set point is often controlled by **negative feedback**. If an increase or decrease is detected in a substance such as glucose, or condition such as body temperature, the body takes action to restore the set point value.

Control of blood glucose concentration

- Involves insulin – which lowers blood glucose concentration – **S** and glucagon
- **S** Insulin:
- secreted when blood glucose concentration rises.
- encourages uptake of glucose by liver and its conversion into glycogen.

Glucagon:

- secreted when blood glucose concentration falls.
- encourages conversion of glycogen into glucose in liver and its release into blood.

Type 1 diabetes results when the pancreas not producing enough insulin. Type 1 diabetes cannot currently be cured but can be managed, by:

- monitoring blood glucose concentration
- insulin injection or insulin pump.

S The skin and homeostasis

- The structure of the skin.

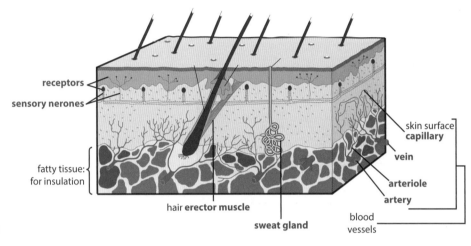

S Controlling body temperature

- Fatty tissue below skin is permanent feature – acts as insulation to reduce heat loss.
- If body gets to hot or cold, receptors detect temperature changes and the brain coordinates the response.If the body gets too hot:
- arterioles in skin dilate (**vasodilation**) ❶ ….. blood flow through skin surface capillaries increased ❷….. more heat is lost ❸.
- sweating is increased ….. evaporation of water from skin's surface transfers energy away from body.

  If the body gets too cold:
- arterioles in skin constrict (**vasoconstriction**) ❶….. blood flow through the skin surface capillaries decreased ❷….. less heat lost ❸.
- sweating decreased ….. reduced evaporation of water from skin's surface and energy transfer from body.
- shivering – heat released by involuntary contraction of muscles warms body.

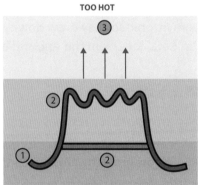

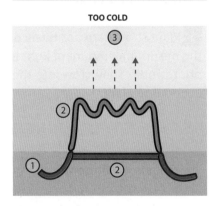

> ## Quick Test

1. Define the term hormone.
2. Describe **one** effect of adrenaline on breathing.
S 3. Draw a diagram to show how insulin and glucagon control blood glucose concentration as it changes from the set point value.
4. Describe how the human body responds to increased temperature.

Tropic responses

Syllabus links:
14.5.1–14.5.3,
S 14.5.4–14.5.5

Learning aims:

- Describe and **S** explain gravitropism and phototropism
- Investigate gravitropism and phototropism
- **S** Explain the role of auxin in controlling shoot growth

Gravitropism

Gravitropism is a response by plants to gravity. Different parts of the plant grow towards gravity, some away from gravity.

- Roots grow towards gravity – they show **positive gravitropism**.
- Shoots grow away from gravity – they show **negative gravitropism**.

> **Key Point**
>
> In all tropisms, parts of a plant grow in a particular direction to the **stimulus**.

S Plant shoots are negatively gravitropic. They grow upwards to obtain the maximum amount of light for photosynthesis. Plant roots are positively gravitropic so they grow downwards. This enables them to obtain water and mineral ions from the soil, and anchors them in the soil.

Phototropism

Phototropism is a response by plants to light. Different parts of the plant grow towards light, some away from light.

- Shoots grow towards light – they show **positive phototropism**.
- Roots grow away from light – they show **negative phototropism**.

S Plant shoots are positively phototropic. They grow upwards to obtain the maximum amount of light for photosynthesis. Plant roots are negatively phototropic. They grow into the soil to obtain water and mineral ions, and to anchor the plant.

> **Practical skills**
>
> Investigate gravitropism
>
> ....
>
> Place germinated seedlings or a plant at different orientations. Observe the seedling/plant over a period of time. Carry out the experiment in the dark to avoid any influence of phototropism.
>
> Investigate phototropism
>
> ....
>
> Place germinated seedlings or a plant in a box - painted black on the inside to reduce reflection of light - with a window cut in one side. Observe the seedlings/plant over a period of time. The angle of curvature of the shoots could be measured.

S Auxins and shoot growth in phototropism

Plant hormones called **auxins** are responsible for the chemical control of plant growth:

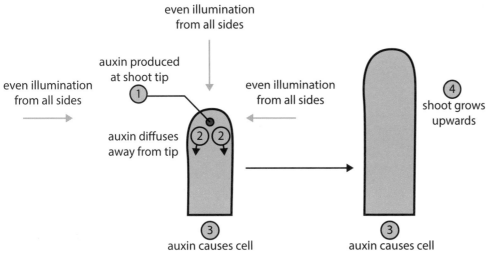

If illumination is from one side, auxin is redistributed:

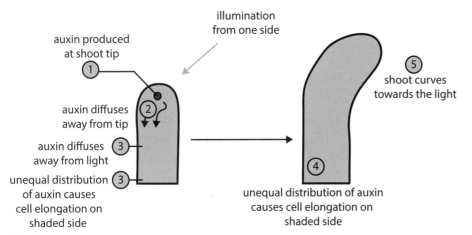

> **Key Point**
>
> Tropisms are examples of how chemicals – in this case, auxins – control plant growth.

S Auxins and shoot growth in gravitropism

Auxin becomes redistributed in gravitropism:

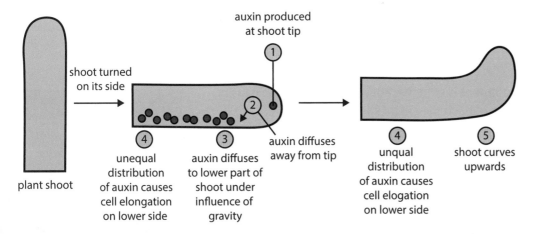

> **Quick Test**
>
> 1. What is the name of a plant's response to gravity?
> S 2. Explain how auxin controls a plant shoot's response to light.

Drugs and medicines

Syllabus links:
15.1.1–15.1.4,
S **15.1.5**

Learning aims:

- Describe a drug
- Describe the use of antibiotics in the treatment of bacterial infections
- State that some bacteria are resistant to antibiotics, reducing their effectiveness, and **S** explain how the development of resistant bacteria can be limited

Drugs

A **drug** is any substance taken into the body that affects or modifies chemical reactions taking place in the body.

Antibiotics

Antibiotics:

- are drugs used to treat infections caused by bacteria
- are taken orally, by a drip into a vein or by injection
- work by killing bacteria or slowing down their growth
- are taken as a course over five days or more.

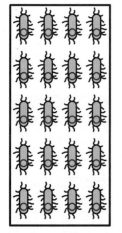

Population of bacteria

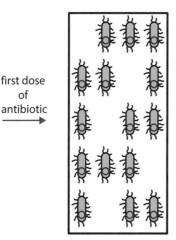

Bacteria most sensitive to antibiotic killed

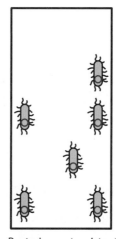

Bacteria most resistant antibiotic not all killed

course of antibiotic is complete

The population of bacteria is killed

first dose of antibiotic → further dose of antibiotic →

Some antibiotics are effective against a wide range of bacteria. Others are effective against specific bacteria.

If the antibiotic chosen for treatment is effective against the bacterium causing the infection, all the population of bacteria will be killed.

Antibiotic resistance

Resistance to antibiotics can develop in populations of bacteria. This resistance reduces the effectiveness of the antibiotic.

- **S** excessive and inappropriate use of antibiotics applies selection pressure for populations of bacteria to develop resistance.

> **Key Point**
>
> Antibiotics will not affect other infectious agents such as viruses because of the way antibiotics work. They should not be used in treating this type of infection.

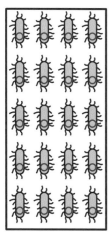

Original population
of bacteria

rapid
reproductive
rate

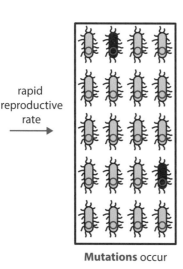

Mutations occur

antibiotic use
leads to
'**natural**'
selection

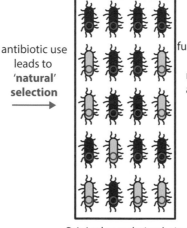

Original population being
killed. Bacteria with
mutations giving resistance
to antibiotic will survive

further, excessive
and
non-essential
antibiotic use

rapid
reproductive
rate

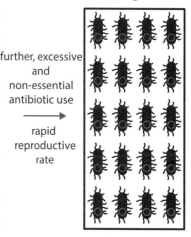

Antibiotic resistance
has spread through the
population of bateria

S In the topic on Selection (on pages 110–111), you also cover how the development of these resistant strains of bacteria is an example of 'natural' selection.

MRSA is one kind of antibiotic-resistant bacterium. The initials MRSA stand for methicillin-resistant *Staphylococcus aureus*, but strains of the bacterium are now resistant to a wider range of antibiotics.

Antibiotics should be used only when essential and not for minor infections. More limited use will limit/slow down the development of resistance.

> ### Key Point
>
> **S** The development of antibiotic resistance will happen anyway. It is their overuse that speeds up the development of bacteria resistant to them.

> ### Quick Test
>
> 1. Describe a drug.
> 2. Describe how antibiotics are used to treat an infection.
> **S** 3. Explain why it is essential to complete a course of antibiotics.

Gas exchange

1 The following shows the breathing system in humans.

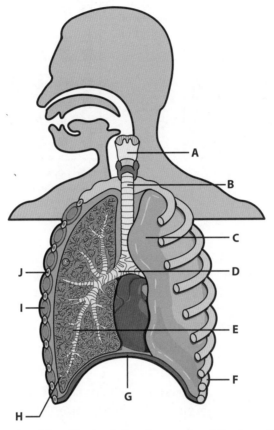

Give the **letters** from the diagram that identify the following parts of the breathing system:

a a bronchus [1]

b the diaphragm [1]

c the trachea [1]

[Total marks 3]

2 A student set up the apparatus shown to investigate the difference between the carbon dioxide concentration in inspired and expired air.

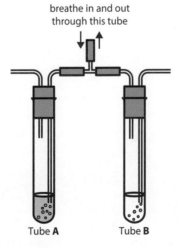

a State the name of the liquid in tubes **A** and **B**. [1]

b The liquid is an irritant.

Suggest **one** safety precaution that could be used when using this liquid. [1]

c Which tube, **A** or **B**, represents the change produced by expired air? Explain your answer. [2]

[Total marks 4]

In questions with a choice between two responses – A or B, or True or False – you are unlikely to get a mark for your choice. It must be correct – unless you could justify it fully – but marks will be awarded for your explanation.

3 One estimate of the total surface area of the alveoli in the human lungs is 70 m^2.

The total surface area of the capillaries supplying the alveoli is estimated at 49 m^2.

a **Suggest** why these values are estimates. [1]

You have not been taught how scientists can measure the surface area of structures in the human body. You must use your knowledge and understanding of lung structure to make a sensible judgment based on this to **suggest** an answer.

b Calculate the percentage surface area of the alveoli that provide exchange surfaces. [2]

Show all your working out. You will be awarded marks for this even if the final answer is incorrect.

> **Show me**

The exchange surface is provided by the contact between the capillaries and the alveoli, so:

percentage surface area of the alveoli for exchange = $\dfrac{\text{area of the capillaries}}{\text{area of the alveoli}} \times 100$

$= \dfrac{\text{..........}}{\text{..........}} \times 100$

$= \text{..........} \%$

c Describe **three** features of the surfaces that make gas exchange efficient. [3]

[Total marks 6]

4 Muscles of the thorax produce the changes that bring about breathing.

a Explain the role of the intercostal muscles and diaphragm during expiration. [6]

b Produce a **sketch** of the thorax identifying the position of the intercostal muscles. [4]

c Explain the differences in rate and depth of breathing when at rest or exercising. [6]

[Total marks 16]

Aerobic and anaerobic respiration

1 ▶ Which of the following statements about energy and respiration is correct?

Tick **one** box.

Respiration involves the release of energy from food using oxygen. ☐

Energy is required to transport substances against a concentration gradient. ☐

The products of respiration are carbon dioxide and oxygen. ☐

Lactic acid is a product of the respiration of yeast. ☐

[1]

2 ▶ The rate of respiration of many organisms can be measured using a respirometer.

A student sets up a respirometer to measure the respiration of germinating seeds. The apparatus includes potassium hydroxide solution to absorb the carbon dioxide produced.

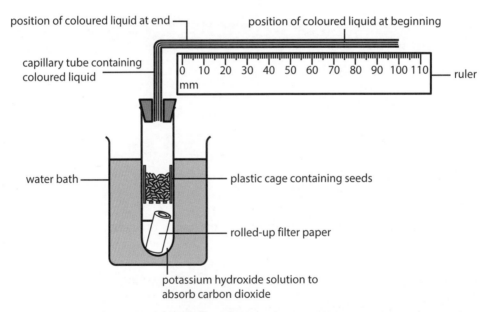

a Suggest why the seeds are placed in a plastic cage. [1]

b Explain why a rolled-up piece of filter paper was placed in the boiling tube. [2]

c The distance moved by a drop of red liquid over 40 minutes was 72 mm.

Calculate the rate of movement of the drop in mm per hour. [3]

d The internal diameter of the capillary tube is 1 mm.

Calculate the rate of respiration, as the volume of oxygen used per hour, using the formula:

volume of oxygen used per hour = rate of movement of drop (from part **c**) × area of capillary tube   [4]

[Total marks 10]

3 Compare aerobic and anaerobic respiration in humans.   [3]

Remember that **compare** means that you should look at similarities as well as differences.

Getting rid of metabolic wastes

1 Which of the following statements about excretion is correct?

Tick **one** box.

Oxygen is an excretory product of the lungs.   ☐

Urea is excreted by the kidneys in urine.   ☐

Urine is taken to the exterior by the ureter.   ☐

Inspired air is taken to the exterior by the trachea.   ☐

[1]

2 The table shows the concentration of dissolved substances as they move from the blood through the kidney and into the urine.

Substance	concentration (g/dm^3)		
	blood plasma	kidney filtrate	urine
water	910.00	990.00	960.00
proteins	80.00	0.00	0.00
glucose	1.00	0.10	0.00
ions	7.50	7.50	15.00
urea	0.30	0.30	20.00

a Identify the substances found in blood plasma but not in the urine.   [2]

b How many times more concentrated is the urea in the urine compared with the urea in the blood plasma?

Show your working.   [2]

c Explain why:

i) no proteins are found in the kidney filtrate [2]

ii) glucose is found in the kidney filtrate but not in the urine. [2]

d In a hospital patient, the rate of production of filtrate from the blood plasma is measured at 120 cm^3 per minute.

Calculate the volume of filtrate, in dm^3, the patient produces in one day. [2]

> **Show me**

The rate given is per minute, so this needs to be converted to a value per hour, then per day.

rate per day = 120 × 60 × 24 = ... cm^3/day

The question requires an answer in dm^3.

1 dm^3 = 1000 cm^3

Therefore, the volume of filtrate the patient produces in one day is the volume calculated divided by 1000.

Check carefully the units you need to give your answer in. Here, you must convert cm^3 to dm^3.

[Total marks 10]

The nervous system

1 Describe the **two** roles of the nervous system. [2]

2 The diagram shows the structure of a neurone.

a Give the letters from the diagram that identify the following parts of the neurone:

i) axon [1]

ii) dendrite [1]

iii) cell body [1]

b State the effector shown by letter **E**. [1]

c Identify the type of neurone shown in the diagram. Explain the reason for your decision. [3]

[Total marks 7]

4 Synapses occur at the junction between neurones. Describe the events that occur at a synapse during the transmission of a nerve impulse.

[5]

5 The diagram shows a person's response when their hand is placed on a hot object.

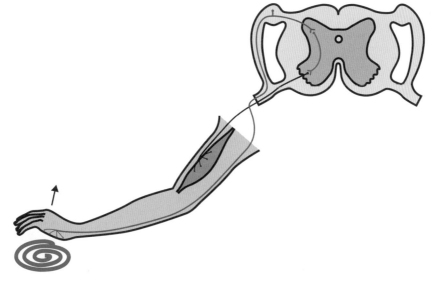

a Describe how the parts of a reflex arc bring about this response.

[8]

b A group of students investigates the speed of nerve impulses.

i) A nerve impulse in the reflex shown took 0.02 seconds to travel from the hand to the spinal cord. The distance of the spinal cord from the receptors in the hand is 0.8 metres.

Calculate the speed of transmission of the nerve impulse in metres per second.

Use the equation:

$$\text{speed} = \frac{\text{distance}}{\text{time}}$$ [2]

> **Show me**

Using the equation:

$$\text{speed} = \frac{\text{distance}}{\text{time}} = \frac{0.8}{0.02} = \text{........................}$$

ii) The students also investigated the transmission of nerve impulses in a neurone of a frog.

The time taken for the nerve impulse to travel along the neurone was 1.5 milliseconds.

The nerve impulse travelled at 30 m/s.

Calculate the length of the neurone in millimetres (mm).

Show your working. [4]

[Total marks 14]

Sense organs

1 State the five stimuli that human sense organs can detect. [2]

2 The diagram shows the human eye.

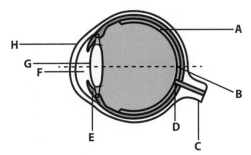

a State the name of:

i) Layer A [1]

ii) Layer H. [1]

b Give the **letters** from the diagram that identify the

i) structures of the eye that refract light rays [1]

ii) structure that carries nerve impulses to the brain. [1]

[Total marks 4]

3 A person walks along a dark street at night and looks into a brightly-lit shop window.

Describe in detail the changes that occur to the iris and pupil. [7]

4 A healthy eye can focus on near and distant objects.

a **Sketch** a diagram to show how the eye focuses light rays from a near object.

Add labels to include the key points. [4]

A sketch is a simple freehand drawing to show the key points. Its features must, however, be in the correct proportions to be meaningful.

b A person reading a book in a garden looks into the sky to watch an aeroplane.

Explain how the person focuses a sharp image of the aeroplane. [5]

[Total marks 9]

5 The graph shows the distribution of rods and cones in a human eye to the left and right of the central axis (0°).

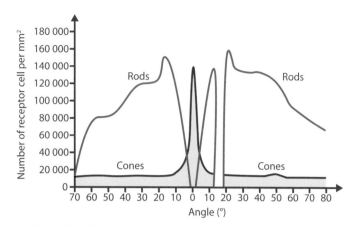

Be careful not to misread the graph when answering this question. It is referring to the number of cones, and not the greatest number of receptor cells, which are rods at 20 °.

a For the cones in the person's eye:

i) State the angle at which the cones are most concentrated. [1]

ii) What is the number of cones found at the point where they are most concentrated?

Give your answer in standard form. [2]

Standard form numbers are written as $A \times 10^n$
Where: A is a number greater than 1 but less than 10.
        It could be decimal number, such as A = 1.8
        or it could be an integer number, such as A = 1.
        If a question requires an answer using standard form, make sure you use it correctly, or you could lose marks.

b The blind spot is the point at which the nerves from receptor cells merge to form the optic nerve. It has no light sensitive cells.

From the graph, suggest the position of the blind spot.

From angle .... to angle .... [3]

c The figure below shows the distribution of receptor cells of the human retina in diagrammatic form.

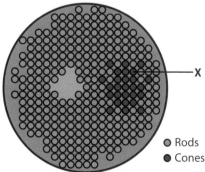

i) On a copy of the figure, mark the position of the blind spot. [1]

ii) State the name of the structure X.

Explain your answer. [2]

[Total marks 9]

Hormones and homeostasis

1 Complete the paragraph using words from the following list:

blood   chemical   electrical
longer   rapid   slower

The nervous system and endocrine system are both involved in the human body's coordination and response.

The nervous system uses .... impulses to communicate. The endocrine

system uses .... substances, secreted into the ....

The responses of the nervous system are ...., while those of the endocrine

system are .... and usually last for a .... period of time.   **[6]**

2 In which endocrine gland is the hormone insulin made?

Tick **one** box.

Adrenal gland ☐

Ovary ☐

Pancreas ☐

Testis ☐

[1]

3 Which letter best matches the effects of adrenaline on the human body?

	Blood glucose concentration	Heart rate	Pupil size
A	decreases	increases	constricts
B	increases	decreases	constricts
C	increases	increases	dilates
D	decreases	increases	dilates

[1]

4 Describe how the human body responds when the body temperature falls.   **[8]**

5 Two patients are thought to be diabetic. They attend a clinic for testing.

Before attending the clinic, medical staff tell the patients to fast for 10 hours. On arrival, staff monitor the concentration of glucose in each patient's blood before the test.

Each patient drinks a solution of glucose. The staff then monitor the patients' blood glucose concentration for several hours.

The results of the tests are shown below.

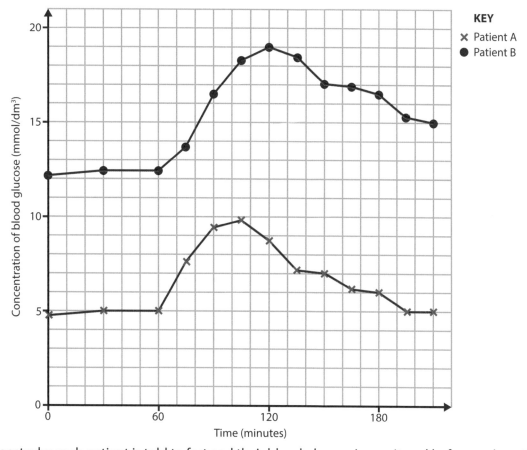

a Suggest why each patient is told to fast and their blood glucose is monitored before undergoing the test. [2]

b Suggest the time at which the glucose solution is drunk. [1]

c For Patient B, what is the concentration of glucose in the person's blood before drinking the glucose solution? [2]

d **Explain** in detail the changes in blood glucose concentration of patient A. [6]

Explain means to give reasons for events that occurred. Several different trends can be seen in the data over the 210 minutes of monitoring. You should describe, then explain, each, if you are asked to explain something in detail, along with the relevant numerical detail, if possible.

e The medical team concludes that one of the patients has type 1 diabetes.

Which person is more likely to be diabetic? Explain your answer. [1]

[**Total marks 12**]

Tropic responses

1 ▸ A student is investigating the effect of gravity on seedlings of maize.

When the seeds have germinated, the student transfers a seedling to an instrument called a klinostat. The instrument rotates, so the seedling is exposed to gravity equally from all directions. The effects of gravity are neutralised.

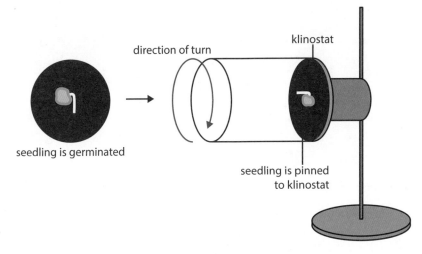

The seedling is pinned to the klinostat so that its root is horizontal.

Predict what will happen to the seedling over the next few days. Explain your answer.　　　[2]

You probably have not used a klinostat in the school lab. **Predict** means to suggest what will happen in the experiment from your knowledge and understanding of gravitropism and the information provided.

2 ▸ Which statements about auxins are correct?

1　Auxin causes cell elongation.

2　Auxin is made at shoot tips only.

3　Auxin is one chemical involved in the control of plant growth.

4　Auxin moves around the plant in the xylem.

A.　1 and 3

B.　1 and 4

C.　2 and 3

D.　2 and 4　　　[1]

3 ▸ A student sets up an experiment to study phototropism.

The student places a newly-germinated seedling into a black plastic canister lined with absorbent foam to keep the seedling moist. The student had cut a window in the canister to allow light to pass through.

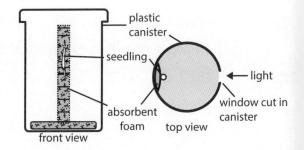

The student then illuminates the plant.

Every 30 minutes, the student opens the canister and measures the angle of the plant stem using a protractor.

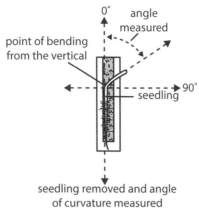

The student's results are shown in the table below.

Time (minutes)	0	30	60	90	120	150	180	210	240
Mean angle of curvature (°)	5	7	9	13	23	39	53	63	70

a Draw a graph of the student's results. [4]

> **Show me**

When drawing graphs, the independent variable almost always goes on the x-axis. The dependent variable – what is being measured – goes on the y-axis.

Label the axes clearly, using identical wording, or sometimes slightly shortened versions, of the headings used in the table of data. Units must be included where appropriate.

Use suitable scales. Work in 1s, 2s, 5s, 10s, 20s, etc. That way, you can work out easily the value of one of the smallest divisions.

The scales you use must be linear – the divisions on the axes represent equal values.

The data you plot should occupy at least half the grid in both directions.

Plot the data accurately. It should be within ± half a small square on your grid.

Then draw a suitable line of best fit. Decide whether the line of best fit should be a straight line or curve.

Do not extend the line of best fit to areas of a graph where data have not been collected – unless you're asked to do so.

b Describe the trend in the data. [3]

c **Suggest** explanations for the trend in the data. [3]

[Total marks 10]

4 Root growth is inhibited by all but very low concentrations of auxin.

Roots are positively gravitropic.

Produce an annotated sketch that explains what happens when a plant root is turned on its side. [6]

5 In the 20th century, plant physiologists in Europe carried out many experiments on phototropism.

a In one experiment, the tip was cut off a plant shoot and a block of gelatine placed between the tip and the stump.

Gelatine is a jelly-like substance that allows the diffusion of water-soluble molecules.

The shoot tip was evenly illuminated.

The diagram summarises the experiment and the response of the plant.

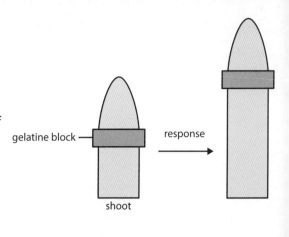

Explain what this tells us about the way in which auxins control plant growth. [4]

b In another experiment, a thin flake of the mineral, mica, was placed in a cut that was made half-way across a plant shoot. Mica prevents the movement of water-soluble molecules.

The plant was illuminated from one side.

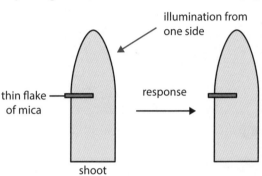

Explain the results fully.

[4]
[Total marks 8]

Drugs and medicines

1 Which statements about drugs are correct?

1 A drug can be any chemical that has an effect on the human body.

2 All human diseases are caused by pathogens.

3 Conservation work is essential as many new drugs are extracted from plants and animals.

4 The term, 'drug', mainly applies to chemicals used as medicines.

A. 1 and 3

B. 1 and 4

C. 2 and 3

D. 2 and 4 [1]

2 Antibiotics are drugs used to treat infections.

a Some antibiotics are designed to slow down the growth of bacteria and not kill them.

Suggest how this helps in the treatment of infections caused by bacteria. [1]

b Suggest **two** circumstances where it is **inappropriate** to give antibiotics against an infection. [2]
[Total marks 3]

3 The scattergraph shows the relationship between the use of an antibiotic called penicillin and resistance to the antibiotic in the bacterium that causes pneumonia. The data are from 18 European countries.

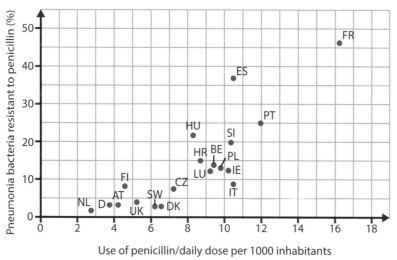

Key
AT = Austria
BE = Belgium
CZ = Czech Republic
D = Germany
DK = Denmark
ES = Spain
FI = Finland
FR = France
HR = Croatia
HU= Hungary
IE = Ireland
IT = Italy
LU = Luxembourg
NL = The Netherlands
PL = Poland
PT = Portugal
SI = Slovenia
SW = Sweden
UK = UK (England only)

a In which country is antibiotic use:

i) the lowest? [1]

ii) the highest? [1]

b What percentage of pneumonia bacteria are resistant to penicillin in Finland? [1]

c Describe the relationship between penicillin use and resistance of the bacterium that causes pneumonia. [3]

> **Show me**

Begin by describing the general trend.

As the daily dose of penicillin (per 1000 inhabitants) ...., the percentage of resistant

pneumonia bacteria ....

Then look for data, called outliers, that do not fit the pattern.

Looking at the pattern in the data, the percentage of resistant pneumonia bacteria for particular doses of penicillin is higher than would be/might be expected in ....

d In some countries, antibiotics can be bought 'over the counter', without a prescription.

i) Suggest **one** country where this practice may occur. [1]

ii) Since the data were collected, some countries have increased their restrictions on the use of antibiotics.

Predict what would happen if antibiotic use continued unchanged. [1]

e Describe how resistance to an antibiotic develops in bacteria. [4]

[Total marks 12]

Reproduction in plants

Learning aims:

- Describe asexual and sexual reproduction
- Describe how the structure of a flower is adapted to the method of pollination
- Describe pollination, fertilisation and germination
- **S** Compare asexual and sexual reproduction
- **S** Compare self-pollination and cross-pollination

Syllabus links:
16.1.1–16.1.2,
16.2.1–16.2.2,
16.3.1–16.3.8, 16.1.3,
16.2.3–16.2.4,
S 16.3.9–16.3.12

Asexual and sexual reproduction

In **asexual reproduction**, offspring are genetically identical to the one parent. Examples include:

Very small animals, like aphids, can also reproduce asexually.

Sexual reproduction involves two parents. It happens in most plants and animals. Offspring are genetically different from each parent.

> **S** Each parent produces a **gamete**. When two different gametes meet, the nuclei fuse to form a **zygote**. This is **fertilisation**. Genetic information from the parents is mixed, causing variation.
>
> Animal gametes are **sperm** and **eggs**.

> **S** Nuclei of gametes are **haploid.** When gametes fuse, the zygote nucleus is **diploid**.

> **Key Point**
>
> Genetically identical offspring can look different if they live in different environmental conditions.

> **Key Point**
>
> Flowering plant gametes are **pollen** and **ovules**.

> **Key Point**
>
> Make sure you know the difference between reproduction and fertilisation.

Advantages and disadvantages

In **asexual reproduction** large numbers of offspring are produced very quickly that are all suited to their environment, but they may not be suited to other environments and environmental change will affect them all.

In **sexual reproduction** offspring may tolerate other environments and some may tolerate changes to their environment, but fewer offspring are produced, and some may not tolerate their environment in a slower process.

Asexual reproduction is used to produce many identical crop plants quickly, which all have known features (for example, good flavour, what pesticides are needed).

Sexual reproduction creates variety. It is used in **selective breeding** to create new varieties of crop plants, which have certain desirable features.

Plant reproduction

All flowers have the same structure.

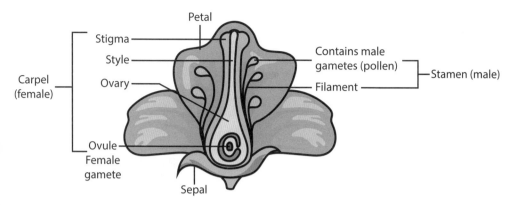

Transfer of pollen from the anther to the stigma by **pollinators** is **pollination**.

Feature	Wind pollination	Insect pollination
Pollen grains	Large amounts of small, smooth, lightweight pollen	Smaller amounts, larger, heavier pollen with sticky or spiked walls
Stigmas	Large feathery often outside flower to catch pollen	Small; inside flower
Anthers	Many, large, often outside flower for easy dispersal	Fewer, smaller, usually inside flower
Nectaries	None	Produce nectar (attracts insects)
Petals	Small or none (easier pollen dispersal).	Large for insects to land on
Colour	Usually green	Bright, colourful (attracts insects)
Scent	none	Scented (attracts insects)

The pollen nucleus fuses with the ovule nucleus during fertilisation.

	Self-pollination	Cross-pollination
Pollen	transferred to the stigma of the same flower or another flower of the same plant	transferred by a pollinator to the stigma of a flower on a different plant of the same species
Gametes	all come from the same parent	come from different parents

S **Self-pollination** is when pollen is transferred to the stigma of the same flower or another flower of the same plant. Gametes all come from the same parent.

Cross-pollination is when pollen is transferred by a pollinator to the stigma of a flower on a different plant of the same species. Gametes come from different parents.

> **Quick Test**

1. **a)** Describe asexual reproduction.
   S **b)** Give one advantage and one disadvantage of asexual reproduction.
2. State the name of the process when a male gamete fuses with a female gamete.
3. Give three features of wind-pollinated pollen grains.

Reproduction in humans

Syllabus links:
16.4.1–16.4.8,
S 16.4.9–16.4.10

Learning aims:

- Identify the parts and their functions of the male and female reproductive systems

- Compare male and female gametes and explain their adaptive features

- Describe development of the zygote into an embryo and then fetus

- **S** Describe the role of the umbilical cord and placenta in the exchange of materials to and from the fetus

Reproductive organs

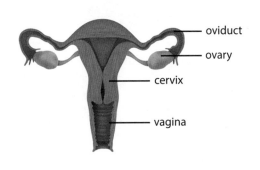
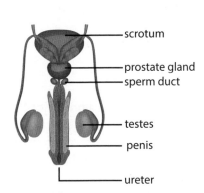

> **Key Point**
>
> The bladder is not part of the reproductive system.

Male organ	Function	Female organ	Function
Testes	Produce sperm	**Ovary**	Produces egg cells
Scrotum	Protect and allow testes to be cooler than body temperature	**Oviduct**	Carry eggs from ovary to the uterus (in which fertilisation occurs)
Sperm ducts	Carry sperm from testes to penis	**Uterus**	Protects and nourishes the zygote/embryo/fetus. Sperm swim through it to reach the oviduct
Prostate gland	Produce fluid to help sperm swim	**Cervix**	Sperm swim up the cervix to the uterus. It widens during birth
Ureter	Tube that sperm leave penis in	**Vagina**	Sperm is released here during sexual intercourse
Penis	Releases sperm into vagina during sexual intercourse		

Sperm and eggs

Sperm have many **mitochondria** to provide energy for the **flagellum** to propel the sperm. Enzymes released by the **acrosome** digest the jelly coat around the egg so the sperm nucleus can enter the egg for fertilisation to happen.

The egg is protected by the jelly coat around it that changes at fertilisation. It also contains food (energy) stores for the developing zygote.

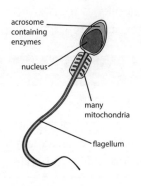
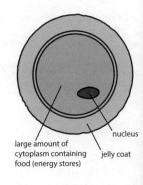

	Sperm (male gamete)	Egg (female gamete)
Size	One of smallest cells (45 micrometres)	One of the largest cells (0.2 mm)
Motility	Swim using flagellum	Cannot move but are wafted along the oviduct by **cilia**
Numbers	Millions produced each day	Ovary contains thousands but usually one released every month at **ovulation**

After fertilisation, the zygote forms a ball of cells called an **embryo**. The embryo **implants** in the uterus lining. After 12 weeks **gestation**, the major organs are formed and the embryo is now called a **fetus.**

> **Key Point**
>
> Fertilisation is the fusion of the nuclei in the gametes (male sperm and female eggs).

The fetus

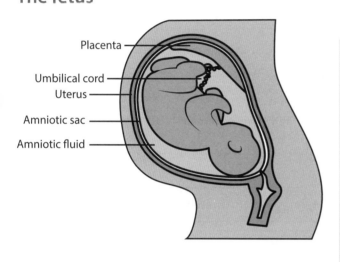

Placenta
Umbilical cord
Uterus
Amniotic sac
Amniotic fluid

Structure	Function
Umbilical cord	Joins placenta to the fetus
Placenta	Allows exchange of materials between mother and fetus
Amniotic sac	Contains amniotic fluid and holds it around the developing fetus
Amniotic fluid	Protects embryo and helps to keep temperature stable

S The circulatory system of the fetus in the placenta and the circulatory system in the mother's uterus wall are not joined. Dissolved substances are exchanged between the blood of the mother and the blood of the fetus:

- Dissolved nutrients and oxygen diffuse from the mother to the fetus.
- Excretory products (including carbon dioxide) diffuse from the fetus to the mother.

Some pathogens and toxins can pass across the placenta and affect the fetus, for example rubella virus, drugs, medicines, alcohol and nicotine.

> **Quick Test**
>
> 1. State the functions of (a) the testes (b) the ovary (c) the oviduct.
> 2. Look at the diagram.
>   a) Name parts **A**, **B** and **C**.
>   b) What is the function of parts **A** and **C**?
> **S** 3. Describe the functions of the placenta.

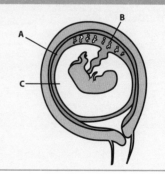

Sex hormones and sexually transmitted infections

Syllabus links:
16.5.1–16.5.2,
S 16.5.3–16.5.4 ,
16.6.1–16.6.5

Learning aims:

- Describe the role of some sex hormones in the body
- **S** Explain the role of some hormones in controlling the menstrual cycle and pregnancy
- Describe HIV as an example of an STI and explain how the spread of these infections is controlled

Sex hormones during puberty

Puberty is when a child develops into an adult (between the ages 10 to 16). Puberty causes a growth spurt, increased muscle development, reproductive organs to grow and develop and underarm and pubic hair to grow. The changes are controlled mainly by two sex hormones:

- **Testosterone** is produced by boys in the testes.
- **Oestrogen** is produced by girls in the ovaries.

Changes during puberty	
Boys	**Girls**
Voice deepens	Hips get wider
Facial and body hair grows	Breasts develop
Testes start producing sperm	Ovaries start producing eggs and the **menstrual cycle** starts

The menstrual cycle is a sequence of changes that take place about every 28 days.

The cycle starts with bleeding called **menstruation (period)** . The ovaries release an egg around Day 14 of the cycle.

If the egg is fertilised in the oviduct, it will implant in the uterus wall and no period occurs.

S Hormones work together to control menstruation and pregnancy. Oestrogen and **progesterone** are produced in the ovaries during the menstrual cycle.

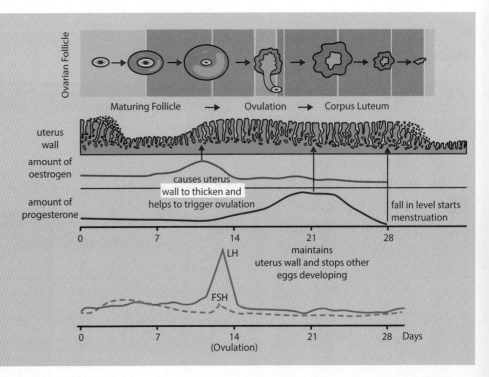

Day in menstrual cycle	Hormones	Effects
1–7	**FSH** (follicle stimulating hormone) increases	1. Egg cell develops 2. Ovaries produce oestrogen
7–14	Oestrogen increases	1. Uterus lining thickens 2. **LH** (luteinising hormone) released 3. Stops release of FSH
14	LH (luteinising hormone) spikes Progesterone increases	Ovulation happens 1. LH (luteinising hormone) and FSH (follicle stimulating hormone) drop to low levels 2. Uterus lining thickens further
Day 14–28: no egg fertilised	Oestrogen and progesterone fall	1. Uterus lining breaks down and period starts 2. FSH (follicle stimulating hormone) levels increase
Day 14–28: egg fertilised	Progesterone and oestrogen (secreted from the placenta (and the ovary) are high	1. Maintains thickened uterus lining 2. Prevents ovulation

Sexually transmitted infections

A **sexually transmitted infection (STI)** is transmitted through sexual contact, for example, during sexual intercourse.

Human immunodeficiency virus (HIV) is a pathogen that causes an STI. The virus can attack the body's immune cells if it is not treated. This may lead to **AIDS**. AIDS is a disease in which the immune system fails, leading to the development of cancers and infections by other pathogens. There is no cure for AIDS at the moment but there may be a cure for HIV if detected early enough.

HIV is spread by sexual contact or exchange of bodily fluids. For example, blood transfer can happen if drug users share needles. HIV can sometimes pass to the fetus through the placenta during pregnancy if the uterus wall is damaged. It can also pass to the baby through breastfeeding.

Antiviral drugs can delay the onset of AIDS.

The spread of STIs, including HIV, can be controlled by:

- not sharing needles after injecting drugs
- not having sex
- only having sex with partners who do not have HIV
- using condoms.

> **Key Point**
>
> HIV is the virus, but AIDS is a condition that can happen because of an HIV infection.

> **Quick Test**
>
> 1. a) Name the organ that produces testosterone.
>   b) Name two changes that are caused by testosterone during puberty.
> 2. Describe ovulation.
> 3. HIV can be spread by sharing needles used to inject drugs. Describe how this happens.

Chromosomes, genes and proteins

Syllabus links:
17.1.1–17.1.4,
S 17.1.5–17.1.12

Learning aims:

- Describe what genes are and where they are found
- Describe the inheritance of sex in humans
- **S** Explain the difference between haploid and diploid cells
- **S** Explain how proteins are made

Chromosomes and genes

Chromosomes are thread-like structures made from **DNA (deoxyribonucleic acid)**, which control inheritance. Each chromosome is made of many **genes**.

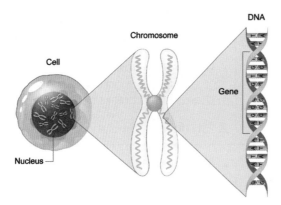

Human body cells have pairs of chromosomes. There may be a different form of the gene on each chromosome. These alternative forms are called **alleles**.

S DNA has two strands twisted into a **double helix** which are connected by pairs of bases:

- **adenine (A)** always pairs with **thymine (T)**
- **cytosine (C)** always pairs with **guanine (G)**.

DNA controls cell functions by controlling protein production. The sequence of bases in a gene determines the sequence of amino acids used to make a specific protein. Each protein has a unique shape which determines its function in the cell, for example, enzymes, membrane carriers or receptors for neurotransmitters.

Sex chromosomes

Human body cells have a pair of **sex chromosomes** that determine the sex of the offspring.

XY is male and XX is female.

Offspring inherit:

- one sex chromosome from the mother. This is always an X chromosome.
- one sex chromosome from the father. This can be an X or a Y chromosome.

The Y chromosome determines the sex of the offspring.

> **Key Point**
>
> It is the chromosomes that are different and not the genes.

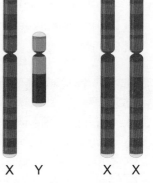

SEX CHROMOSOMES

X   Y   X   X
Male   Female

S The haploid nucleus of the gametes contains a single set of chromosomes. When gametes fuse, the diploid nucleus contains two sets of chromosomes. In diploid cells, there is a pair of each type of chromosome. Humans have 23 pairs in a diploid cell.

Making proteins

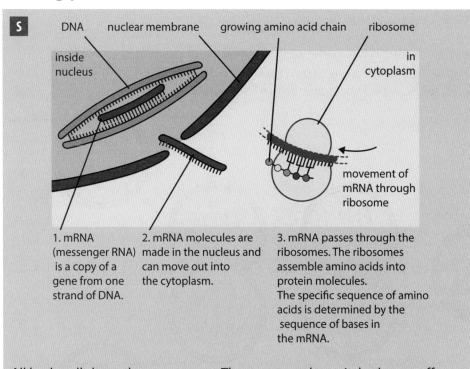

1. mRNA (messenger RNA) is a copy of a gene from one strand of DNA.

2. mRNA molecules are made in the nucleus and can move out into the cytoplasm.

3. mRNA passes through the ribosomes. The ribosomes assemble amino acids into protein molecules.
The specific sequence of amino acids is determined by the sequence of bases in the mRNA.

> **Key Point**
>
> Genes (DNA) cannot leave the nucleus, so **mRNA (messenger RNA)** copies the gene and takes it from the nucleus to the ribosome in the cytoplasm.

All body cells have the same genes. The genes can be switched on or off depending on the proteins the cell needs. For example, cells produced in shoot tips can become leaf cells or flower cells or stem cells. Each cell type needs different specific proteins so only the genes making the necessary specific proteins are expressed (or switched on).

> **Quick Test**
>
> 1. Describe the difference between a gene and an allele.
> 2. Describe how sex is inherited in humans.
> S 3. Describe how different shaped proteins are made.
> S 4. How are genes transported from the nucleus to the ribosomes in the cytoplasm?
> S 5. How many chromosomes are in a haploid cell?

S Mitosis and meiosis

Learning aims:

- S Describe mitosis and its importance
- S Explain what stem cells are
- S Describe meiosis and its importance

Syllabus links:
S 17.2.1–17.2.5,
17.3.1–17.3.2

Mitosis

Mitosis is a type of nuclear division that produces two genetically identical **daughter cells**. Before cell division occurs, the cell needs to grow and increase the number of sub-cellular structures, for example, ribosomes and mitochondria.

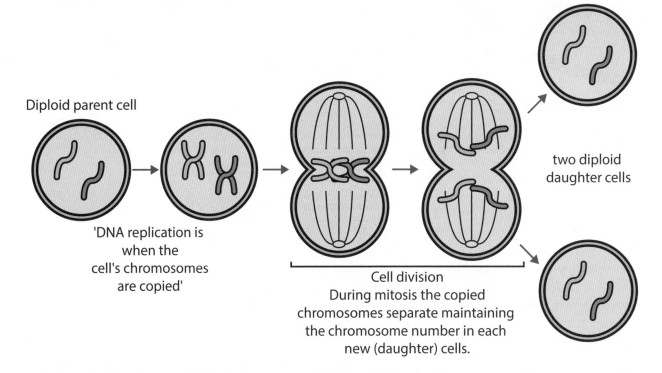

Diploid parent cell

'DNA replication is when the cell's chromosomes are copied'

two diploid daughter cells

Cell division
During mitosis the copied chromosomes separate maintaining the chromosome number in each new (daughter) cells.

The exact **replication** of chromosomes happens before mitosis in the parent cell. Mitosis ensures that all cells are genetically identical to the parent cell.

The uses of mitosis are:

- growth in multicellular organisms
- replacing dead or worn-out cells
- repairing damaged tissues
- asexual reproduction in single-celled organisms.

Specialised cells in the body lose their ability to produce different types of cells. **Stem cells** are **unspecialised cells** found in many tissues in the body. Stem cells divide by mitosis to produce daughter cells within the tissue. They can become specialised for specific functions, for example, to repair tissues and in growth and development.

Meiosis

Meiosis is a reduction division where the chromosome number is halved from diploid to haploid. This results in genetically different cells.

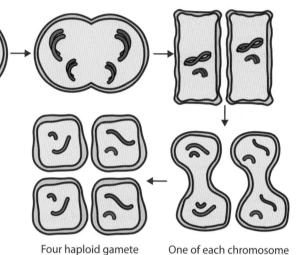

Diploid parent cell with two pairs of chromosomes.

DNA replication is when the cell's chromosomes are copied.

The copied chromosomes separate maintaining the chromosome number in each new (daughter) cells.

Cell divides to form two diploid daughter cells.

Four haploid gamete cells are formed with a single set of chromosomes.

One of each chromosome pair separate and the cells divide again.

Meiosis produces the gametes. When the gametes fuse at fertilisation, the zygote is diploid.

Comparing mitosis and meiosis

Mitosis	Meiosis
Forms body cells	Forms gametes
One cell division	Two cell divisions
Two diploid cells produced	Four haploid cells produced
New cells contain the original number of chromosomes	New cells contain half the original number of chromosomes
New cells are identical to the parent cell	New cells are different to parent cell
Used in asexual reproduction	Used in sexual reproduction

> **Quick Test**

S **1.** Define mitosis.

S **2.** State two uses of mitosis.

S **3.** What are stem cells?

S **4.** Define meiosis.

S **5.** What type of cell is produced during meiosis?

Monohybrid inheritance

Syllabus links:
17.4.1–17.4.12,
S 17.4.13–17.4.18

Learning aims:

- Describe key terms used in genetics
- Interpret and draw genetic diagrams
- **S** Explain the use of a test cross
- **S** Use genetic diagrams to predict the results of monohybrid crosses involving codominance or sex linkage

Key terms in monohybrid inheritance

Inheritance is the transmission of genetic information from generation to generation.

Genotype	Genetic make-up of an organism, for example, Bb where B and b are the alleles for a gene
Phenotype	Observable features of an organism
Homozygous	Two identical alleles for a feature are present, for example, BB or bb
Heterozygous	Two different alleles are present, for example, Bb
Dominant allele	Expressed when present in the genotype (BB or Bb)
Recessive allele	Only expressed when no dominant allele is present in the genotype (bb)
S Codominance	All alleles in heterozygous organisms contribute to the phenotype
S Sex-linked characteristic	Gene responsible for a feature is located on a sex chromosome. The characteristic is then more common in one sex

When two identical homozygous individuals breed together it is **pure breeding.** Heterozygous individuals (for example, Bb) will not be pure breeding because they have different alleles.

Genetic crosses

Pedigree diagrams show the inheritance of a trait through generations of a family. A **monohybrid cross** involves one gene for a specific **trait**. **Genetic diagrams**, including **Punnett squares**, are used to show genetic crosses, offspring combinations from the parents and their probability.

Parent genotype	PW		PW	
Gametes	P	W	P	W
Offspring	PP	WP	PW	WW

Ratio: 3:1

Phenotype: Purple: White

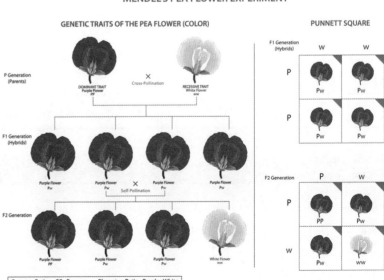

MENDEL'S PEA FLOWER EXPERIMENT

S A **test cross** is used to determine if a dominant phenotype, for example, purple pea flower, is homozygous (PP) or heterozygous (PW):

- If parent is homozygous, all offspring will express the dominant phenotype.
- If parent is heterozygous, half the offspring have the dominant phenotype and half have the recessive.

> **Key Point**
>
> Use the alleles given in genetic questions. Do not make up your own.

S Codominance

An example of codominance is blood group type. There are three alleles of this gene. Alleles I A (produces Antigen A) and I B (produces Antigen B) are codominant. Allele I O (produces no antigens) is recessive to both I A and I B.

Phenotype	Genotype	An example of a genetic diagram for codominance
A	$I^A I^A$ or $I^A I^O$	
B	$I^B I^B$ or $I^B I^O$	
AB	$I^A I^B$	
O	$I^O I^O$	

S Sex linkage

Colour blindness is a sex-linked characteristic caused by a recessive allele on the X chromosome. This makes it more common in males because they only need one copy of the allele as the Y chromosome has no equivalent allele.

		Father's gametes	
		X^R	Y
Mother's gametes	X^R	$X^R X^R$ (female, colour vision)	$X^R Y$ (male, colour vision)
	X^r	$X^R X^r$ (female, colour vision [carrier])	$X^r Y$ (male, colour blind)

X^R is the allele for normal colour vision and X^r is the colour-blind allele.

> **Quick Test**
>
> 1. Describe what terms mean: (a) recessive allele; (b) phenotype; (c) homozygous.
> 2. Pea plants can be tall (T) or short (t).
>   a) Which is the dominant allele?
>   b) Copy and complete a punnet square to show the offspring from two tall heterozygous (Tt) pea plants.
>   c) What is the ratio of tall:short pea plants?
> **S** 3. Describe codominance.
>
> Male parent alleles
>
> | | T | t |
> |---|---|---|
> | T | | |
> | t | | |
>
> Female parent alleles

Variation and adaptation

Syllabus links:
18.1.1–18.1.8,
S 18.1.9–18.1.10 ,
18.2.1–18.2.2,
S 18.2.3

Learning aims:

- Describe and give examples of different types of variation
- Describe what a mutation is and its causes
- Describe and give examples of adaptive features

Variation

Variation is the differences between individuals of the same species.		
Types:	**Continuous/Phenotypic**	**Discontinuous/Genotypic**
Description	Range of phenotypes between two extremes (i.e. no distinct properties) Usually **quantitative** 	Limited number of phenotypes with no intermediates (i.e. distinct categories with no intermediate values) Usually **qualitative**
Examples:	Body length Body mass Leaf length Heart rate	ABO blood groups Eye colour Seed colour in peas Seed shape in peas
Cause:	Both genes and the environment, for example, the potential height of a tree is decided by genes from its parents. Shaded conditions can result in the tree not reaching this height.	Usually by a single or small number of genes. Genetic variation is caused by meiosis (gametes formation) and then the random fusion of male and female gametes.

> **Practical skills**

To investigate variation:

- use a large **random** sample size
- select features and categories to measure
- record data and analyse it, for example, calculate the proportion of individuals for each feature, identify features that are continuous or discontinuous variation, etc.

Mutation

A **mutation** is a rare random genetic change that forms new alleles. Ionising radiation can cause:

- uncontrolled cell division resulting in cancer (**tumours**)

- **sterility** when the testes or ovaries are exposed or damage genes in the gametes which will affect foetal development
- **leukaemia** (white blood cell cancer) in the children of workers at nuclear power stations.

Some chemicals (for example, those found in cigarette smoke) also increase the rate of mutation.

People with **cystic fibrosis** have a mutation in their DNA that causes the secretion of thick, sticky mucus which causes severe breathing difficulties. A child must inherit one copy of the faulty allele from each of their parents. The parents will not usually have cystic fibrosis, because they have one normal dominant allele. They are called **carriers**.

> **S** The sources of genetic variation in a population are:
> - gene mutation (a random change in the base sequence of DNA)
> - meiosis
> - random mating
> - random fertilisation.

Adaptive features

Adaptive features are the inherited features of an organism that increase its chances of survival. This allows it to reproduce and pass on its genes to its offspring.

S

	Hydrophytes	**Xerophytes**
Environment:	aquatic	arid and dry
Examples of adaptations:	Wide and flat leaves and large internal air spaces allow leaves to float Thin waxy cuticle as no need to prevent water loss	Small needle-shaped, rolled/spine-like leaves and thick waxy cuticle reduce water loss by transpiration Tap roots go deep into soil to find water

> **Quick Test**
>
> 1. What causes variation?
> **S** 2. Name two causes of genetic variation in a population.
> 3. What is a mutation?
> 4. What is an adaptive feature?

Selection

Syllabus links:
18.3.1–18.3.3,
S 18.3.4–18.3.6

Learning aims:

- Describe the natural selection process
- Describe selective breeding in certain animals and plants
- **S** Describe how antibiotic-resistant bacteria arise
- **S** Compare natural and artificial selection

Natural selection

Natural selection is when certain traits become more common in a population over time:

- Many offspring are produced in the population.
- Genetic variation occurs within populations.
- Organisms compete for limited resources to survive.
- Organisms better adapted to their environment have a greater chance of survival. This is called **survival of the fittest**.
- Surviving organisms reproduce and pass their favourable alleles to the next generation.

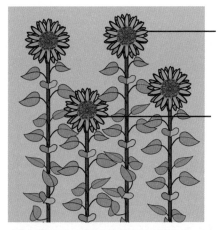

Taller plants capture more sunlight for more photosynthesis. More food and seeds are made and allele for tall height is passed to their offspring.

Shorter shaded plants photosynthesise less, make less food and produce fewer seeds.

> **Key Point**
>
> Natural selection usually occurs over very long time periods.

S **Adaptation** is the process that results from natural selection when populations become more suited to their environment over many generations. For example, if taller plants produce more seeds, the allele for tall plants will be more frequent in the population.

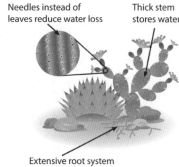

Needles instead of leaves reduce water loss

Thick stem stores water

Extensive root system to take in water

S Antibiotic resistant bacteria

Antibiotic resistant bacteria develop when:

- a random mutation happens in the DNA of an individual bacterial cell
- the mutation protects the bacterium against the effects of an antibiotic, for example penicillin; it is now antibiotic-resistant
- bacteria without the mutation die
- surviving resistant bacteria have less competition for food; they grow, reproduce, and pass the advantageous allele on to their offspring.

Over time, bacteria have developed resistance to many antibiotics, making some bacterial infections difficult to treat.

Selective breeding

The **selective breeding** (**artificial breeding**) process is repeated over many generations to improve:

- all crop plants to increase yield and improve shape, size and ease of peeling and taste of fruits; new colours or shapes of flowers.
- cows, sheep and goats for meat or milk; dog and cat breeds with specific features; larger eggs from chickens; thickness of coat in sheep, etc.

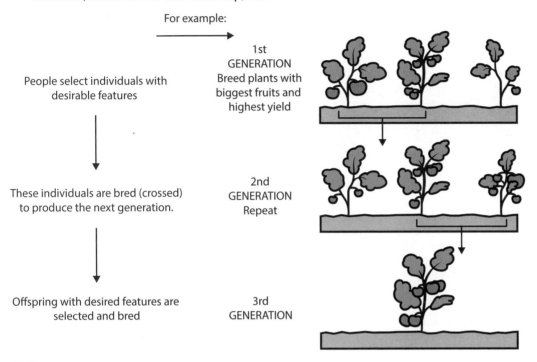

For example:

People select individuals with desirable features

These individuals are bred (crossed) to produce the next generation.

Offspring with desired features are selected and bred

1st GENERATION Breed plants with biggest fruits and highest yield

2nd GENERATION Repeat

3rd GENERATION

S Natural versus artificial selection

	Natural selection	Artificial selection
Found in	Natural populations	Domesticated/controlled populations
Survival chances	Increase with good adaptive features	Might be at risk if conditions change
Speed of change	Slow process over many generations	Faster process in short periods of time
Traits	Inherited adaptive features	Humans select desirable features
Affects	Entire population	Selected individuals
Diversity	Increase in genetic diversity	Decrease in genetic diversity
Evolution	Causes evolution over many generations	Does not allow evolution to occur
Effort	None	Often labour-intensive and expensive
Examples	a) Selection of long-necked giraffes b) Changes in size and shape of birds' beaks depending on feeding habits	a) dog breeding b) crossbreeding in cash crops, for example coffee, wheat and rice

> **Quick Test**

1. What is adaptation?
2. Describe what selective breeding is.
3. **S** How does the speed of change differ in natural selection and artificial selection.

Reproduction in plants

1 ▸ Strawberry plants grow runners. New strawberry plants start to form along the runner.

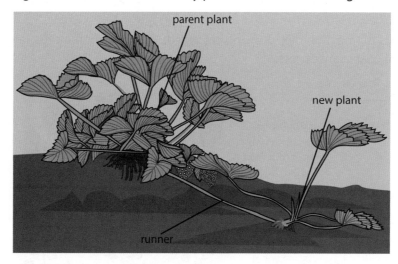

parent plant

new plant

runner

a Look at Fig 16.3. Is this sexual or asexual reproduction? [1]

b Give another example of an organism that reproduces asexually. Describe the process. [2]

> **Show me**

Another organism that reproduces asexually is .... It does this

by ....

c State **two** differences between sexual reproduction and asexual reproduction. [2]

S **d** Farmers cut the runners and put them in pots to sell.

Suggest the advantages of the farmer producing new strawberry plants in this way. [2]

> If there are two marks available, you must give two responses

S **e** Suggest why strawberry plants also use sexual reproduction. [2]

[Total marks 9]

S **2** ▸ **a** Fertilisation happens in sexual reproduction. Describe fertilisation. [3]

> **Show me**

Fertilisation is the .... of the .... of the ....

b Name the structure formed at fertilisation. [1]

S **c** Explain why the structure formed at fertilisation is diploid. [2]

[Total marks 6]

3 The following figure shows the parts of a flower.

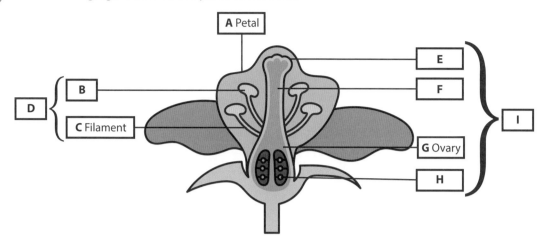

a | Name the parts of the plant labelled **B**, **D**, **E**, **F**, **H** and **I**. | [3]

b | State the function of parts **B**, **E** and **H**. | [3]

c | Name **two** haploid parts of the flower. | [1]

d | Name the diploid part of the flower formed at fertilisation. | [1]

e | Describe pollination. | [1]

f | Why is cross-pollination useful in a habitat in which conditions often change? | [2]

> **Show me**

Cross-pollination mixes .... from two .... This means that there is ....

.... in the offspring which is a survival ....

g | The figure shows a flower that is pollinated by small animals, such as bees.

Name **two** features of wind pollinated flowers that help make pollination more successful. | [2]

h | Look at the flower again. Where does fertilisation occur? | [1]

[Total marks 14]

4 Some students are investigating germination of seeds. They use the apparatus shown below.

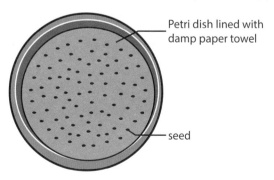

Petri dish lined with damp paper towel

seed

a | Describe how the students can investigate the effect of temperature on seed germination and have reliable results. | [6]

In an investigation description you must name the different variables and the process to follow.

b   Predict the result of the investigation. Explain why you think this.   **[3]**

> **Show me**
>
> I think that the .... the temperature the seeds are in, the .... they
>
> will germinate. This is because ....

[Total marks 9]

Reproduction in humans

1   The diagram shows the female reproductive system.

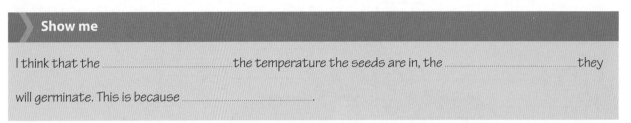

a   Name the organs labelled A, B, C and D.   **[4]**

b   **i)**   Name the organ where the embryo implants.   **[1]**

      ii)   Name the organ where eggs are produced.   **[1]**

      iii)   Name the organ where fertilisation happens.   **[1]**

c   Describe fertilisation.   **[1]**

d   Describe the difference between an embryo and a fetus.   **[1]**

[Total marks 9]

2   **a**   The boxes on the left show the names of some parts of the male reproductive system.

The functions of the parts are in the boxes on the right.

Copy the boxes and draw four lines to link each part of the male reproductive system with its function.

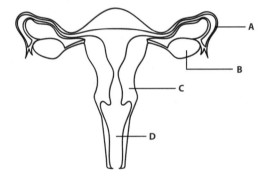

Part	Function
Testes	Carry sperm from testes
Scrotum	Transfer sperm into vagina
Sperm ducts	Produce sperm
Urethra	Carry sperm to vagina
Penis	Keep testes cooler than body temperature

One line has been drawn for you. Draw the additional lines.   **[4]**

> Four marks are available so you must draw four lines

b   **i)**   State how eggs are similar to sperm.   **[1]**

      ii)   Give two ways in which sperm are different to eggs.   **[2]**

[Total marks 7]

3 The diagram shows a developing fetus.

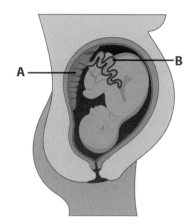

a Name parts A and B. [2]

b Name **two** substances that pass from the mother to the fetus. [1]

If there is only one mark available, you must give two responses to get the mark.

c Describe how substances pass to the fetus. [2]

[Total marks 5]

Sex hormones and STIs

1 Girls produce more oestrogen during puberty. Puberty causes changes in a girl's body. One of these changes is that girls start to menstruate/have periods.

a Name **three** other changes caused by oestrogen that only happen in a girl's body. [3]

b State the day of the monthly cycle when:

i) a period starts [1]

ii) an egg is released. [1]

c Describe what happens to the uterus wall during the monthly cycle. [2]

d Name the hormone that causes a boy's body to change during puberty. [1]

[Total marks 8]

2 **a** The boxes on the left show the names of some female hormones.

The functions of the hormones are in the boxes on the right.

Copy the diagram and draw lines to link each hormone with its function.

Hormone	Function
FSH	Uterus lining breaks down
LH	Maintains uterus lining
Progesterone	Causes release of egg
	Causes egg to develop

[3]

There are only three marks available, so only draw three lines.

b What happens to FSH and LH levels when progesterone levels increase? **[1]**

[Total marks 4]

3 HIV is an infectious disease.

a State the type of pathogen that causes HIV. **[1]**

b Describe the link between HIV and AIDS. **[2]**

c Discuss how HIV can be spread and how it can be prevented. **[4]**

There are four marks here, but you must give some ways HIV can be spread and some ways it can be prevented to get all four marks.

[Total marks 7]

Chromosomes, genes and proteins

1 **a** Copy and complete the sentences below:

i) A .... is a thread-like structure found in the nucleus made of DNA. **[1]**

ii) DNA has a .... structure. **[1]**

iii) A length of DNA that codes for a protein is called a .... **[1]**

iv) Alternative forms of a gene are .... **[1]**

S **b** Look at the diagram of DNA.

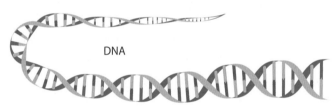

DNA

Describe the structure of DNA. **[3]**

> **Show me**

DNA has .... strands twisted into a .... The strands are

connected by pairs of ....

c The diagram shows a section of one length of DNA.

Copy and complete the boxes to show the structure of the second length of DNA. One has been done for you.

Strand 1	A	A	C	T	G	G
Strand 2	T					

[1]

[Total marks 8]

2 The sex of an organism is determined at fertilisation.

a i) Name the chromosomes found in the nucleus of body cells in a woman that determine sex. [1]

ii) Describe how these structures are different in a man. [1]

iii) Describe how the female and male parents determine the sex of the offspring. [1]

S **b** i) How many chromosomes are found in body cells in humans? [1]

ii) Explain how the number of chromosomes remains the same as all body cells after fertilisation. [4]

Use appropriate keywords when writing explanations.

[Total marks 8]

3 **a** Describe how proteins are made. [6]

b What are the functions of proteins in the cell? [2]

c Explain why DNA replication is important. [1]

[Total marks 9]

4 Some cells produced in shoot tips can become leaf cells or flower cells or stem cells.

Explain why it is important that only some of the genes are expressed in these cells. [3]

5 **a** Look at the diagrams below.

A   B   C

Put the structures in order of size starting with the smallest. [1]

b Name the structure where bases code for a gene. [1]

S **c** If adenine forms 22 per cent of the bases in a length DNA, how much guanine will be present? [1]

[Total marks 3]

S Mitosis and Meiosis

1 **a** There are two types of cell division: mitosis and meiosis.

The table has statements about cell division.

For each statement, copy and complete the table to show the type of cell division that is described.

One has been completed for you.

Statement	Type of cell division described by the statement
Genetically identical cells produced	Mitosis
How cells for growth are produced	
How gametes are made	
How genetic information is copied	
How the zygote divides to grow	
Every division produces four daughter cells	

[3]

b   Name the type of cell division used in asexual reproduction.   [1]

c   **i)**   What are stem cells?   [1]

     ii)   Why are stem cells important in the body?   [1]

[Total marks 6]

2   Look at the table showing the number of chromosomes in the body cells of some living organisms.

Organism	Number of chromosomes
Sweet potato	90
Rice plant	24
Earth worm	36
Elephant	56

a   Most living organisms have an equal number of chromosomes. Explain why.   [2]

b   **i)**   When a cell divides by meiosis, how many cells are produced?   [1]

     ii)   How many chromosomes will be present in these cells:

       a.   elephant sperm?

       b.   sweet potato pollen?

       c.   earthworm muscle cells?   [3]

[Total marks 6]

Monohybrid inheritance

1   **a**   Organisms in a species have different phenotypes.

Copy and complete the sentence below to explain the meaning of phenotype.

Phenotype describes the .... an organism has.   [1]

b The differences in organisms are caused by genes.

i) Each gene has two different alleles. What is an allele? [1]

ii) Match each type of allele to the correct definition.

> 1. There are more than two alleles for the gene
>
> 2. Each chromosome has two alleles for the gene

(A) Homozygous

> 3. One chromosome has two alleles for the gene and the other has none
>
> 4. The two alleles for the gene are different

(B) Heterozygous

> 5. The gene is found on the male chromosome only
>
> 6. The two alleles for the gene are the same

[1]

c Short pea plant height is caused by a recessive gene **(t)**. Both parent plants are tall.

Explain how you can use a test cross to identify the parental genotypes. [4]

d Both parents are heterozygous for this feature.

What is the probability of their offspring being tall or short?

Use **t** for the recessive allele and **T** for the dominant allele.

Copy and complete the genetic diagram to help you.

Male parent alleles

Female parent alleles		

[3]

[Total marks 10]

2 Fur colour is inherited in leopards.

- The allele for spotted fur is B.
- The allele for black coat is b.

Here is a pedigree diagram of the inheritance of fur colour in a family of leopards.

a Compare the genotype of Leopard 1 and Leopard 2. [2]

> The command word **compare** tells you that you must mention both the things that you are comparing.

b   Describe the phenotypes of leopards 5 and 8.   [2]

c   In generation 1, state the phenotypic ratio of spotted fur to black leopards.   [1]

d   Leopard 5 breeds with a black leopard.

     i)   Will the offspring be pure bred or not pure bred?   [1]

     ii)   State the genotype and phenotype of the offspring.   [2]

     [Total marks 8]

S 3   Red–green colour blindness is an inherited condition found mainly in men.

It prevents people being able to tell the difference between red and green.

a   Explain why more men are colour blind than women.   [4]

b   A man with normal colour vision has the genotype $X^R Y$.

His partner is colour blind with the genotype $X^r X^r$.

Predict the probability of their offspring having colour vision or being colour blind.

Use a genetic diagram to help you.

Include:

- Parental gametes
- Offspring genotypes and phenotypes.   [3]

     [Total marks 7]

Variation and adaptation

1   Some students are investigating variation in tomatoes. Look at the picture of some different types of ripe tomatoes.

a   What is variation?   [1]

b   Name one type of discontinuous and one type of continuous variation in tomatoes.   [2]

c   Why is variation in a species important?   [2]

d   The students collected data on the length of some ripe tomatoes from one plant.

Length (cm)	4.1	4.2	4.3	4.4	4.5	4.6	4.7	4.8	4.9
Number of tomatoes	2	5	8	13	21	11	7	4	1

     i)   Plot a graph to show this data   [3]

     ii)   What is the range of values of tomato length from the plant?   [1]

     iii)   Five tomatoes on one stem of the plant have lengths of 4.4, 4.5, 4.8, 4.1 and 4.7 cm.

        Calculate the average length of the tomatoes. Show your working out.   [3]

> You are asked to show your working, so show it.

     [Total marks 12]

2 Tree frogs are adapted to not being eaten by predators. The picture shows a tree frog on a leaf.

a What is an adaptive feature? [4]

> **Show me**
>
> It is an .... feature that helps an organism to .... and
>
> .... in its ....

b Explain how the tree frog being green is an adaptive feature. [2]

[Total marks 6]

3 Marram grass grows on sand dunes. Water drains through sand dunes very quickly.

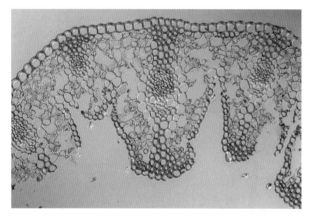

Suggest and explain some adaptive features of marram grass leaves to their windy, dry environment. [6]

To get six marks, you must make suggest and explain at least **three** points in your answer.

4 Peppered moths are found all over the UK. The moths rest on tree trunks and are food for birds. Before 1848, there were only light moths. There are now two varieties of peppered moths: light and dark.

Light and dark pepper moth shape adaptation

a   The first dark moths appeared from 1848. Suggest what caused the dark form of the peppered moth.   [1]

b   Name the type of variation seen in these peppered moths: continuous or discontinuous.   [1]

c   After 1848, trees in polluted areas had dark bark. By 1895, most of the peppered moths found in Manchester were dark coloured. Explain why dark moths increased and pale moths decreased.   [6]

> **Show me**

When there is pollution, the light moths are no longer .... on the dark trees so they

are .... by birds and could not .... The dark moths were

.... so they .... and could pass on their ....

to their offspring.

[Total marks 8]

Selection

1 ▶ A farmer has a herd of milk cows.

Some cows produce more milk than others. The farmer has two bulls: one born to a high yield milk cow and one to a lower yield milk cow.

a   Describe how the farmer can have a herd with all the cows producing a high milk yield.   [6]

b   A rose grower also uses the selective breeding process. Roses have stems with thorns.

Suggest **three** features of roses that the farmer may want to improve in his plants.   [3]

[Total marks 9]

2 ▷ Plants are found in many habitats including dry, desert climates.

a   What name is given to plants adapted to survive in dry desert climates?   [1]

b   How are these plants adapted to find and preserve absorbed water?   [6]

c   Which word(s) describes when an organism has a feature that helps it survive in its environment?   [1]

mutation   phenotype   survival of the fittest   adaptation   natural selection

[Total marks 8]

3 ▷ Bacterial infections can be treated with antibiotics.

Penicillin is an antibiotic used to kill many different bacteria.

How has the overuse of antibiotics led to some bacteria becoming antibiotic-resistant?   [3]

Write your ideas in a sensible order, using good English and scientific terms.

4 ▷ Living organisms have many features which allow them to survive in the environment where they live.

Penguins live in very cold climates and eat fish. They stand up all of the time and often rock back on their heels using their tails to balance. Unlike most birds, penguins cannot fly but can swim.

a   What is adaptation?   [3]

b   Explain **three** adaptations of penguins that increase their chances of survival.   [6]

[Total marks 9]

Energy flow, food chains and food webs

Syllabus links:
19.1.1–19.1.2,
19.2.1–19.2.14,
S 19.2.15–19.2.19

Learning aims:

- Use and interpret food chains and food webs
- Identify and describe different trophic levels
- Use and interpret pyramids of number, biomass **S** and energy
- **S** Explain the effects of inefficient energy transfers

Food webs and trophic levels

Energy from the Sun is transferred by light and trapped during **photosynthesis**. Plants store this energy as 'chemical energy' in their **biomass** ('living mass'). The arrows in a **food chain** show how this energy transfers through other organisms in a **habitat**.

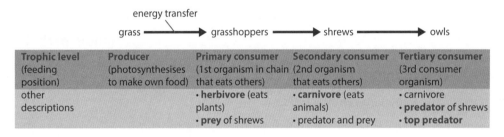

energy transfer

grass ⟶ grasshoppers ⟶ shrews ⟶ owls

Trophic level (feeding position)	Producer (photosynthesises to make own food)	Primary consumer (1st organism in chain that eats others)	Secondary consumer (2nd organism that eats others)	Tertiary consumer (3rd consumer organism)
other descriptions		• **herbivore** (eats plants) • **prey** of shrews	• **carnivore** (eats animals) • predator and prey	• carnivore • **predator** of shrews • **top predator**

> **Key Point**
>
> Make sure you understand all the terms used in the diagram.

Other trophic levels are **quaternary consumer** and **decomposer**. Decomposers (for example, fungi) break down dead organisms and their wastes.

Linked food chains form a **food web**, which shows:

- **omnivores**
- organisms feeding at more than one trophic level
- **competition** between organisms for food.

We use food chains and webs to model the effects of human activity, such as:

- using **pesticides** (e.g. killing grasshoppers increases the amount of grass but reduces shrew numbers)
- putting new species in a habitat (e.g. adding lizards, which eat grasshoppers, reduces food for the shrews)
- harvesting for human food (e.g. fishing for too many of one type of fish).

S Efficiency of energy transfers

A lot of energy is lost to the environment (especially as heat from respiration) at each trophic level. Energy losses reduce the energy available further along a food chain, so:

- chains usually have fewer than five trophic levels
- it can be more efficient for humans to eat crop plants than to eat animals fed on crop plants.
-

38 units released by respiration and eventually transferred to environment as heat

2 units of energy stored in new sheep biomass

60 units of energy transferred to environment stored in substances in faeces and urine

sheep gains **100 units** of energy in the biomass of the grass that it eats

Ecological pyramids

In a **pyramid of numbers**, the length of a trophic level bar shows the number of organisms.

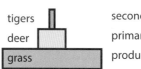

tigers — secondary consumers
deer — primary consumers
grass — producers

Very large or very small organisms can give an inverted shape in a pyramid of numbers. A **pyramid of biomass** is not affected by organism size and so usually avoids this problem. Each bar shows the dry mass of the organisms (the mass without water, since water is not made by organisms).

birds
caterpilliars
trees

secondary consumers
primary consumers
producers

birds
caterpilliars
trees

An inverted pyramid of numbers   **A pyramid of energy biomass**

S Pyramids of energy

In the food web below, the pyramid of biomass for the:

* orange food chain is pyramid-shaped because the total mass of pondweed at any one time is large
* blue food chain is inverted because the total mass of tiny algae at any one time is small.

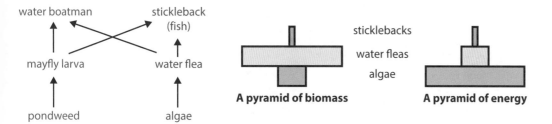

water boatman   stickleback (fish)
mayfly larva   water flea
pondweed   algae

sticklebacks
water fleas
algae

A pyramid of biomass   **A pyramid of energy**

However, algae are constantly reproducing, so the amount of energy they supply to the primary consumers over a period of time is similar to the plant. For this reason, the best way to show how efficiently energy is transferred is in a **pyramid of energy**. The trophic level bars show the energy per area per time (giving units such as kJ/km^2/year).

> **Quick Test**

1. Look at the food web in the last section. Identify the:
   a) secondary consumers
   b) herbivores.
2. Sketch a food chain showing organisms A, B, C and D.
   * A is a top predator
   * B is a herbivore
   * C is a secondary consumer
   * D is a producer
S 3. State a reason why energy is lost from a trophic level.
4. Sketch a pyramid of numbers for the food chain at the top of the previous page.

Carbon cycle and nitrogen cycle

Learning aims:

- Describe the carbon cycle
- **S** Describe the nitrogen cycle
- **S** State the roles of microorganisms in the nitrogen cycle

The carbon cycle

Most substances in living things are **organic** compounds, which contain many carbon-carbon and/or carbon-hydrogen bonds. Carbohydrates, fats and proteins are all organic molecules.

The **carbon cycle** summarises how carbon atoms are recycled.

> ### Key Point
>
> Carbon dioxide does not have C–C or C–H bonds; it is an **inorganic** molecule.

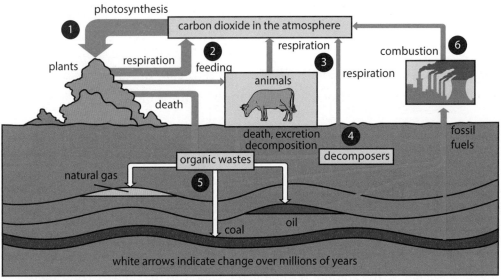

1. During **photosynthesis**, plants and algae take in carbon dioxide to make glucose. This organic molecule is then used to make other organic compounds.

2. Carbon is transferred through food chains when organisms feed.

3. During **respiration**, organisms release carbon dioxide into the atmosphere.

4. During **decomposition**, decomposers feed on the organic compounds in animal wastes and dead organisms. The respiration of decomposers also releases carbon dioxide.

5. Some dead organisms become trapped underground and do not decompose. Instead, they slowly become fossil fuels over millions of years.

6. **Combustion** of organic compounds, including fossil fuels and wood, produces carbon dioxide.

S The nitrogen cycle

The **nitrogen cycle** summarises how nitrogen atoms are recycled.

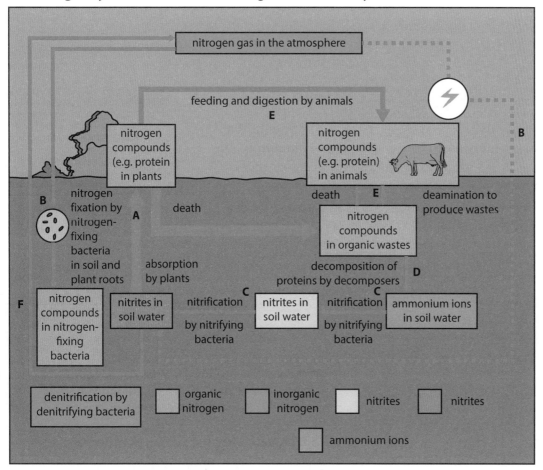

A Plants need nitrogen to make amino acids and proteins. This gas cannot be used from the air because it is unreactive, so plants absorb it as **nitrate ions** (NO_3^-) from the soil.

B **Nitrogen-fixing bacteria** live in nodules on some plant roots and carry out **nitrogen fixation** (a process that makes nitrate ions using nitrogen). Nitrogen is also 'fixed' by lightning.

C **Nitrifying bacteria** in the soil carry out **nitrification**, in which ammonium ions (NH_4^+) are used to make **nitrite ions** (NO_2^-) and then nitrate ions.

D **Decomposers** make ammonium ions (NH_4^+) as they digest urea and proteins in dead organisms.

E Nitrogen passes along food chains as organisms feed and digest proteins into amino acids (used to make new proteins). Excess amino acids cannot be stored and are broken down by **deamination**. This produces nitrogen-rich molecules that become **urea** (excreted in urine).

F **Denitrifying bacteria** convert nitrates into nitrogen gas during **denitrification**.

Quick Test

1. Give **two** examples of different types of organic molecules found in living things.
2. In which process is carbon:
   a) removed from the atmosphere by living organisms?
   b) released into the atmosphere by living organisms?
3. Explain the effect of burning fossil fuels on the concentration of gases in the air.
S 4. Draw a flow chart to explain how a nitrogen atom in cow urine can end up back in the cow's food.
S 5. Give the name of the bacteria that carry out a process that is *opposite* to nitrogen-fixing.

Populations

Learning aims:

- Define the terms population, community, ecosystem
- State the factors affecting population growth and identify growth curve phases
- **S** Explain the shape of a growth curve

Syllabus links:
19.4.1–19.4.6,
S 19.4.7

Ecosystems

The number of individuals of one species living in an area is its **population**. All the populations of the different species in the area form the **community**. The community and all the environmental factors that affect the organisms (e.g. temperature, food supply) form an **ecosystem**.

Population size factors

Populations are affected by changes in **physical factors** (e.g. temperature, light) and living or **biological factors** (e.g. food supply). The table shows some effects of biological factors.

Biological environmental factor	Increase in factor can cause population ...	Reason
food supply	increase	More food means fewer organisms starve and organisms are healthier, making them more likely to reproduce.
disease	decrease	**Pathogens** can kill organisms or make them less healthy so they cannot reproduce.
competition	decrease	When organisms compete, one species may get more of a resource, meaning that another does not get enough.
predation	decrease	Increasing **predator** numbers reduces the numbers of their **prey** (and so there are fewer prey organisms to reproduce).

Predators and prey

The effects of predation are clearly seen when a community has only a few species, and so one organism depends almost entirely on another for its food.

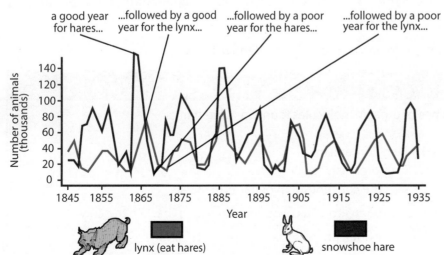

a good year for hares... ...followed by a good year for the lynx... ...followed by a poor year for the hares... ...followed by a poor year for the lynx...

lynx (eat hares)   snowshoe hare

> ### Key Point
>
> Plant species compete for light, (gases from the) air, water, nutrients (mineral ions), space. Remember LAWNS. Animal species compete for food, water and space.

Growth curves

The effect of a limited resource (for example, food supply) on population growth can be shown on a **growth curve**. It has a sigmoid shape, which is easily seen in lab conditions (for example, using a yeast population). It is less common in nature because many factors affect population growth.

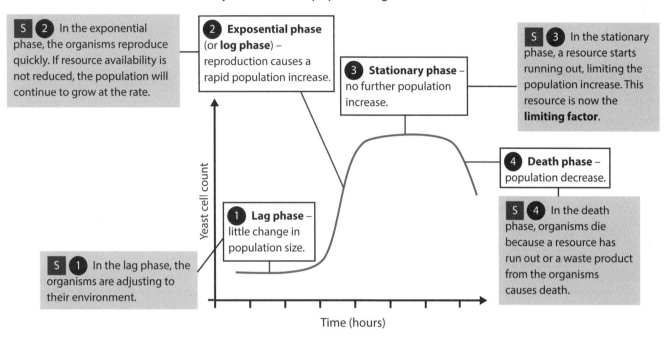

S 2 In the exponential phase, the organisms reproduce quickly. If resource availability is not reduced, the population will continue to grow at the rate.

2 Exponential phase (or **log phase**) – reproduction causes a rapid population increase.

3 Stationary phase – no further population increase.

S 3 In the stationary phase, a resource starts running out, limiting the population increase. This resource is now the **limiting factor**.

4 Death phase – population decrease.

S 4 In the death phase, organisms die because a resource has run out or a waste product from the organisms causes death.

1 Lag phase – little change in population size.

S 1 In the lag phase, the organisms are adjusting to their environment.

Measuring populations

Counting all the individuals of a species in an area takes too long. So, we use more samples give more accurate estimates but take longer, and larger areas need more samples since organisms are not evenly spread out. Samples are taken at **random** to avoid the experimenter affecting the counting and causing **bias**.

Practical skills

1. Extend two measuring tapes (A and B) at right angles.
2. Generate a random number from 0 to 9 (for example, using a computer).
3. Person A walks this number of metres along tape A.
4. Generate another random number from 0 to 9.
5. Person B walks this number of metres along tape B.
6. Both people walk at right angles until they meet.
7. Place the middle of a **quadrat** at this point.
8. Count the number of the organism under investigation.
9. Repeat until enough samples are collected.
10. Estimate the population.
    $$\text{estimated population} = \text{number in sample} \times \frac{\text{study area (m}^2)}{\text{sample area (m}^2)}$$

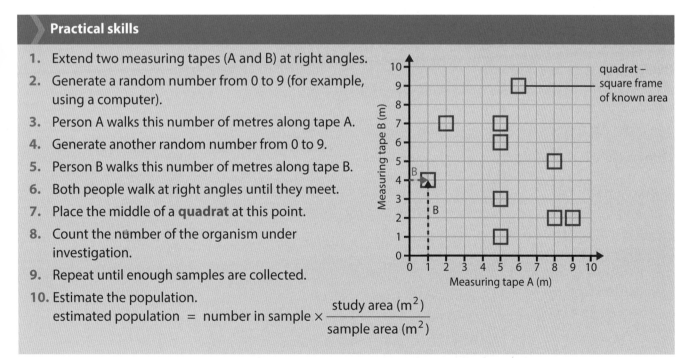

Quick Test

1. Explain how predation affects the prey population in an ecosystem.

S 2. State two reasons why a yeast population growing in glucose solution may start to decrease.

Factors affecting biodiversity

Learning aims:

- Describe ways to increase food production, their advantages and disadvantages
- Describe the effects of habitat destruction
- Explain the consequences of deforestation

Food supply

Farming methods increase **yields** (the amount of useful product obtained from crop plants and livestock). Increased food production is needed to support growing numbers of people in the world.

Farming method	Reason it increases yield
agricultural machinery	quicker than using people, increasing the amount of crop grown
larger fields	allow larger agricultural machinery, which is more efficient
chemical fertilisers	add mineral ions to the soil to boost crop growth
insecticides	kill insects to reduce damage to crops (and improve their quality)
herbicides	kill 'weeds' to stop them competing with crop plants
selective breeding	provides new crop plants and livestock breeds that give better yields

Important terms in ecology

An **ecosystem** describes all the interactions between a community of species and the physical factors in an area. A **habitat** is the name of the place where organisms live (e.g. forest, pond).

Biodiversity describes the number of different species in a community. If there are many different species, an area is very 'biodiverse'.

Monoculture

Monoculture means planting large areas with just one crop.

Advantages include:
- the same chemicals are applied to the whole crop
- it is easier to harvest one large area of one crop.

Disadvantages include:
- it reduces biodiversity, limiting food supply for other organisms
- it destroys habitats, reducing other resources (e.g. shelter)
- **pesticides** kill insects and plants that are not **pests**
- all the plants are usually genetically identical, meaning that pests and diseases are easily spread
- all the plants use up the same mineral ions from the soil
- pollution is caused by chemicals used to control pests and add mineral ions.

In Malaysia, huge areas of rainforests have been cleared for palm oil monoculture.

Intensive livestock farming

Intensive livestock farming means keeping animals in temperature-controlled barns (not in fields).

Advantages include:

- animals use less energy to move and keep warm, and so have more energy for growth
- animals are better protected from predators
- it is easier to treat all the animals for diseases
- it is easier to ensure that all the animals have a good diet.

Disadvantages include:

- pollution caused by animal wastes
- animals are close together, so diseases spread easily (including to wild animals)
- pollution caused by chemicals used to control diseases
- animals produce a lot of carbon dioxide/methane (which contributes to climate change).

> ### Key Point
>
> Monoculture and intensive farming can increase yields and so increase profits.

Chickens are often intensively farmed.

Habitat destruction

Habitats are destroyed by:

- using land for housing and farming
- extracting natural resources (for example, quarries for stone)
- water pollution (for example, from oil spills, plastics, animal wastes, farm chemicals).

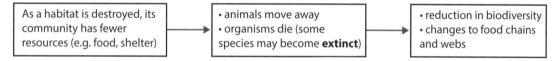

As a habitat is destroyed, its community has fewer resources (e.g. food, shelter)	• animals move away • organisms die (some species may become **extinct**)	• reduction in biodiversity • changes to food chains and webs

Deforestation (removal of forest habitats) *also* causes:

- increased carbon dioxide in the air (due to burning trees and less photosynthesis)
- soils to wash away (since they are no longer held together by tree roots)
- flooding (due to lack of soil to soak up water).

> ### Quick Test
>
> 1. **a)** Give a reason why rainforests are removed.
>   **b)** State the term used to describe this removal.
>   **c)** Explain how this affects the biodiversity in an area.
> 2. Choose two chemicals used in farming and explain why they are used.

Pollution and conservation

Learning aims:

- Describe pollution of land, air and water **S** including eutrophication
- Describe some sustainable resources **S** and explain how they are sustained
- Explain why organisms become endangered or extinct
- Describe conservation methods **S** and why they are important

Syllabus links:
20.3.1– 20.3.3,
20.4.1–20.4.4,
S 20.3.4, 20.4.5–
20.4.9

Plastic pollution

Non-biodegradable plastics do not quickly rot in the environment. So, they takes up space in **landfill sites** and pollute land and water habitats. Plastic waste can also release poisonous chemicals and trap animals.

> **Key Point**
>
> **Pollution** is when any substance reaches a concentration that causes harm.

Water pollution

Untreated sewage and excess fertiliser both contain nutrients that can cause uncontrolled growth of organisms in water, causing fish and other animals to die.

S Eutrophication is when water becomes over-full of nutrients.

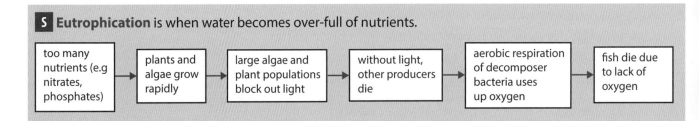

too many nutrients (e.g nitrates, phosphates) → plants and algae grow rapidly → large algae and plant populations block out light → without light, other producers die → aerobic respiration of decomposer bacteria uses up oxygen → fish die due to lack of oxygen

Air pollution

Greenhouse gases (e.g. carbon dioxide, methane) trap heat in the atmosphere. Pollution by these gases increases this **greenhouse effect** causing **global warming**, which leads to **climate change**.

- Methane increases due to oil exploration, more farm animals and rice paddy fields.
- Carbon dioxide increases due to burning **fossil fuels**.

> **Key Point**
>
> Remember what causes what. Greenhouse effect → global warming → climate change.

Endangerment and extinction

Extinction is when a species ceases to exist. **Endangerment** is the risk of extinction, often caused by:

- climate change (can make habitats unsuitable)
- pollution
- habitat destruction (see Topic 37)
- hunting animals (for food, fur or 'medicines', or to protect farms)
- introducing new species into a habitat that compete with **native** species
- overharvesting (not using resources sustainably).

S There is less genetic variation in smaller populations, which limits how well a population can change (**evolve**) if the environment changes. Smaller populations are more likely to die out.

Sustainable resources

A **sustainable resource** is replaced as fast as it is used, so it does not run out. Obtaining wood and fish can both be sustainable.

S Sustainability method	Forests	Fish
Stop people using some areas (all the time or when organisms are reproducing)	✓	✓
Only allow a certain amount to be taken – a **quota**	✓	✓
Monitor population sizes, to change amount of replanting or quota size	✓	✓
Use nets that catch just one species, with large meshes to let young fish escape		✓

Conservation

Conservation is trying to stop organisms and habitats disappearing. Conservation methods include:

- educating people to live more sustainably and to respect nature
- monitoring populations of organisms to find those that are declining
- saving seeds in seed banks (to be planted if endangerment or extincting occurs)
- stopping people harming certain species or habitats
- breeding organisms in captivity.

S Some animals do not breed well in captivity, so we use:

- artificial insemination (AI) – placing sperm directly into a female's uterus
- in vitro fertilisation (IVF) – **gametes** are mixed in a lab, producing embryos that are implanted in females.

These techniques are also useful when males and females are in breeding centres that are far apart, and help to increase genetic variation in the different centres.

Conservation programmes can:

- maintain or repair biodiversity (releasing captive-bred animals into the wild)
- reduce extinction
- protect habitats (setting up nature reserves)
- avoid harming ecosystems that might affect our futures, by preserving:
  - the cycling of carbon, nitrogen and water (e.g. so rain continues to fall in an area)
  - food supply
  - organisms that may contain unknown useful substances (e.g. new medicines)
  - fuel supplies (e.g. wood)
  - genetic variation (useful for selective breeding and genetic modification).

> ### Quick Test

1. a) Give two examples of greenhouse gases.
   b) For each gas, give a reason why its levels in the atmosphere are increasing.
S 2. The quota for cod in the North Sea is 22 000 tonnes/year.
   a) Explain how using a quota helps sustainable fishing.
   b) Describe how fishing boats avoid catching young cod.

Biotechnology

Syllabus links: 21.1.1, 21.2.1– 21.2.4, S 21.1.2, 21.2.5–21.2.7

Learning aims:

- Describe the use of yeast in making bread and biofuels
- Describe and investigate the uses of enzymes in foods and washing powders
- Describe why bacteria are useful for biotechnology S and explain their ease of use
- S Explain the use of fermenters to make useful products using microorganisms

Yeast

Biotechnology is using biological processes to make useful products.

Yeast (single-celled fungi) produce carbon dioxide and ethanol in anaerobic respiration.

$$\text{glucose} \rightarrow \text{carbon dioxide} + \text{ethanol}$$

The feeding and respiration of yeast (often called **fermentation**) is used to make:

- bread – carbon dioxide bubbles make the dough rise before baking
- ethanol **biofuel** – some vehicles use pure ethanol, but it is normally mixed with petrol.

Enzymes

Enzymes in washing powders break down substances in stains.

- **Amylase** digests starch.
- **Protease** digests proteins.
- **Lipase** breaks down fats.

> ### Key Point
>
> Enzymes are biological catalysts, and so allow effective washing at low temperatures.

> ### Practical skills
>
> 1. Make wells in agar plates containing starch + iodine, or milk, or vegetable oil + indicator.
> 2. Make suspensions of different washing powders in water.
> 3. Heat some of each suspension at 95 °C to **denature** the enzymes for the **controls**.
> 4. Fill different wells with heated and unheated washing powder suspensions.
> 5. Leave for 1 hour.
> 6. Measure and compare the 'zones of digestion' (colourless areas) for each well.

Pectin strengthens apple cell walls and sticks them together. **Pectinase** is used to extract apple juice because it digests pectin.

> ### Practical skills
>
> 1. Add 50 g of crushed apples to two beakers.
> 2. Add distilled water to one beaker (the control) and an equal volume of pectinase solution to the other.
> 3. After 30 minutes, filter the mixtures.
> 4. More juice comes from pectinase-treated apples. The juice is also clearer because the loss of pectin makes bits of apple tissue fall apart.

> S Some people cannot digest a sugar called **lactose** because their bodies do not make **lactase**, which splits lactose into glucose and galactose. Lactase is added to milk to make it lactose-free.

Fermenters

Bacteria are useful for biotechnology because:

- they reproduce very quickly
- they make complex molecules
- they are easy to genetically modify.

S **Plasmids** are easy to move into and out of bacteria and plasmid DNA is simple to genetically modify. So, producing GM bacteria is quick and straightforward.

Using bacteria does not raise **ethical issues** (e.g. how they are cared for). The need to treat animals with respect makes genetically modifying them and using them in biotechnology quite complicated.

GM bacteria are grown in large-scale **fermenters**, and produce useful substances (e.g. **insulin**, **penicillin**). These huge tanks are also used to grow yeast and other fungi, such as those that make **mycoprotein** (a high-protein, low-fat food).

Before a fermenter is used, it is **sterilised** (all microorganisms are killed) using high-pressure steam. This ensures that no other microorganisms grow inside it and produce unwanted substances.

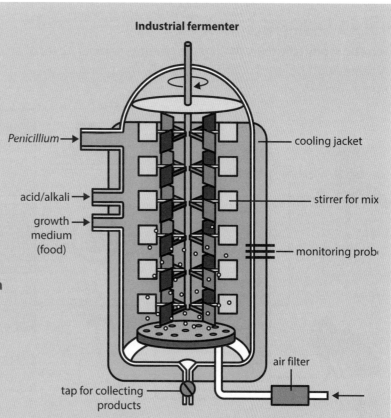

Industrial fermenter

Penicillium →

acid/alkali →

growth medium (food) →

cooling jacket

stirrer for mix

monitoring prob.

air filter

tap for collecting products

Conditions in a fermenter are carefully controlled to give microorganisms the best conditions for growth.

Condition	Reason for control
temperature	Optimum temperature for enzymes is used (respiration increases temperature).
pH	Optimum pH for enzymes is used.
oxygen	Oxygen for respiration is constantly added.
nutrients	Food substances, vitamins and minerals are added for growth and health.
wastes	Wastes (e.g. carbon dioxide) are removed so that they do not poison the cells.

> **Quick Test**

1. Write out the word equation for anaerobic respiration in yeast.
2. Give the reason that enzymes are added to washing powders.
3. Explain why using pectinase helps to extract more juice from apples.
S 4. Give one reason bacteria are useful for biotechnology.

Genetic modification

Learning aims:

Syllabus links:
21.3.1–21.3.2,
S 21.3.3–21.3.4

- Outline some examples of genetic modification
- S Describe the process of making GM bacteria that make human proteins
- S Discuss the advantages and disadvantages of GM crops

GM and its uses

Genetic modification is altering the genetic material (DNA) of an organism by removing, changing or inserting genes. This produces genetically modified organisms (GMOs).

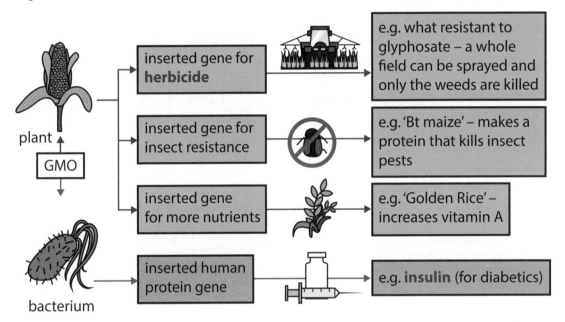

S GMO bacteria

Genes contain instructions for making proteins. Once the human gene responsible for a specific protein has been identified, it is cut out of a DNA molecule using **restriction enzymes**. These leave unpaired bases either side of the gene, called **sticky ends**.

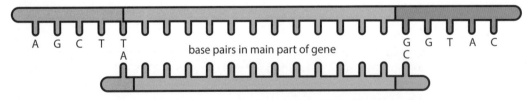

A plasmid is then cut open using the same restriction enzymes to leave **complementary** sticky ends.

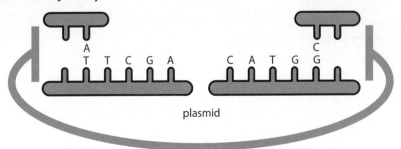

The sticky ends of the plasmid and gene pair together, and the DNA is re-joined using **DNA ligase** (an enzyme). The reformed loop is a **recombinant plasmid** (it contains DNA from another organism).

The recombinant plasmid is inserted into bacteria, which multiply to produce many more bacteria containing the recombinant plasmid. **Gene expression** occurs (a gene carries out its function) and the human protein is produced by the bacteria.

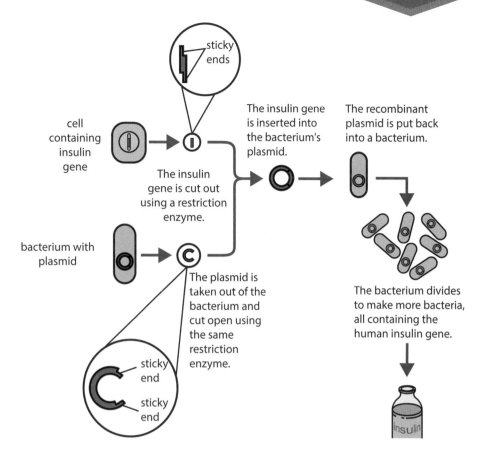

cell containing insulin gene

The insulin gene is cut out using a restriction enzyme.

sticky ends

The insulin gene is inserted into the bacterium's plasmid.

The recombinant plasmid is put back into a bacterium.

bacterium with plasmid

The plasmid is taken out of the bacterium and cut open using the same restriction enzyme.

sticky end

sticky end

The bacterium divides to make more bacteria, all containing the human insulin gene.

insulin

ⓢ Pros and cons of GM crops

Advantages	Disadvantages
less chemical use (e.g. pesticides)	more expensive seeds
increased **yield**	farmers become dependent on using certain chemicals (e.g. glyphosate herbicide)
development of more nutritious crops for poorer parts of the world	risk of genes being transferred to wild plants (e.g. making herbicide-resistant weeds)
new varieties produced much quicker than selective breeding	GM plants or their offspring cause unforeseen problems

> **Quick Test**

1. What does GMO stand for?
2. State why scientists might want to insert human genes into bacteria.
ⓢ 3. What are the following enzymes used for?
   a) DNA ligase
   b) restriction enzymes.
ⓢ 4. Give the name for a loop of bacterial DNA that contains a foreign gene.
ⓢ 5. Explain how a GM crop could produce more yield than the non-GM version.

Energy flow, food chains and food webs

1 ▷ Look at the food web.

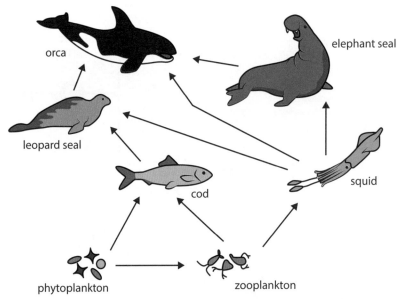

a The only organism that can photosynthesise in this food web is phytoplankton. Give the name of the trophic level that these organisms are in. [1]

b From this food web, give the name of:

i) a quaternary consumer

ii) an organism that feeds at two trophic levels. [2]

c Identify the organisms that compete for squid. [1]

d State what the arrows in the food web show. [1]

e Predict two effects on other organisms of overfishing cod. Give a reason for each effect. [4]

f Sketch a food chain that includes the elephant seal. [1]

g Sketch a pyramid of numbers for your food chain. [2]

S h Explain the shape of your pyramid of numbers. [3]

> In an **explain** question, you often need to state what happens and then give the reasoning why. In this case, there are two marks for that reasoning, so you need to make two points.

> **Show me**

As you go further up the pyramid, the bars become ....

This is due to their being less .... as you go up the pyramid because . . . .

[Total marks 15]

2 ▷ Animals feeding at which tropic level feed on dead organisms and wastes?

A. decomposers

C. producers

B. primary consumers

D. quaternary consumers [1]

3 Explain how energy from the Sun becomes stored in the biomass of a herbivore. [3]

4 Give the reason why it is more energy efficient for humans to eat corn rather than to eat chickens fed on corn. [1]

Carbon cycle and nitrogen cycle

1 Look at the food web in question 1 on page 138.

a Explain how phytoplankton changes the concentration of carbon dioxide dissolved in seawater. [2]

b How do organic molecules in phytoplankton end up in the elephant seal? [1]

c Name the process by which wastes from these animals are removed from the water. [1]

d i) When sea organisms die, they can form layers that become buried and trapped underground. Give the name of a useful product that these layers form. [1]

ii) Explain one problem caused by the product you have chosen. [2]

> You need to use your answer to part (i) here. Do not write about something else!

e Suggest how phytoplankton get their nitrogen. [1]

> In a **suggest** question, you must apply what you know to a new situation.

[Total marks 8]

2 Carbon dioxide is an inorganic molecule. What does this mean?

A. it contains many carbon–carbon bonds and/or carbon–hydrogen bonds

B. it contains many carbon–carbon bonds but not carbon–hydrogen bonds

C. it contains many carbon–hydrogen bonds but not carbon–carbon bonds

D. it contains neither carbon–hydrogen bonds nor carbon–carbon bonds [1]

3 The diagram shows part of the carbon cycle.

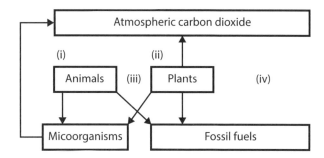

Give the letter of the arrow missing at each point (i)–(iv). [4]

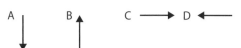

S **4** Use these terms to complete each sentence about the nitrogen cycle. Each word can be used once or not at all.

| ammonium | bacteria | deamination | decomposers |

nitrate   nitrification   nitrifying   nitrite

nitrogen-fixation   proteins

a Amino acids are nitrogen-containing molecules that are needed to make ....

b .... happens in some bacteria and also when there is lightning.

c During nitrification ...., ions are used to make NO_2^- and NO_3^- .

d Plants absorb nitrogen as .... ions from the soil.

e Urea is made from the products of .... during which amino acids are broken down. **[5]**

S **5** Describe the process of denitrification in soils. **[2]**

This is worth two marks, so you need two points. In this question, there is one mark for the name of the organism that carries out the process and one mark for a description of what happens.

> **Show me**

.... bacteria convert nitrates into ....

Populations

1 Look at the food web in question 1 on page 138.

a Predict and explain what will happen to the elephant seal population if many more orcas suddenly move into the ecosystem. **[2]**

b Describe the competition between cod and squid. **[1]**

c Elephant seals and leopard seals both live on land and go hunting in the sea. Apart from food supply, suggest one other way in which these two species compete. **[1]**

d Suggest and explain what will happen to the populations of squid and cod if a new fish disease enters the ecosystem. **[4]**

You need to suggest what happens and then give your reasoning. Try to link your suggestion with your reasoning using a word such as 'because'.

e Apart from biological factors, there are physical factors that affect these organism populations. Explain how one physical environmental factor will affect the phytoplankton population. **[2]**

[Total marks 10]

2 Which of these is a biological environmental factor?

A. predation

B. rainfall

C. soil moisture content

D. temperature **[1]**

3 A farmer wants to know if she should spray herbicide to kill dandelions in a field that is 15 m wide and 10 m long. It is only worth spraying if there are more than seven dandelion plants per m².

Wire frames of area 0.5 cm² were placed randomly at 15 positions in the field. The total number of dandelion plants in the sample area was 20.

a Use this formula to estimate the population. [2]

$$\text{estimated population} = \text{number in sample} \times \frac{\text{study area (m}^2)}{\text{sample area (m}^2)}$$

> **Show me**
>
> First calculate all the values you need. Then put them into the formula.
>
> Number in sample = ...   Study area = 15 × 10 = ... m²
>
> Sample area = ... m²

b Give the name of the wire frames used. [1]

c Give the reason why the wire frames were placed at random. [1]

d A student suggests that more samples should be taken. Evaluate this idea. [5]

[Total marks 9]

> There are a lot of marks here. You need to write down the advantages and disadvantages of the idea and then use evidence to reach a decision.

4 The changes in the numbers of yeast cells growing in a solution of glucose and water were measured each day for two weeks. There was a small increase in yeast cell numbers between days 0 and 3. There was then a very rapid and large increase in cell numbers between days 4 and 7. There was little change in the numbers between days 8 and 9. After day 10, the numbers of yeast cells started to decrease.

a **i)** Give the name of the phase between Days 8 and 9. [1]

S **ii)** Suggest the limiting factor that has caused this phase. [1]

b Suggest an explanation for what happened after Day 10. [2]

[Total marks 4]

Factors affecting biodiversity

1 In the diagrams, a star represents an individual organism. Which diagram shows the greatest biodiversity? [1]

A   B   C   D

2 Four different grapevine plants of similar sizes were each covered with 150 grapevine aphids. Each plant was treated with the same amount of four different insecticides. After five days, there were 166 aphids on the vine treated with insecticide W, 210 on the vine treated with insecticide X, 3 on the vine treated with insecticide Y and 285 on the vine treated with insecticide Z.

a Identify the best insecticide to increase the yield of grapes. [1]

b Explain how an insecticide increases yield. [2]

c Calculate the percentage change in the numbers of aphids when using insecticide X. [1]

> **Show me**

Percentage change is worked out using this formula.

$$\text{percentage change} = \frac{(\text{value at end} - \text{value at start})}{\text{value at start}} \times 100$$

d Explain a problem with using insecticides when growing crops. [2]

[Total marks 6]

3 Discuss how intensive farming can damage the environment. [3]

> Look at the number of marks. Your answer should contain three different points.

4 Explain how deforestation can lead to increased flooding in an area. [3]

5 Outline two ways in which deforestation leads to global warming. [2]

Pollution and conservation

1 Which word means 'to change gradually over time'?

A. endanger **B.** evolve **C.** select **D.** sustain [1]

2 **a** Carbon dioxide is a natural component of the atmosphere. Give the reason it can be a pollutant. [1]

b The Bramble cay melomys was a tiny mouse-like animal that only lived on one small low-lying island off the coast of Australia (its highest point was three metres above sea level).

The melomys became extinct in 2019. Explain how atmospheric carbon dioxide could have caused this. [3]

[Total marks 4]

3 Humans first arrived on the island of Madagascar about 1500 years ago. Grandidier's giant tortoise lived on the island but became extinct about 1250 years ago.

A similar tortoise, the Aldabra giant tortoise, was found on a small island near Madagascar. Scientists discovered that it likes eating the fruits of a tree found only on Madagascar (not on the small island). Some Aldabra tortoises are now being bred in captivity in Madagascar, to be released into the wild.

a Suggest why the Grandidier's giant tortoise became extinct. [1]

b Describe how the release of Aldabra tortoises may affect the ecosystem. [3]

c Suggest **one** way in which the Aldabra tortoises could be protected once released. [1]

d The population of Aldabra tortoises is very small. Suggest and explain a potential problem for the species if it is released into the wild in Madagascar. [2]

[Total marks 7]

4 Near intensive farms, rivers often turn green and the fish die. Explain how intensive farming can cause the fish to die. [5]

Biotechnology

1 Which biofuel is made using yeast?

A. biodiesel B. carbon dioxide C. ethanol D. petrol [1]

2 Outline why yeast is used to make bread. [2]

It may help to write down the equation for anaerobic respiration in yeast.

3 To make yoghurt, *Lactobacillus bulgaricus* bacteria are added to milk and left in a warm place for several hours. The bacteria feed on the milk and respire. Give the reason that yoghurt-making is an example of biotechnology. [1]

4 Some students investigated different washing powders for their ability to digest starch, proteins and lipids (fats and oils). The students mixed each washing powder with water. They added the mixtures to different wells in various types of agar jelly. Each well was 5 mm in diameter.

After an hour, the students recorded the results (which are shown in the table).

Substances added to agar	Washing powder	Diameter of well + zone of digestion/mm			
		1st well	2nd well	3rd well	Mean
starch + iodine	X	15	17	13	15
starch + iodine	Y	20	20	23	21
starch + iodine	Z	5	5	5	5
milk	X	10	12	11	11
milk	Y	8	8	11	9
milk	Z	5	5	5	5
oil + indicator	X	17	11	14	
oil + indicator	Y	12	13	17	14
oil + indicator	Z	5	5	5	5

a Describe the appearance of the zone of digestion in the agar containing starch and iodine. [1]

b Calculate the missing mean value. [1]

Do not forget the units!

c   Give the reason for calculating a mean.   [1]

d   One of the washing powders was 'non-biological'. Identify and explain which of the washing powders this was.   [3]

e   **i)**   Explain which washing powder was the most effective at removing proteins.   [2]

       ii)   If this washing powder is used in a high-temperature wash, its ability to remove protein stains is reduced. Explain this observation.   [2]

[Total marks 10]

5   Some students added different concentrations of pectinase to apple pulp. After 30 minutes, the students compared the amount of juice collected. The table shows the results.

Pectinase concentration (g/100 cm^3)	Amount of juice collected by filtration after 30 minutes (cm^3)
0 (distilled water)	3.5
0.1	3.7
0.2	4.4
0.3	4.4
0.4	4.9

a   Explain the purpose of adding only distilled water to one sample of apple pulp.   [2]

b   Explain the effect of increasing the concentration of pectinase on the amount of juice collected.   [4]

c   Calculate the percentage increase in juice obtained using 0.4 g/100 cm^3 pectinase compared with using 0 g/100 cm^3 pectinase.   [1]

> **Show me**
>
> Use this formula:
>
> $$\% \text{ increase in juice volume} = \frac{\text{volume with pectinase} - \text{volume without pectinase}}{\text{volume without pectinase}} \times 100$$

d   Suggest two control variables for this experiment.   [2]

[Total marks 9]

S   **6**   Lactase is produced in fermenters using a fungus called kōji mold.

a   Explain why the fermenter is treated with high-pressure steam before the mold is grown.   [2]

b   Explain why the temperature in a fermenter needs to be controlled using a cooling water jacket.   [2]

c   Paddles in the fermenter constantly mix its contents. Suggest and explain why this is necessary.   [2]

d   Explain why lactase is added to some milk sold in supermarkets.   [2]

e   Give the name of a food product produced in a similar way, using a fungus.   [1]

[Total marks 9]

Genetic modification

1 Which of the following best describes genetic modification?

    A. adding genes to an organism

    B. adding or changing genes in an organism

    C. adding or changing or deleting genes in an organism

    D. breeding organisms with new combinations of genes that make them more useful to humans   **[1]**

2 Compare DNA ligase and restriction enzymes.   **[2]**

> If a biological word has -ase at the end, it indicates that it is an enzyme.

3 The diagram shows a sticky end from a gene that has been cut out of human DNA.

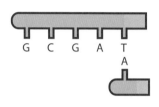

    Which is the complementary sticky end?   **[1]**

    A.   C C C T

    B.   C G C T

    C.   A A A G

    D.   G C G A

4 Suggest two traits (**features**) which could be desirable to add to a crop plant using genetic modification.   **[2]**

5 Suggest why someone who farms a small piece of land may not grow GM crops.   **[1]**

6 A bacterium called *Bacillus thuringiensis* produces a toxic protein. Explain **one** advantage and **one** disadvantage of genetically modifying a crop to contain the gene for this toxin.   **[4]**

> This is worth four marks, so you need to state an advantage and a disadvantage and provide an explanation of each. Think about using linking words and phrases to link your statements to your explanations, such as 'because', 'due to', 'and so'.

> **Show me**
>
> An advantage is that .... and so ....

7 **a** Many people with diabetes need to inject themselves with insulin. In the past, insulin was obtained from pigs. Today, it is mainly obtained from genetically modified bacteria. State **two** advantages of using bacteria.   **[2]**

  b Outline the process by which bacteria can be genetically modified to produce insulin.   **[6]**

                                                        [Total marks 8]

Mixed exam-style questions

1 The diagram shows a lion.

Which term describes a lion?

A arthropod

B carnivore

C pathogen

D producer [1]

In multiple-choice questions, one way of working out the correct answer is by eliminating the incorrect options.

2 Which type of cell contains a large vacuole?

A human egg cell

B neurone

C palisade mesophyll cell

D red blood cell [1]

3 Which chemical reaction uses energy from light?

A carbon dioxide + water → glucose + oxygen

B glucose → alcohol + carbon dioxide

C glucose → lactic acid

D glucose + oxygen → carbon dioxide + water [1]

4 Which organ secretes enzymes **and** hormones?

A adrenal gland

B kidney

C liver

D pancreas [1]

Make sure you take special note of words in **bold**. In this question, you need to choose an organ that secretes both things.

5 Which term describes the removal of undigested food from the body?

    A   active transport   **C**   egestion

    B   digestion   **D**   excretion   **[1]**

> Some words that have specific scientific meanings may be used differently in everyday language. In examination questions, make sure you stick to the scientific meanings of words.

6 Which part of the movement of water through a plant occurs by osmosis?

    A   from the soil into plant root hair cells

    B   from the surface of mesophyll cells into air spaces in leaves

    C   out of leaves through stomata

    D   through xylem vessels   **[1]**

7 How do heart rate and breathing change during physical activity?

	heart rate	breathing rate	depth of breathing
A	decreases	decreases	decreases
B	decreases	increases	decreases
C	increases	decreases	increases
D	increases	increases	increases

   [1]

8 Which process does **not** use energy released by respiration?

    A   contraction of the muscular wall of the heart

    B   passage of nerve impulses along a neurone

    C   swimming of sperm cells to an egg cell

    D   transpiration of water vapour from plant leaves   **[1]**

> Take special care if you see the word **not**. You're unlikely to choose the correct answer if you ignore it.

9 Which row correctly compares nervous and hormonal control?

	nervous control	hormonal control
A	acts quickly	longer-lasting effects
B	acts slowly	short-lived effects
C	longer-lasting effects	acts slowly
D	short-lived effects	acts quickly

   [1]

10 What can kill bacteria but **not** viruses?

A   antibiotics

B   antibodies

C   pathogens

D   platelets   [1]

11 What term describes the joining of the nuclei of two gametes?

A   fertilisation

B   germination

C   pollination

D   reproduction   [1]

12 What is the name of the pathogen that causes AIDS?

A   ECG

B   HIV

C   PNS

D   STI   [1]

13 Which process increases genetic variation?

A   asexual reproduction

B   inheritance

C   mutation

D   natural selection   [1]

14 Which trophic level are herbivores?

A   primary consumers

B   producers

C   secondary consumers

D   tertiary consumers   [1]

S 15 Which groups of organisms have the most similar DNA base sequences?

A   birds and mammals

B   dicotyledons and fish

C   insects and reptiles

D   protoctists and viruses   [1]

S 16 Which structure is **not** made of protein?

A   antibody

B   DNA

C   enzyme

D   virus coat   [1]

S 17 Which statement describes the function of bile?

A   breaking down carbohydrates in the small intestine

B   increasing the acidity of food as it leaves the stomach

C   increasing the surface area of fats and oils for chemical digestion

D   lubricating the passage of food through the small intestine   [1]

18 Through which transport vessels does translocation occur?

    A blood capillaries   **C** phloem vessels

    B lacteals   **D** xylem vessels   **[1]**

19 Which biological process does **not** involve the joining of two molecules with complementary shapes?

    A antibodies binding to antigens

    B mRNA molecules attaching to ribosomes

    C neurotransmitter molecules binding to receptor proteins

    D the formation of enzyme-substrate complexes   **[1]**

20 Which statement describes mitosis?

    A cell division always giving rise to stem cells

    B cell division giving rise to genetically different cells

    C nuclear division giving rise to genetically identical cells

    D reduction division giving rise to genetically identical cells   **[1]**

21 The diagrams show different types of cell.

Which type of cell is formed by meiosis?

A

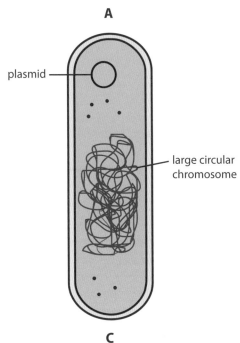

plasmid

large circular chromosome

B

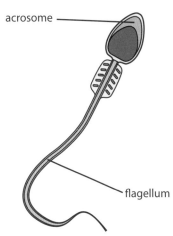

acrosome

flagellum

C

haemoglobin

D

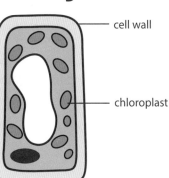

cell wall

chloroplast

not to scale   **[1]**

S **2** How do strains of antibiotic-resistant bacteria develop?

   A genetic modification

   B natural selection

   C random mating

   D selective breeding [1]

S **23** Which process involves the removal of the nitrogen-containing part of amino acids to form urea?

   A deamination

   B denitrification

   C nitrification

   D nitrogen fixation [1]

S **24** Why are bacteria useful in biotechnology and genetic modification?

   A They contain nuclei into which DNA can be inserted.

   B They contain plasmids into which DNA can be inserted.

   C They have a nervous system that can sense pain.

   D They reproduce slowly but at a constant rate. [1]

S **25** What is the function of restriction enzymes?

   A breaking down lactose to produce lactose-free products

   B breaking down the jelly coat of an egg cell

   C cutting DNA leaving free ends

   D joining lengths of DNA together [1]

26 **a** **Table 26.1** shows some of the nutrients that make up a balanced diet, some of their principal dietary sources and their importance in the body.

Table 26.1

nutrient	examples of dietary sources	importance of nutrient
proteins	beans, eggs, fish, meat, milk, seeds	provide amino acids to make new proteins for enzymes and growth
	butter, cheese, fish, meat, nuts	energy store for respiration
vitamin D		for strong bones and teeth
iron	green leafy vegetables, red meat	

Complete **Table 26.1** by writing the name of the missing nutrient, **one** example of the missing dietary sources and **one** example of the missing importance.

The first row has been completed for you. [3]

b **Fig. 26.1** shows a section through a human molar tooth.

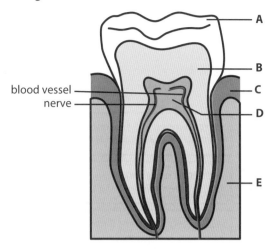

blood vessel
nerve

Fig. 26.1

State the letter on **Fig. 26.1** that identifies:

the enamel .... the pulp .... [2]

c Complete the sentences. Use terms from the list.

Each term can be used once, more than once, or not at all.

chemical	**larger**	**physical**
smaller	**surface area**	**thickness**

Molar teeth chew food, making the pieces of food .... This is an example of

.... digestion and increases the .... of the food for the

action of enzymes in .... digestion. [4]

d A tooth became infected by bacteria.

The nerves in the tooth carried impulses, leading to a feeling of pain.

i) Identify **two** terms from the list that can be used to describe the type of nerve cells that carry impulses away from the infected tooth.

effectors   **motor neurones**

peripheral nerves   **relay neurones**   **sensory neurones** [2]

Sometimes, in questions like this, you may be asked to 'circle' the correct answers. Other times, you may need to write them down.

ii) A dentist treated the bacterial infection with antibiotics.

State **one** reason **for**, and **one** reason **against**, treating a tooth infection with antibiotics. [2]

State means to give a clear, straightforward answer or answers.

[Total: 13]

27 **a** The boxes on the left show some ecological terms.

The meanings of some ecological terms are in the boxes on the right.

Link each ecological term with its meaning.

One link has been drawn for you. Make **four** additional links.

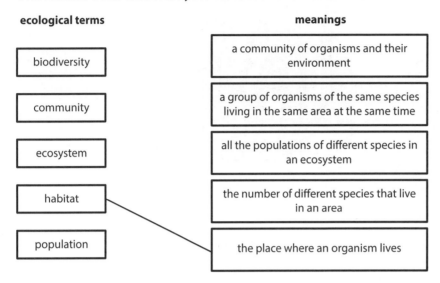

ecological terms		meanings

[3]

b One example of habitat destruction is deforestation.

State **two** reasons for deforestation. [2]

c One undesirable effect of deforestation is that more species become endangered or extinct.

i) State **two other** undesirable effects of deforestation. [2]

ii) Describe how captive breeding programmes can help conserve endangered species in their natural environments. [1]

> **Show me**

After you have bred a species in captivity to increase its numbers, some of these ....

Describe means you have to state the main point or points.

iii) In captive breeding programmes, males with higher levels of testosterone are more successful at producing offspring than males of the same species with lower levels of testosterone.

Suggest **one** reason why males with higher testosterone levels are more successful breeders. [1]

Suggest means you have to apply what you know or understand to propose a possible answer or answers. This may mean using knowledge or ideas from other parts of your Biology course.

d Deforestation in an ecosystem decreases the flow of energy through the ecosystem.

Explain why deforestation decreases the flow of energy through an ecosystem. [2]

Make sure you look at how many marks there are for a question. Usually, you'll need to make at least the same number of different points in your answer to get full marks.

[Total: 11]

28 A student tested some pasta for the presence of starch and reducing sugars such as glucose.

a **i)** Describe the test for the presence of starch. [2]

> **Show me**
>
> To test for starch, add ....
>
> If starch is present, the colour changes from brown to ....

ii) Describe the test for the presence of a reducing sugar. [3]

b The tests showed that the pasta contained starch but no reducing sugars such as glucose.

The student then ate some of the same type of pasta.

The concentration of glucose in the student's blood was monitored after eating the pasta. The results are shown in **Fig. 28.1**.

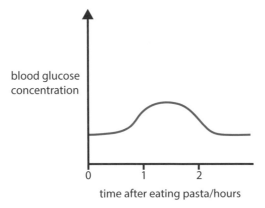

Fig. 28.1

i) Explain why, in **Fig. 28.1**, the student's blood glucose concentration increased soon after eating the pasta. [3]

Explain means you have to give the reason or reasons.

ii) State **two** reasons why, in **Fig. 28.1**, the student's blood glucose concentration later decreased. [2]

S **iii)** Explain how **Fig. 28.1** shows an example of homeostatic control by negative feedback. [2]

If a question refers you back to an earlier part of the question, as here, make sure you do look back to help you answer.

[Total: 12]

29 Farmers use fertilisers to provide mineral ions, such as nitrates, to plant crops.

a State why farmers provide mineral ions to plant crops. [1]

b State which part of a plant absorbs mineral ions. [1]

c Explain why plants need nitrate ions. [2]

d Plants also absorb mineral ions that have been released from dead or waste organic material.

Describe how mineral ions are released from dead or waste organic material. [2]

S **e**   Plants absorb mineral ions by active transport.

Explain why mineral ions have to be absorbed by active transport.   [2]

S **f**   Sometimes, fertilisers put on fields of plant crops can lead to the deaths of fish and other animals in streams and rivers near to the fields.

Explain how the fertilisers can lead to these deaths.   [6]

> **Show me**
>
> If more fertiliser is put on the field than is absorbed by the crops, then the .... fertiliser can .... into nearby streams and rivers.
>
> In the water, the mineral ions cause an increased growth of .... When these die, ...
>
> The increased number of decomposers .... reducing the level of ....

[Total: 14]

30 **a**   **Fig. 30.1** shows a section through the human eye.

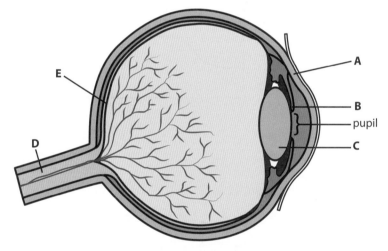

Fig. 30.1

Table 30.1 shows some parts of the eye, some letters from **Fig. 30.1** and some functions of parts of the eye.

Table 30.1

part of eye	letter from Fig. 30.1	function of part of eye
iris	B	controls how much light enters the pupil
lens		
	D	
		contains light receptors

Complete **Table 30.1** by writing the names of the missing parts of the eye, letters from **Fig 30.1** and functions of parts of the eye.

The first row has been completed for you.   [6]

b In bright light, the pupil becomes smaller.

In dim light, the pupil becomes larger.

This is known as the pupil reflex.

    i) Outline what is meant by the term reflex action. [2]

Outline means to set out the main points.

    ii) Explain the benefit of the pupil reflex in **dim** light. [2]

S   **iii)** Explain how circular and radial muscles in the iris act during the pupil reflex in **bright** light. [2]

Always try to use the correct scientific terms in your answers.

c **Fig. 30.2** shows some seedlings that have been grown in a light-proof box, **X**. Other seedlings have been grown in a similar box, **Y**, that has one side missing so light can enter. All other conditions in each box are the same.

X   Y

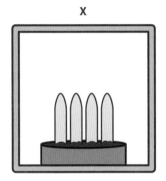 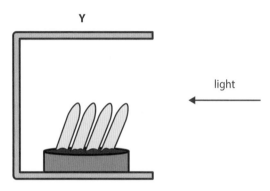

light

Fig. 30.2

    i) State the name of the response shown by the seedlings in box **Y** that is **not** shown by the seedlings in box **X**. [1]

S   **ii)** Explain the role of auxin in the response shown by the seedlings in box **Y**. [4]

> **Show me**

Auxin is made in the .... From there it .... becoming more

concentrated on ....

Auxin stimulates .... which causes the shoots to curve and grow
towards the light.

[Total: 17]

S **31** **a** The lining of the small intestine is covered with many villi.

Fig. 31.1 shows a section through a single villus.

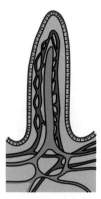

Fig. 31.1

i) The mean width of a villus is about 0.06 mm.

Give this value in μm (micrometres). [1]

> **Give** means you have to state a clear, straightforward, often short, answer.

ii) Describe **and** explain **three** ways that villi are adapted for the efficient absorption of nutrients from the small intestine into the blood. [6]

> **Describe and explain** means you have to state the main point, or points, and then give a linked reason(s).

b After leaving the small intestine, blood flows to the liver.

Fig. 31.2 shows the main blood vessels taking blood to and from the liver.

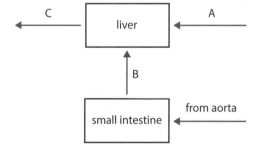

Fig. 31.2

i) Identify the blood vessels labelled **A**, **B** and **C** in **Fig. 31.2**. [3]

> **Identify** can mean to name (as here) or to select the correct answer from several possibilities.

ii) Suggest **one** reason why blood from the small intestine goes to the liver before passing around the rest of the body. [1]

c i) In mammals, blood flows in a double circulation.

Describe what is meant by the term double circulation. [1]

ii) Blood is transported at a higher pressure in arteries than in veins.

Describe **and** explain **one** way the structure of arteries is related to this higher pressure. [2]

[Total: 14]

Practice Paper 1: Multiple Choice (Core)

Instructions

- There are 40 questions on this paper. Answer **all** questions.
- For each question, circle **one** of the four possible answers, **A**, **B**, **C** and **D**.
- You may use a calculator.
- The total mark for the paper is 40.

1 Which statement describes respiration?

    A. chemical reaction in cells that produces glucose

    B chemical reaction in cells that releases energy

    C uses carbon dioxide and produces oxygen

    D uses oxygen and produces carbon dioxide

2 The diagram shows a section through an animal cell.

What is part X?

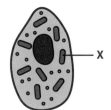

    A chloroplast

    B mitochondrion

    C nucleus

    D plasmid

3 The diagrams show sections through different types of cell.

Which cell is adapted for efficient water absorption?

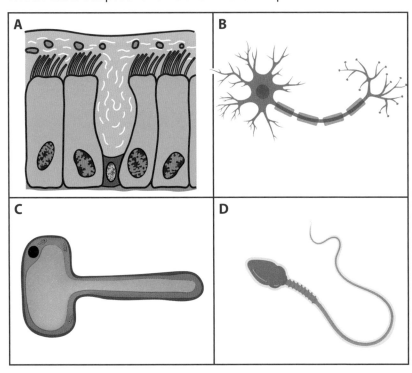

4 Which can be produced by anaerobic respiration in yeast?

A biological washing powders

B bread

C fruit juice

D glucose

5 Identify the process by which carbon dioxide enters leaf cells and water moves out from them?

A active transport

B diffusion

C osmosis

D transpiration

6 Which statement is correct?

A Amino acids make up proteins.

B Fatty acids make up carbohydrates.

C Glucose molecules make up fats.

D Glycogen molecules make up sugars.

7 Identify the substance that is a biological catalyst.

A enzymes

B hormones

C neurones

D plasmids

8 Photosynthesis can be described as:

carbon dioxide + water → X + Y

What are X and Y?

A oxygen + sunlight

B oxygen + glucose

C oxygen + energy

D sunlight + energy

9 Where are nutrients absorbed into the blood?

A large intestine

B liver

C small intestine

D stomach

10 The diagram shows the mammalian heart.

What is part X?

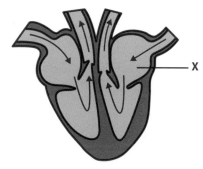

A   left atrium

B   left ventricle

C   right atrium

D   right ventricle

11 Which features are all risk factors for coronary heart disease?

A   lack of exercise, smoking, healthy weight

B   some exercise, overweight, age 20–30 years

C   stressful lifestyle, healthy diet, overweight

D   stressful lifestyle, over 50 years old, overweight

12 What process is shown in the diagram?

A   clotting

B   feeding

C   phagocytosis

D   respiration

13 Which is the pathway of oxygen into the blood?

A   alveoli → bronchioles → bronchus → trachea

B   bronchus → trachea → bronchioles → alveoli

C   trachea → alveoli → bronchioles → bronchus

D   trachea → bronchus → bronchioles → alveoli

14 Which substance is **not** removed from the body by excretion?

A   carbon dioxide

B   faeces

C   urea

D   water

15 The diagram shows a section through the eye.

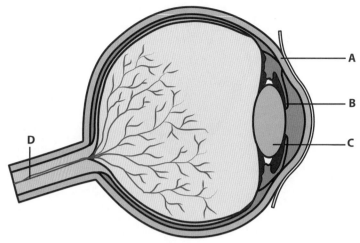

Which part of the eye focuses light onto the retina?

16 The body is under nervous and hormonal control.

Which statement about nervous control is correct?

A It is fast and lasts for a longer duration than hormonal control.

B It is fast and lasts for a short duration.

C It is slow and lasts for a longer duration than hormonal control.

D It is slow and lasts for a short duration.

17 The diagram shows a section through a flower.

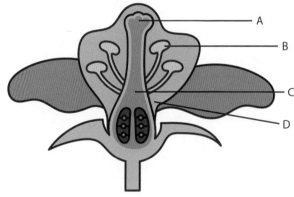

Where are the male gametes formed?

18 The bar chart shows all the number of different coloured rose flowers in a garden.

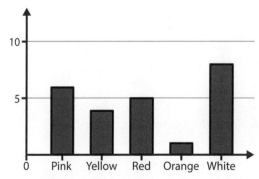

What type of variation is shown by rose flower colour?

A continuous   **C** limited

B discontinuous   **D** random

19 The diagram shows part of the carbon cycle.

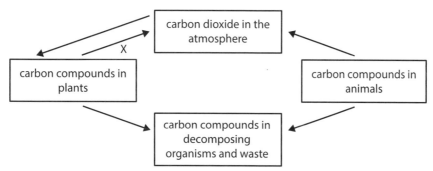

What is the process shown by arrow X?

A   decomposition

B   feeding

C   photosynthesis

D   respiration

20 What is an ecological community?

A   a group of organisms of one species, living in the same area, at the same time

B   all of the populations of different species in an ecosystem

C   the populations of different species living in different habitats in different areas

D   two or three species living in the same area, at the same time

21 Which of these actions will **not** cause habitat destruction?

A   building a quarry to extract marble

B   increasing the area of land to grow crops

C   designating a natural environment as a nature reserve

D   releasing waste water from factories into local rivers

22 How can an animal species be protected from becoming endangered or extinct?

A   cutting down local forests and vegetation where the animal lives

B   educating local people about the species and what it needs

C   introducing another animal species in their habitat that eats the same foods

D   organising hunting tours for the animal in the local area

23 Why are bacteria used in biotechnology?

A   They are very small.

B   They contain few mitochondria compared to other cells.

C   They reproduce by sexual reproduction.

D   They reproduce very quickly.

24 What are the main features of reptiles?

A dry scaly skin, lay eggs on land

B dry scaly skin, lay eggs in water

C moist skin, lay eggs on land

D moist skin, lay eggs in water

25 The diagram shows a cell at ×1500 magnification.

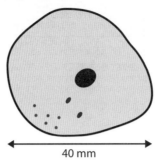

40 mm

The width of the image is 60 mm.

What is the actual width of the cell?

A 0.25 mm

B 2.5 mm

C 0.004 mm

D 0.04 mm

26 Which statement is true for osmosis and diffusion?

	Needs a partially permeable membrane	Needs energy from the cell	Molecules move from a dilute to a more concentrated solution
A	✓	X	X
B	X	✓	✓
C	X	X	X
D	X	X	✓

27 A student investigated the effect of temperature on enzyme activity.

The results showed that there was no activity above 40 °C.

Which statement explains the results?

A The active site of the enzyme changed shape, and the substrate no longer fitted into it.

B The enzyme died and the substrate was left unchanged.

C The substrate and the active site of the enzyme had changed shape.

D The substrate changed shape and no longer fitted into the active site of the enzyme.

28 The biuret test can be used to test for protein in urine samples.

What colour will the urine change to if protein is present?

A blue

B blue-black

C purple

D orange

29 Why do plants need magnesium ions?

A to make chlorophyll

B to make proteins

C to release carbon dioxide

D to use in active transport

30 Where in the digestive system is amylase secreted?

A pancreas and salivary glands

B pancreas only

C salivary glands only

D stomach wall and salivary glands

31 Which process is **not** an example of genetic modification?

A breeding together two animals with desirable genes so their offspring have the same genes as the parents

B inserting genes into crop plants to improve their nutritional quality

C inserting genes into crop plants to make them resistant to herbicides

D inserting human genes into bacteria to produce insulin

32 Which is the pathway of water through a plant?

A root hair cells → phloem → mesophyll cells → stomata

B root hair cells → xylem → mesophyll cells → stomata

C stomata → mesophyll cells → phloem → root hair cells

D stomata → mesophyll cells → xylem → root hair cells

33 Two students are running in a 100 m race.

Student X has trained for the race, but student Y has **not** trained.

What will happen to their heart rates during the race?

A The heart rates of both students will increase but X's will be lower than Y's.

B The heart rates of both students will increase but Y's will increase at a slower rate than X's.

C The heart rates of both students will increase by the same amount.

D The heart rate of student Y will increase but student X's stays the same.

34 Some students investigated the effect of temperature on respiration in yeast.

The temperatures used were 5, 15, 25 and 35 °C.

Which flask was kept at 25 °C?

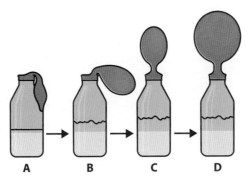

sugar and yeast fermentation experiment

35 Which is the order of a reflex arc?

A   effector → sensory neurone → relay neurone → motor neurone → receptor

B   receptor → motor neurone → relay neurone → sensory neurone → effector

C   receptor → relay neurone → sensory neurone → motor neurone → effector

D   receptor → sensory neurone → relay neurone → motor neurone → effector

36 Some students are investigating plant growth. They put a growing plant on its side.

The diagram shows the result after a few days.

Which statement describes the plant growth?

	Shoot	Root
A	Negatively phototropic	Negatively geotropic
B	Negatively phototropic	Positively geotropic
C	Positively phototropic	Negatively geotropic
D	Positively phototropic	Positively geotropic

37 Peas can have smooth skin or wrinkled skin.

The allele for smooth skin is R and the allele for wrinkled skin is r.

The diagram shows a monohybrid cross.

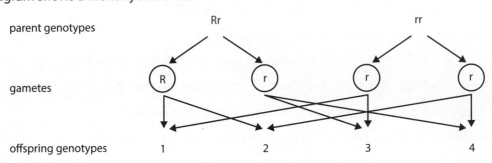

Which offspring have wrinkled skin?

A   1 and 3   B   2 and 4   C   2 and 3   D   3 and 4

38 The picture shows a polar bear.

Polar bears live in the Arctic. They hunt prey such as seals.

Which adaptation helps it to survive?

A big tail to swat flies away

B can swim slowly to catch prey in water

C have white fur, so they are not camouflaged on land

D large ears to reduce heat loss

39 A farmer wants to breed cattle to improve milk yield.

The farmer has two bulls:
- bull X's mother had mean milk yield in the herd
- bull Y's mother had the highest milk yield in the herd.

Which is the best mating to improve milk yield?

A bull X with an unrelated mean milk producer

B bull X with the highest milk producer

C bull Y with a mean milk producer

D bull Y with the highest unrelated milk producer

40 The diagram shows a food chain.

tree → caterpillars → small birds → hawks → fleas

Which is the correct pyramid of numbers for this food chain?

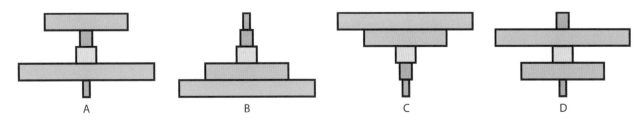

Practice Paper 2: Multiple Choice (Extended)

Instructions

- There are 40 questions on this paper. Answer **all** questions.
- For each question, (circle) **one** of the four possible answers, **A**, **B**, **C** and **D**.
- You may use a calculator.
- The total mark for the paper is 40.

1 When plants photosynthesise, which characteristic of living organisms are they showing?

  A movement

  B nutrition

  C reproduction

  D sensitivity

2 The photograph shows a centipede.

Which group of organisms are centipedes part of?

  A arachnids

  B crustaceans

  C insects

  D myriapods

3 The diagram shows an animal cell.

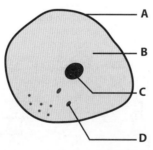

Which part of the cell is the cytoplasm?

4 What is 0.0002 mm in µm?

  A 0.002 µm

  B 0.2 µm

  C 2 µm

  D 200 µm

5 Which change will increase the rate of diffusion of oxygen into a cell?

    A   a decrease in temperature

    B   a decrease in the cell's surface area

    C   a decrease in the oxygen concentration inside the cell

    D   a decrease in the oxygen concentration outside the cell

6 What test is used for the presence of fats and oils?

    A   Benedict's solution test

    B   biuret test

    C   ethanol emulsion test

    D   iodine solution test

7 How do the bases in DNA pair up together?

    A   A with A, and C with C

    B   A with C, and G with T

    C   A with G, and C with T

    D   A with T, and C with G

8 Which statement about an enzyme's active site is correct?

    A   It has a complementary shape to its product.

    B   It has a complementary shape to its substrate.

    C   It has an identical shape to its product.

    D   It has an identical shape to its substrate.

9 The graph shows the results of an investigation into the effects of light intensity and carbon dioxide concentration on the rate of photosynthesis.

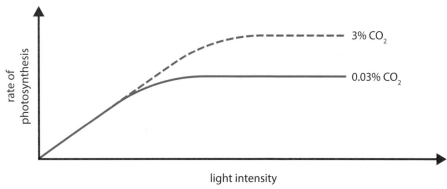

Which statement correctly describes the graph?

    A   As light intensity increases, carbon dioxide concentration becomes the limiting factor.

    B   Increasing carbon dioxide concentration always increases the rate of photosynthesis.

    C   Increasing light intensity always increases the rate of photosynthesis.

    D   When light intensity is low, carbon dioxide concentration is the limiting factor.

10 The diagram shows a section through part of a leaf.

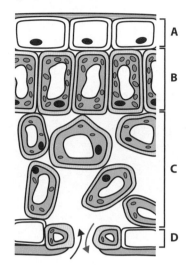

Where does most photosynthesis occur?

11 What is the correct order of the organs that food goes through as it passes along the alimentary canal?

A   mouth → oesophagus → stomach → large intestine → small intestine

B   mouth → oesophagus → stomach → small intestine → large intestine

C   mouth → stomach → oesophagus → small intestine → large intestine

D   mouth → stomach → small intestine → oesophagus → large intestine

12 Which statement about bile is correct?

A   Bile acts in the large intestine.

B   Bile chemically digests fats and oils.

C   Bile emulsifies proteins.

D   Bile is made in the liver.

13 Which statement about the enzyme trypsin is correct?

A   Trypsin breaks down carbohydrates in the mouth.

B   Trypsin breaks down fats and oils in the small intestine.

C   Trypsin breaks down proteins in the small intestine.

D   Trypsin breaks down proteins in the stomach.

14 The diagram shows a section through part of the lining of the small intestine.

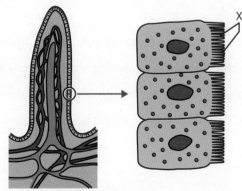

What is the name of the structures labelled X?

A capillaries

B lacteals

C microvilli

D villi

15 The diagram shows a section through a plant root.

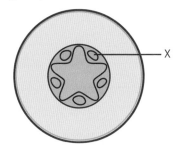

Which row is correct?

	name of part X	function of part X
A	phloem	transports sucrose and amino acids
B	phloem	transports water and mineral ions
C	xylem	transports sucrose and amino acids
D	xylem	transports water and mineral ions

16 When will a plant wilt?

A when the rate of transpiration is equal to the rate of water uptake

B when the rate of transpiration is greater than the rate of water uptake

C when the rate of transpiration is less than the rate of water uptake

D when transpiration stops

17 The diagram shows the single blood circulatory system of a fish.

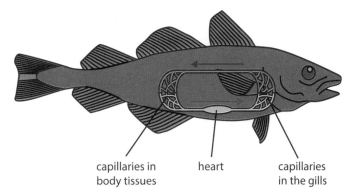

capillaries in   heart   capillaries
body tissues   in the gills

Which statement correctly describes a single circulatory system?

A Blood collects oxygen once on each complete circulation.

B Blood collects oxygen twice on each complete circulation.

C Blood is at a higher pressure than in a double circulatory system.

D Blood is pumped twice by the heart during each complete circulation.

18 Why does the heart rate increase during physical activity?

   A to keep blood pressure constant

   B to reduce body temperature

   C to supply blood more quickly to the brain

   D to supply oxygen more quickly to muscles

19 A student wrote some notes describing arteries.

They wrote:

'Arteries have …1… walls to withstand the high …2… of blood pumped from the heart into the aorta and the rest of the body.

Artery walls have …3… to maintain blood pressure.'

Complete the above paragraph by using the words in the table below.

	1	2	3
A	thick	oxygen content	valves
B	thick	pressure	elastic recoil
C	thin	oxygen content	elastic recoil
D	thin	pressure	valves

20 What is the function of lymphocytes?

   A to engulf pathogens

   B to produce antibodies

   C to produce antigens

   D to produce blood clots

21 Cholera bacteria cause chloride ions to enter the small intestine. This can lead to severe diarrhoea and dehydration.

Which statement explains these symptoms?

   A Chloride ions cause water to be absorbed from the small intestine into the blood.

   B Chloride ions cause water to enter the small intestine by osmosis.

   C Chloride ions in the small intestine disrupt the effective function of bile.

   D Chloride ions reduce thirst.

22 The diaphragm is involved in breathing.

Which row describes the diaphragm during inspiration?

	action of diaphragm	change in shape of diaphragm
A	contracts	becomes domed
B	contracts	becomes flattened
C	expands	becomes domed
D	expands	becomes flattened

23 The diagram shows apparatus used to compare the composition of inspired and expired air. The test-tubes contain limewater.

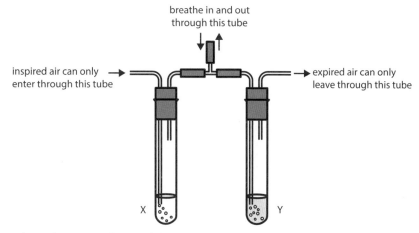

When a student breathes in and out of the apparatus, the limewater in test-tube Y becomes cloudy compared with the limewater in test-tube X.

What conclusion can be made from these results?

A Expired air contains less oxygen than inspired air.

B Expired air contains more carbon dioxide than inspired air.

C Expired air contains more water than inspired air.

D Expired air is warmer than inspired air.

24 What is produced by goblet cells to protect the breathing system from pathogens?

A acid

B antibiotics

C antibodies

D mucus

25 What is the equation for anaerobic respiration in muscles?

A glucose → alcohol + carbon dioxide

B glucose → carbon dioxide + lactic acid

C glucose → carbon dioxide + water

D glucose → lactic acid

26 What organ excretes urea?

   A kidney

   B liver

   C lung

   D rectum

27 Where do motor neurones carry electrical impulses to?

   A brain and spinal cord

   B muscles and glands

   C receptors

   D relay neurones

28 Which response is caused by the hormone adrenaline?

   A decreased breathing rate

   B decreased heart rate

   C increased pupil diameter

   D increased secretion of testosterone

29 The diagram shows seedlings growing towards light.

What is the name of this response?

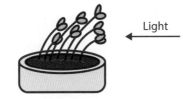

   A germination

   B gravitropism

   C homeostasis

   D phototropism

30 The diagram shows some of the stages of sexual reproduction in plants.

Three of the stages are labelled X, Y and Z.

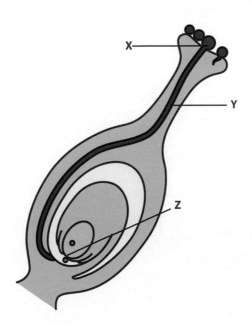

Which row shows correct descriptions of the three stages?

	X	Y	X
A	nucleus from the pollen grain enters the ovule	pollen grain on the stigma grows a pollen tube	pollen tube grows towards the ovule
B	pollen grain on the stigma grows a pollen tube	nucleus from the pollen grain enters the ovule	pollen tube grows towards the ovule
C	pollen grain on the stigma grows a pollen tube	pollen tube grows towards the ovule	nucleus from the pollen grain enters the ovule
D	pollen tube grows towards the ovule	pollen grain on the stigma grows a pollen tube	nucleus from the pollen grain enters the ovule

31 Which statement describes a function of the umbilical cord during pregnancy?

A   preventing pathogens and toxins passing to the fetus

B   producing hormones

C   transporting dissolved nutrients from the mother to the fetus

D   transporting dissolved oxygen from the fetus to the mother

32 The graph shows the relative amounts of two hormones during the menstrual cycle.

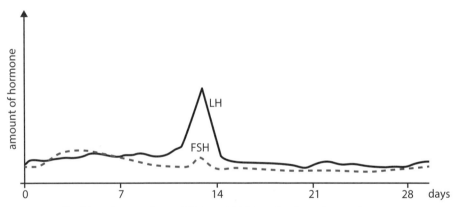

What event is controlled by the peaks in FSH and LH just before day 14?

A   fertilisation

B   implantation

C   menstruation

D   ovulation

33 What travels from the nucleus of a cell to the cytoplasm to control the production of proteins?

A   DNA

B   enzymes

C   mRNA

D   ribosomes

34 The Punnett square shows a monohybrid cross between two mice.

			male gg white fur	
			gametes	
			g	g
female Gg grey fur	gametes	G	Gg grey fur	Gg grey fur
		g	gg white fur	....

Which genotype and phenotype complete the Punnett square?

A Gg grey fur

B Gg white fur

C gg grey fur

D gg white fur

35 What genotype or genotypes cause blood group A?

A I^A only

B $I^A I^A$ only

C $I^A I^A$ and $I^A I^O$

D $I^A I^B$, $I^A I^B$ and $I^A I^O$

36 What causes discontinuous variation?

A environment and genes

B environment only

C genes only

D selective breeding

37 Which process adds nitrogen gas to the atmosphere?

A decomposition

B denitrification

C nitrification

D nitrogen fixation

38 A student wrote some notes about the eutrophication of water.

They wrote:

'Eutrophication …1… the availability of ions such as nitrates which eventually …2… the amount of dissolved oxygen and leads to the …3… of organisms needing dissolved oxygen to survive.'

Complete the above paragraph by using the words in the table below.

	1	2	3
A	decreases	decreases	growth
B	decreases	increases	growth
C	increases	decreases	death
D	increases	increases	death

39 How can fish stocks be conserved?

A decreasing closed seasons

B decreasing protected areas

C increasing net mesh size

D increasing quotas

40 During genetic modification, what type of enzyme joins DNA sticky ends together?

A lactase

B ligase

C pectinase

D restriction enzyme

Practice Paper 3: Theory (Core)

Instructions

- Answer **all** questions.
- Write your answer to each question in the space provided.
- You may use a calculator.
- The total mark for the paper is 80.

1 ▸ Fig. 1.1 shows some glasshouses used to grow plant crops.

Fig. 1.1

a State why it is important that the plants in the glasshouses receive a lot of light.

.... **[1]**

b Fig. 1.2 shows a section through some cells from a leaf.

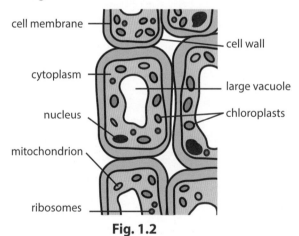

Fig. 1.2

Identify which part of a plant cell absorbs the light the plant needs.

.... **[1]**

c The plants are provided with water containing mineral ions such as magnesium.

State why plants need magnesium.

.... **[1]**

d When the temperature drops, heaters can be used to keep the temperature stable inside the glasshouses. Some heaters release carbon dioxide which the plants can absorb.

i) State which part of a plant absorbs carbon dioxide.

.... **[1]**

ii) State the name of the process by which plants absorb carbon dioxide.

.... **[1]**

(e) Fig. 1.3 shows a section through a leaf.

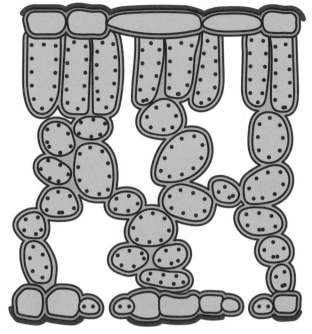

Fig. 1.3

Identify and explain **two** adaptations of a leaf to carry out its functions.

adaptation 1

....

explanation

....

adaptation 2

....

explanation

.... **[4]**

[Total: 9]

3 (a) Describe what is meant by the term asexual reproduction.

....

....

.... **[2]**

(b) Describe what is meant by the term sexual reproduction.

....

....

.... **[2]**

c During sexual reproduction in plants, a zygote is formed in a flower.

i) State the name of the process that forms a zygote.

.... [1]

ii) Identify where in a flower a zygote is formed.

.... [1]

d Humans reproduce by sexual reproduction.

Fig. 2.1 shows a diagram of a human egg cell.

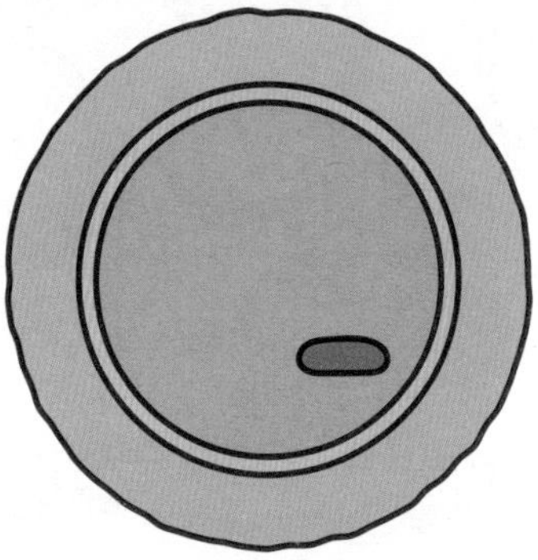

Fig. 2.1

Describe **two** ways that an egg cell is specialised for its function.

1 ....

2 .... [2]

e Compare eggs cells and sperm cells in terms of their number and size.

number

....

size

.... [2]

f State the names of **two** structures that are found in plant cells but **not** in animal cells.

1 ....

2 .... [2]

[Total: 12]

3 **a** Describe what is meant by the term physical digestion.

....

....

.... [2]

b Teeth are involved in physical digestion.

Describe the functions of incisors, canines and molar teeth.

incisors

....

canines

....

molars

.... [3]

c **i)** State the name of the chemical test used to detect proteins.

.... [1]

ii) State the colour change seen if protein is present.

.... [1]

d Fig. 3.1 shows a diagram of the human digestive system.

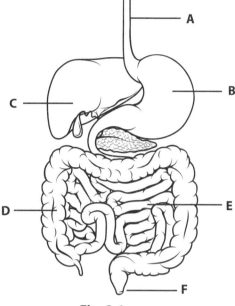

Fig. 3.1

i) Give **one** letter that shows where protease enzyme is secreted.

.... [1]

ii) Give **one** letter that shows where absorption occurs.

.... [1]

e Some students investigated the rate of an enzyme-controlled reaction at different temperatures.

Fig. 3.2 shows a graph of their results.

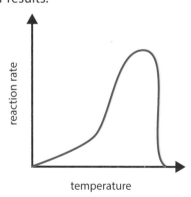

Fig. 3.2

Use Fig. 3.2 to describe the effects of changes in temperature on enzyme activity.

....

....

....

....

.... [4]

[Total: 13]

4 **a** The boxes on the left show some organisms found in food chains.

The boxes on the right show descriptions of some organisms found in food chains.

Draw **five** lines to link each organism to its correct description.

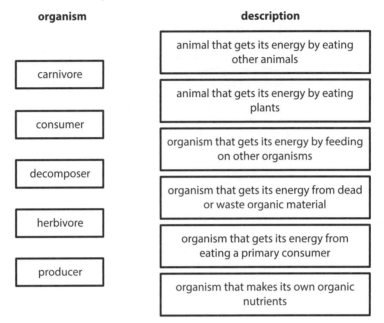

organism

description

carnivore

consumer

decomposer

herbivore

producer

animal that gets its energy by eating other animals

animal that gets its energy by eating plants

organism that gets its energy by feeding on other organisms

organism that gets its energy from dead or waste organic material

organism that gets its energy from eating a primary consumer

organism that makes its own organic nutrients

[4]

b Fig. 4.1 shows a food web.

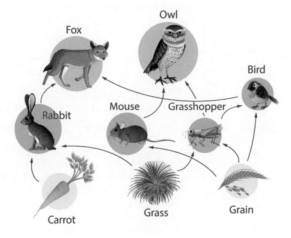

Fig. 4.1

Identify **one** food chain from Fig. 4.1 made of **four** organisms.

.... [2]

c Fig. 4.2 shows an African food chain.

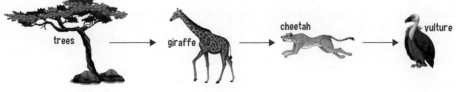

Fig. 4.2

Sketch a pyramid of biomass for this food chain. Label the stages of the pyramid. [2]

d Scientists sometimes find it difficult to collect the data needed to accurately draw a pyramid of biomass.

Suggest **one** reason why.

.... [1]

e Vulture populations have been decreasing for many years.

   i) Suggest **two** reasons for the decrease in vulture populations.

   1 ....

   .... [2]

   ii) Describe **one** way that endangered vultures can be conserved.

   .... [1]

[Total: 12]

5 Fig. 5.1 shows two species of fox.

The Arctic fox, *Vulpes lagopus*, lives in the Arctic and the fennec fox, *Vulpes zerda*, lives in the deserts of North Africa.

Arctic fox   Fennec fox

Fig. 5.1

a Identify **two** adaptive features of the fennec fox that make it different from the Arctic fox. Suggest how these features help the fennec fox survive in its environment.

adaptive feature 1

....

how this feature helps survival

....

adaptive feature 2

....

how this feature helps survival

.... [4]

b Different individual fennec foxes have slightly different shades of coat colour.

State the type of variation seen in fennec fox coat colour.

.... [1]

c Identify **one** visible feature that identifies the two fox species as mammals.

.... [1]

d State the genus of the two fox species.

.... [1]

e The coat colour of the Arctic fox has evolved by natural selection.

Outline how this has happened.

....

....

....

.... **[3]**

[Total: 10]

6 **a** Fig. 6.1 is a diagram of the human breathing system.

Fig. 6.1

State the name of each structure labelled **A** to **E** in Fig. 6.1.

A ....

B ....

C ....

D ....

E .... **[5]**

b Describe **three** ways inspired air is different from expired air.

1 ....

2 ....

3 .... **[3]**

c Describe **two** features of gas exchange surfaces.

1 ....

2 .... **[2]**

d Compare the processes of aerobic and anaerobic respiration in humans.

....

....

....

.... **[4]**

[Total: 14]

7 **a** The boxes on the left show some genetic terms.

The boxes on the right show the meanings of some genetic terms.

Draw **three** lines to link each genetic term to its correct meaning.

genetic term   meaning

| having two different alleles of a particular gene |

genotype

| having two identical alleles of a particular gene |

homozygous

| observable features of an organism |

phenotype

| the alleles present |

[3]

b Flower colour in pea plants is controlled by a single allele.

The dominant allele **F** causes the flowers to be purple.

The recessive allele **f** causes the flowers to be white.

A farmer crosses a pea plant with white flowers with a heterozygous pea plant with purple flowers.

Complete the Punnett square and the phenotypic ratio for this cross.

	purple flowers	
white flowers		

phenotypic ratio .... white : .... purple

[3]

c **i)** Describe the meaning of the term mutation.

....

.... [1]

ii) State **two** factors that increase the rate of mutation.

1 ....

2 .... [2]

iii) Describe the effect of mutation on variation.

.... [1]

[Total: 10]

Practice Paper 4: Theory (Extended)

Instructions

- Answer **all** questions.
- Write your answer to each question in the space provided.
- You may use a calculator.
- You can use a copy of the Periodic Table.
- The total mark for the paper is 80.

1 Fig. 1.1 shows a section through a flower.

Fig. 1.1

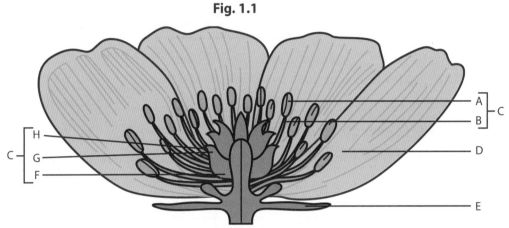

a Table 1.1 shows some functions of different parts of the flower.

Complete Table 1.1 by stating the name of each part of the flower and giving the letter that identifies it.

Table 1.1

function of part of flower	name of part of flower	letter on Fig. 1.1
produces pollen grains		
contains the ovule		
protects the flower while in bud		

[3]

b The flower in Fig. 1.1 is insect-pollinated.

i) State the meaning of the term pollination.

....

.... [1]

ii) Describe **three** differences between the structure of the flower in Fig. 1.1 and a wind-pollinated flower.

1 ....

....

2 ....

....

3 ....

.... [3]

c Explain **one** advantage and **one** disadvantage of cross-pollination compared with self-pollination.

advantage ....

....

disadvantage ....

.... [2]

d Insecticides are used to control insect pests that would otherwise affect the quality and yield of crops.

Many people are concerned that insecticides are also affecting pollinators such as bees.

Fig. 1.2 shows the results of some research on the effects of a type of insecticide called a neonicotinoid on queen bees. Concentrations used in the investigation were similar to those found in the environment.

Fig. 1.2

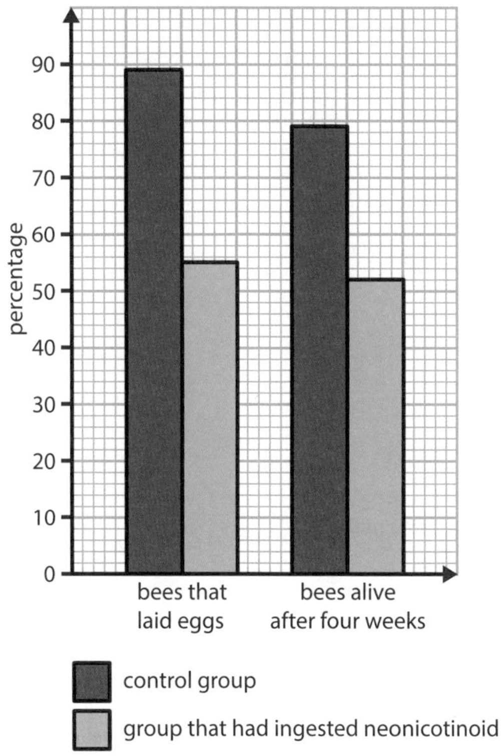

i) Describe the results of the investigations shown in Fig. 1.2.

....

....

....

....

.... [2]

185

ii) Neonicotinoids work by affecting the transmission of nerve impulses across synapses in insects.

Describe the events that occur as a nerve impulse is transmitted across a synapse in humans.

....

....

....

....

....

....

....

.... **[3]**

[Total: 14]

2 Viruses can enter the cells of a host and cause disease.

a State **three** of the body's defences against microorganisms.

1 ....

2 ....

3 .... **[3]**

b Vaccinations are used to protect people from transmissible diseases.

Outline the process of vaccination.

....

....

....

....

....

.... **[3]**

c Measles is a transmissible disease caused by a virus.

Fig. 2.1 shows the numbers of measles cases in England and Wales recorded over a number of years.

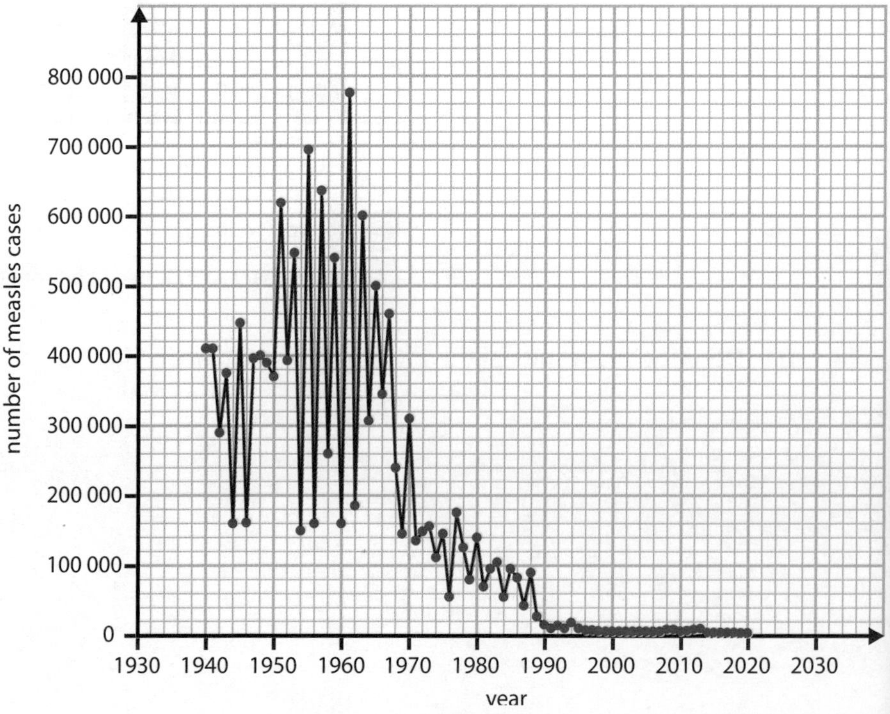

Fig. 2.1

i) State the time period over which data were collected.

.... [1]

ii) State the maximum number of measles cases in one year during that time period.

Give your answer to the nearest 10 000.

.... [1]

iii) The first measles vaccination in the UK was in 1968.

A vaccine used to protect against three serious diseases, measles, mumps and rubella (**MMR**), was introduced in 1988.

Using Fig. 2.1, describe the effects of vaccination in the control of measles.

....

....

....

....

....

.... [2]

d The disease COVID-19 is also caused by a virus.

One of the areas of research to protect people from the virus was to prevent its reproduction.

Researchers investigated the effects of amino acids on the virus.

Describe the role of amino acids in the reproduction of a virus.

....

....

....

....

.... [2]

[Total: 12]

3 Plants use the process of photosynthesis to synthesise carbohydrates and other molecules.

a State the chemical symbol equation for photosynthesis. [2]

b Some of the substances involved in photosynthesis are transported to and from the leaf in the xylem and phloem.

Fig. 3.1 shows a section through the stem of a dicotyledonous plant.

Stem cross-section

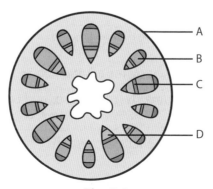

Fig. 3.1

i) State the letter on Fig. 3.1 that identifies the phloem.

.... [1]

ii) Other than water, state **one** molecule that is transported in the phloem.

.... [1]

c Farmers can increase yields by increasing the rate of photosynthesis of crop plants.

Scientists have investigated how different concentrations of carbon dioxide in a greenhouse can affect the rate of photosynthesis.

The results of one investigation are shown in **Fig. 3.2**.

Fig. 3.2

i) Describe the results of the investigation shown in Fig. 3.2.

....

....

....

....

....

....

....

....

.... [4]

ii) Explain the results for species **B** shown in Fig. 3.2.

....

....

....

....

.... [2]

d Another method of increasing crop yield is by the addition of nitrate fertilisers.

Excess nitrates can be washed into streams, rivers and lakes and cause eutrophication of water.

Explain the process of eutrophication in aquatic ecosystems.

....

....

....

....

....

....

....

....

....

....

                                                                                        [5]

                                                                                   [Total: 15]

4 ▶ Fig. 4.1 shows the golden lion tamarin, *Leontopithecus rosalia*.

Fig. 4.1

The golden lion tamarin is a type of New World monkey that lives in the Atlantic Forest area of Brazil.

a State the genus name of the golden lion tamarin.

....   **[1]**

b By 1970, the population of golden lion tamarins in the wild had fallen to about 200. The species was almost extinct.

The population had decreased because of deforestation, hunting and capture of the monkeys for the pet trade.

Apart from leading to the extinction of organisms, explain **three other** undesirable effects of deforestation.

1 ....

....

2 ....

....

3 ....

....   **[3]**

(c) The golden lion tamarin was part of a captive breeding programme in 30 zoos in Northern Europe and America.

Captive-bred golden lion tamarins were reintroduced into the wild from 1984 to 2000.

i) Suggest **two** precautions that must be taken before reintroducing captive-bred animals into the wild.

1 ....

....

2 ....

.... [2]

ii) Fig. 4.2 shows data collected during the reintroduction programme.

Fig. 4.2

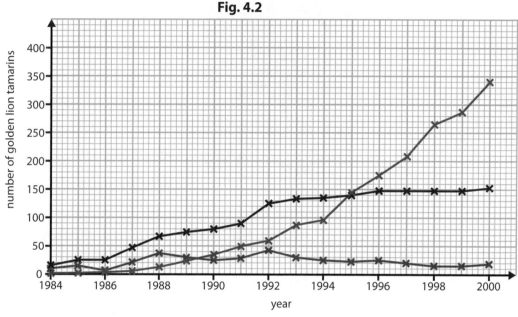

✖ cumulative total of golden lion tamarins reintroduced
✖ total reintroduced still alive
✖ total born in wild still alive

Using Fig. 4.2, state the total number of captive-bred golden lion tamarins reintroduced into the wild from 1984 to 2000.

.... [1]

iii) Using Fig. 4.2, state the year in which the number of golden lion tamarins born in the wild exceeded the total number reintroduced.

.... [1]

iv) Using Fig. 4.2, calculate the number of golden lion tamarins born in the wild as a percentage of the total number in the population in 2000.

Give your answer to the nearest whole number.

....% [2]

d Fig. 4.3 shows the evolutionary relationships of New World monkeys based on their evolutionary relationships.

Fig 4.3

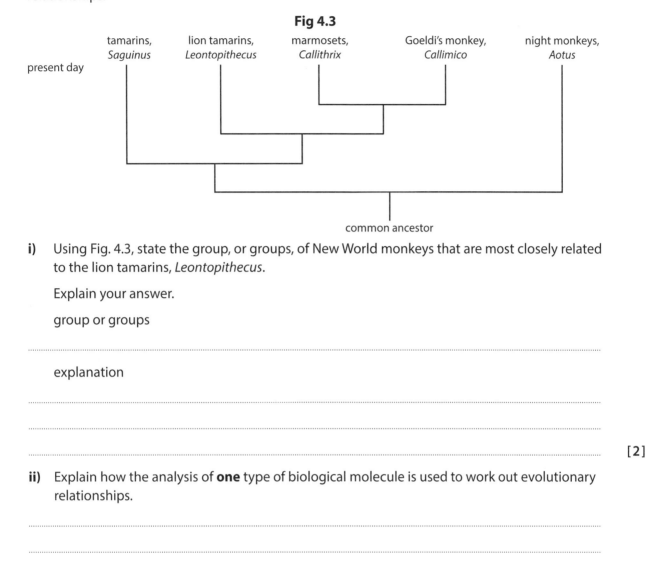

i) Using Fig. 4.3, state the group, or groups, of New World monkeys that are most closely related to the lion tamarins, *Leontopithecus*.

Explain your answer.

group or groups

....

explanation

....

....

.... [2]

ii) Explain how the analysis of **one** type of biological molecule is used to work out evolutionary relationships.

....

....

....

.... [2]

[Total: 14]

5 Insulin is a hormone that helps regulate the concentration of glucose in the blood.

a Insulin can be produced on a large scale using the bacterium, *Escherichia coli* (*E. coli*), or yeast, *Saccharomyces cerevisiae* (*S. cerevisiae*).

i) Table 5.1 compares the production of insulin by *E. coli* and by *S. cerevisiae*.

Table 5.1

		Microorganism	
		E. coli	*S. cerevisiae*
factor in insulin production	concentration of product / mg insulin per dm^3 medium	9.00	75.00
	production rate / mg insulin per dm^3 medium per h	4.01	1.04
	final mass of cells / g microorganism per dm^3 medium	1.20	5.00

Using the data in Table 5.1, suggest **one** reason for selecting *E. coli* to produce insulin and **one** reason for selecting *S. cerevisiae* to produce insulin.

E. coli

....

....

....

S. cerevisiae

....

....

....

[2]

ii) Fig. 5.1 shows the population growth of *E. coli* during insulin production.

Fig. 5.1

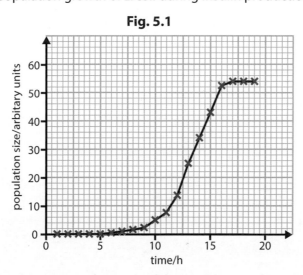

Describe and explain the pattern of growth of the population of *E. coli* in Fig. 5.1.

....

....

....

....

....

....

....

....

....

....

....

....

.... [6]

b Insulin can be produced on a large scale in fermenters.

Fig. 5.2 shows a fermenter used in insulin production.

Industrial fermenter

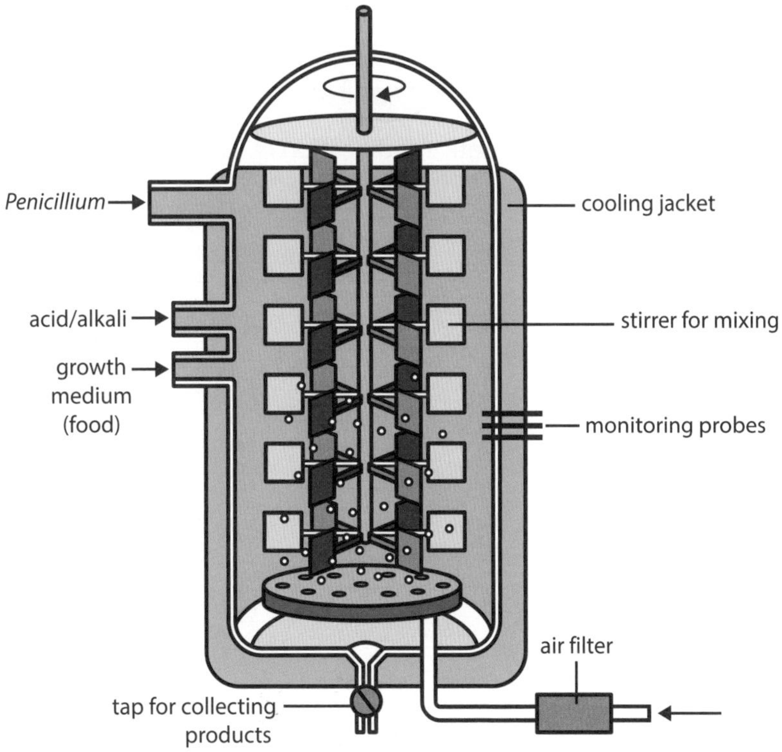

Fig. 5.2

i) Suggest why the water-filled outer jacket is required to maintain the temperature of the fermenter at 37 °C.

....

....

.... [1]

ii) One of the probes monitors temperature.

Suggest **one other** condition that the other probes monitor.

.... [1]

c The *E. coli* used to produce insulin has been genetically modified.

Fig. 5.3 shows a simplified version of part of the technique used.

Fig. 5.3

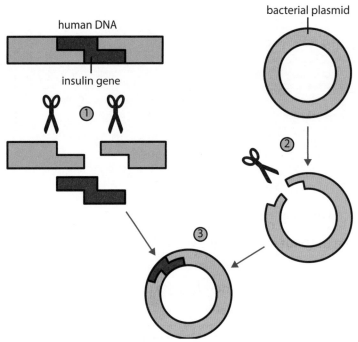

i) Outline the processes involved in genetic modification in stages **1**, **2** and **3** in Fig. 5.3.

stage 1

....

....

....

stage 2

....

....

....

stage 3

....

....

.... **[4]**

ii) Outline what happens to the plasmid **after** stage **3**.

....

....

.... **[1]**

[Total: 15]

6 **a** The human eye is able to see objects in dim light.

i) Explain how the muscles of the iris change the size of the pupil when light becomes dimmer.

....

....

....

.... **[3]**

ii) Rods are the receptor cells used for vision in dim light.

Cones are the receptor cells used for colour vision.

Fig. 6.1 shows rods and cones with their connecting neurones.

Fig. 6.1

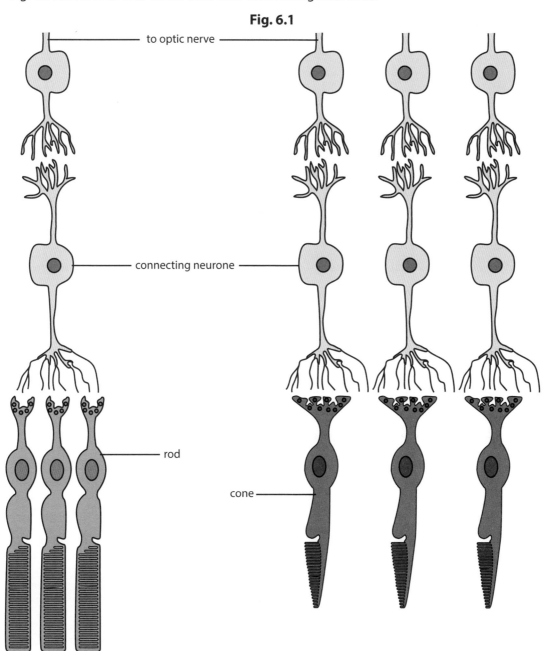

Suggest how the arrangement of rods and their connecting neurones increases their sensitivity for night vision.

....

....

.... **[1]**

b Red-green colour blindness is caused by cones that **cannot** distinguish between red and green light.

Colour vision and red-green colour blindness are controlled by a gene on the X chromosome.

There are two alleles of the gene for colour vision:

- the allele for colour vision, which can be represented by X^B
- the allele for red-green colour blindness, which can be represented by X^b.

Fig. 6.2 is a pedigree diagram showing the inheritance of red-green colour blindness in a family.

Fig. 6.2

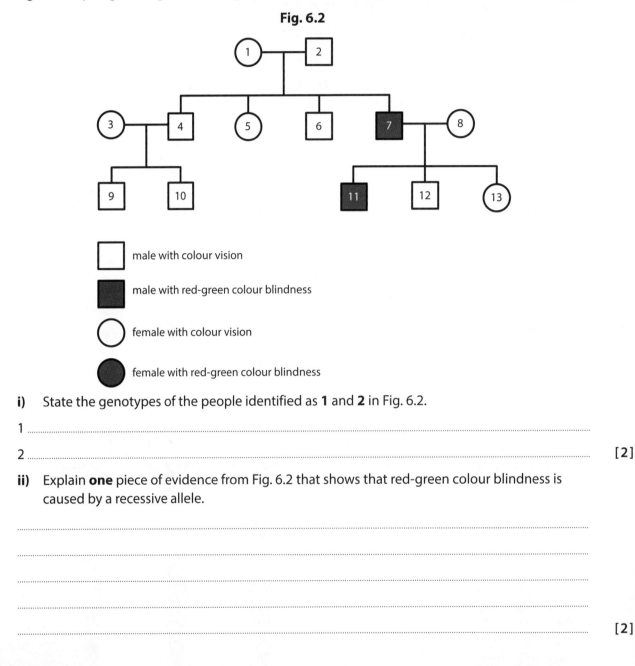

i) State the genotypes of the people identified as **1** and **2** in Fig. 6.2.

1 ....

2 .... [2]

ii) Explain **one** piece of evidence from Fig. 6.2 that shows that red-green colour blindness is caused by a recessive allele.

....

....

....

....

.... [2]

iii) In the UK, red-green colour blindness affects, to some extent, 1 in 12 males and 1 in 200 females.

Explain why red-green colour blindness is far less common in females than in males.

....

....

....

....

.... **[2]**

[Total: 10]

Practice Paper 6: Alternative to Practical

Instructions

- Answer all the questions.
- You may use a calculator.
- You should show your working and use appropriate units.
- The total mark for this paper is 40.

1 Two students investigated the effect of exercise on their pulse rates.

Pulse rates can be used to measure heart rate.

Fig. 1.1 shows how the students measured their pulse rates.

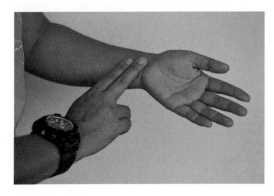

Fig. 1.1

The pulse rate of student **A** at rest = 64 beats per minute

The pulse rate of student **B** at rest = 76 beats per minute

The students then exercise.

Immediately after the exercise, the students measure their pulse rates again, and then at 1-minute intervals.

a State the independent variable in this investigation.

.... [1]

b State **two** variables that should have been kept constant in this investigation.

1 ....

2 .... [2]

c The students' results are shown in Fig. 1.2.

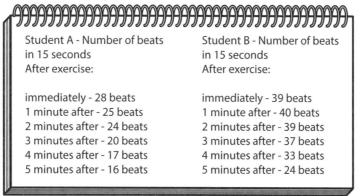

Student A - Number of beats
in 15 seconds
After exercise:

immediately - 28 beats
1 minute after - 25 beats
2 minutes after - 24 beats
3 minutes after - 20 beats
4 minutes after - 17 beats
5 minutes after - 16 beats

Student B - Number of beats
in 15 seconds
After exercise:

immediately - 39 beats
1 minute after - 40 beats
2 minutes after - 39 beats
3 minutes after - 37 beats
4 minutes after - 33 beats
5 minutes after - 24 beats

Fig. 1.2

Prepare a table and record the results shown in Fig. 1.2.

[3]

d A pulse can be felt from the blood in an artery as the artery passes over bone or muscle.

Fig. 1.3 shows a section through a small artery when viewed with a light microscope.

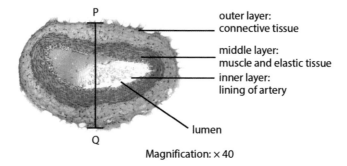

P

outer layer:
connective tissue

middle layer:
muscle and elastic tissue

inner layer:
lining of artery

lumen

Q

Magnification: × 40

Fig. 1.3

i) Draw a diagram of the section through the artery.

[4]

    ii)   The magnification of the artery in Fig. 1.3 is ×40.

         Line PQ shows the width of the artery.

         Measure the length of line **PQ** from Fig. 1.3.

         The length of line **PQ** = ... mm

         Calculate the actual width of the artery using the formula:

$$\text{width of artery} = \frac{\text{length of line PQ}}{\text{magnification}}$$

         Give your answer to **two** significant figures.

.... mm   **[3]**

e   Heart rate can also be recorded as an electrocardiogram (**ECG**).

      Fig. 1.4 shows part of a person's ECG.

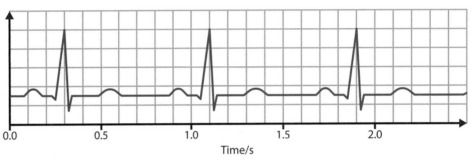

Time/s

Fig. 1.4

    i)   Determine the duration of a single heartbeat using information from Fig. 1.4.

.... **[1]**

    ii) Using your answer from part (**i**), calculate the person's heart rate.

        Space for working.

.... beats per minute   **[2]**

f   Give **one** reason why:

    i)   taking a manual pulse rate, as in Fig. 1.1, would be preferred to measuring heart rate using an ECG.

.... **[1]**

    ii) using an ECG to measure heart rate would be preferred to measuring a pulse rate manually.

.... **[1]**

[Total: 18]

2 A group of students measured the rate of transpiration of a leafy plant shoot in the laboratory.

The rate of transpiration of a leafy plant shoot can be measured using a potometer, as shown in Fig. 2.1.

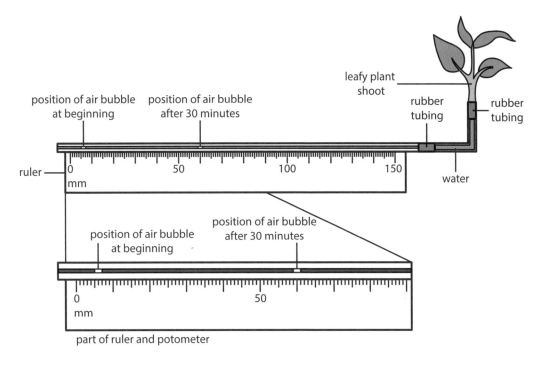

Fig. 2.1

a Record the position of the air bubble from Fig. 2.1 at the beginning of the experiment and after 30 minutes.

Position of air bubble at beginning .... mm

Position of air bubble after 30 minutes .... mm [1]

b Calculate the distance moved by the bubble in 30 minutes.

Write your answer in Table 2.1.

Table 2.1.

Time /minutes	Distance moved by bubble /mm
0	0
5	9
10	18
15	28
20	35
25	45
30	

[1]

(c) Plot a line graph on the grid to show the distance moved by the bubble in 30 minutes. [4]

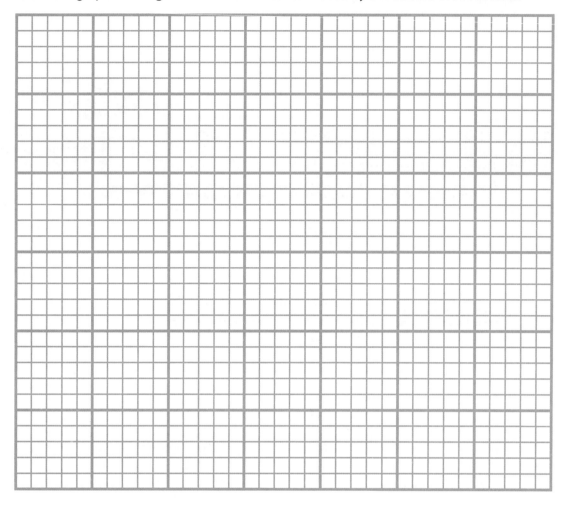

(d) Describe the relationship between time and the distance moved by the bubble.

....

.... [2]

(e) Other groups of students measured the rate of transpiration in other plant shoots.

All the groups follow an identical method.

The temperature of the laboratory is a constant 20 °C. Other conditions were the same throughout the laboratory.

Describe **one other** variable the groups of students need to control to be able to make valid comparisons between their data.

.... [1]

(f) A student stated that:

'The rate of transpiration will be affected by light intensity.'

Plan an investigation to test this statement.

....

....

....

....

....

....

....

....

....

....

....

....

....

....

....

[6]

(g) One student said that:

"What we really measured in this experiment was the rate of water uptake and not the rate of transpiration".

Evaluate the claim made by this student.

....

....

[1]

h Transpiration occurs through stomata in the leaf epidermis.

Students examined the lower epidermis of a leaf with a light microscope.

They made four counts of the stomata they saw.

Their counts, as seen with the microscope, are shown in Fig. 2.2.

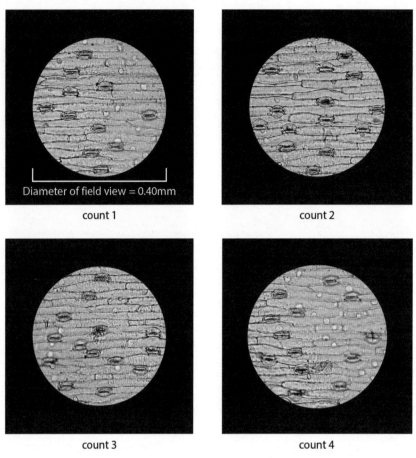

Fig. 2.2

i) Calculate the mean number of stomata in the field of view from Fig. 2.2.

.... [1]

ii) Calculate the number of stomata per mm^2 of leaf.

π = 3.14

Number of stomata per mm^2 = ... [3]

iii) The number of stomata per mm^2 calculated in part **(ii)** is an estimate of the true value.

Suggest two ways the data collection could be improved to increase the accuracy of the estimate.

1 ....

....

2 ....

.... **[2]**

[Total: 22]

Page 6-7 Section 1 Revise Questions

Page 7: Classifying living organisms
1 plant
2 insect; arthropod; invertebrate; animal
3 *Rosa*
4 **S** species E

Page 8-9 Section 2 Revise Questions

Page 9: Cells, tissues, organs, organisms
1 a) mitochondria/mitochondrion
   b) cytoplasm
2 ciliated epithelial cells
3 large surface area to absorb water/mineral ions quickly
4 a) 0.04 mm (unit symbol is needed)
   b) **S** 40 μm (unit symbol is needed)

Page 10-13 Section 3 Revise Questions

Page 11: Diffusion and active transport
1 • net/overall movement of particles
   • down a concentration gradient OR from higher to lower concentration
2 a) increases rate of diffusion
   b) decreases rate of diffusion
   c) increases rate of diffusion
   d) decreases rate of diffusion
3 from the kinetic energy of the particles
4 a) active transport
   b) root hair cell

Page 13: Osmosis
1 water
2 two of: cores of the same size/diameter/length/surface area, length of time core is in solution, solute (sucrose) always the same, cores are dried before measuring their masses, temperature of solution.
3 **S** the water potentials are equal

Page 14-15 Section 4 Revise Questions

Page 15: Important molecules in living things
1 glucose
2 a) biuret (solution/reagent)
   b) (pale) blue → purple
3 carbon, hydrogen, oxygen
4 **S** ATG GGC
   TAC CCG

Page 16-17: Section 5 Revise Questions

Page 17: Enzymes and how they work
1 metabolic (reactions)
2 active site
3 a) pH8
   b) **S** • fastest reaction rate
       • because active site is the correct/best shape
4 • no reaction/activity/colour change
   • because the enzyme is denatured

Pages 18-25: Section 1-5 Practice Questions

Page 18: Classifying living organisms
1 respiration/nutrition [1]
2 D [1]
3 a) amphibians [1]; b) B [1]
4 **S** a) bases changed/sequence of bases changed (answer must use the term 'base') [1]; b) C [1] its base sequence is the most similar to A/only one base is different [1]

Page 18: Cells, tissues, organs, organisms
1 a) all the cells are the same [1]
   b) to make features/cell walls/nuclei/cytoplasm easier to see [1]
   c) • neat pencil drawing of an onion cell with *no* broken lines [1]
       • correct labels to two of: nucleus, cell wall, cell membrane, cytoplasm [2]
   d) chloroplast [1]
   e) i) two of: ribosomes, mitochondria, cell membrane [2]
       ii) two of: making proteins (ribosomes), aerobic respiration (mitochondria), control of substances into and out of cells (cell membrane) [2]
   f) ×40
   g) 0.01 × 40 = 0.4 mm (do not forget the unit symbol) [1]
   h) **S** length is 60 μm, width = 10 μm (do not forget the unit symbols) [2]
2 Two of:
   • both use DNA as genetic material
   • animal cells have nuclei (bacterial cells do not)
   • bacterial cells have DNA in a large circular loop/chromosome (animal cells do not)
   • bacterial cells have DNA in small plasmids (animal cells do not) [2]
3 • cell division
   • to increase number of cells for growth/repair [2]
4 • carries oxygen
   • large surface area/contains haemoglobin/no nucleus [2]

Page 19: Diffusion and active transport
1 • slowest between Q and T
   • least difference in concentration between these two regions [2]
2 a) • increases rate of diffusion
       • because particles take less time to move between points that are closer together [2]
   b) • decrease in rate of diffusion
       • because the net movement of particles is reduced when there is less difference between the concentrations [2]
3 a) down the concentration gradient/oxygen concentration is higher in the lungs than the blood [1]
   b) • (the blood containing oxygen is swiftly removed) to maintain the concentration gradient
       • the greater the concentration gradient, the greater the rate of diffusion [2]
4 a) any sensible precaution with a reason, for example:
       • wear eye protection
       • to reduce the risk of eye damage
       OR
       • quickly rinse off acid if it splashes on skin
       • to reduce the risk of skin damage [2]
   b) i) size/surface area of cube [1]
       ii) time taken for cube to go colourless [1]
       iii) one of: concentration of acid/type of acid/volume of acid/type of agar/concentration of alkali in agar/concentration of phenolphthalein/temperature [1]

c) i) 6 cm² [1]
    ii) As the surface area increases, the time for the cube to change colour completely increases. [1]
    iii) The surface area to volume ratio decreases and it takes longer for the acid to diffuse all the way through the cube. [1]
5 a) two from:
       • particles move from place to place
       • diffusion is passive/does not require energy, active transport is active/requires energy
       • particles diffuse down a concentration gradient, in active transport they move against a concentration gradient
       • active transport always requires a membrane, diffusion need not involve a membrane [2]
   b) **S** carrier proteins [1]

Page 20: Osmosis
1 diffusion, solvent, permeable [3]
2 • dissolves/is a solvent [1]
   • urea/substances in urine [1]
3 a) C [1]
   b) sugar [1]
   c) it will rise [1]
   d) **S** • the dilute sugar solution has a higher water potential/concentration of water molecules than the concentrated sugar solution [1]
       • (net) flow of water from higher to lower water potential/concentration of water molecules; there is a (net) flow of water molecules down their concentration gradient [1]
   e) **S** lowered [1]
   f) **S** • greater (net) flow of water (molecules); liquid in thistle funnel rises even higher [1]
       • (because there is …) an increase in concentration gradient/an increase in the difference between the water potentials [1]
4 a)

Concentration of solute in solution (%)	Percentage change in mass (%)
10	50
20	25
30	-30
40	-30

[2 – lose one mark for each incorrect to a minimum of 0]
   b) the starting masses of the cores are not all equal [1]
   c) pure water [1]
   d) can calculate a mean (for a more accurate result)/can check readings to avoid anomalies [1]
   e) two of: cores of the same size/diameter/length/surface area, length of time core is in solution, solute (sucrose) always the same, cores are dried before measuring their masses, temperature of solution. [2]
5 a) • cytoplasm/vacuole contain a lot of water
       • which causes a pushing force (of the cell membrane) against the cell wall. [2]

b) **S** • water is lost from the cell (by osmosis)
  • (and so) the cell membrane pulls away from the cell wall/the cell becomes floppy **[2]**

6 **S** • higher water potential outside the cell compared with inside/greater concentration of water molecules outside the cell compared with inside
  • there is a (net) flow of water (molecules) … from higher to lower (water potential/water concentration)/down their concentration gradient
  • so the cell swells/bursts **[3]**

Page 22: Important molecules in living things

1 A **[1]**
2 D **[1]**
3 a) vitamin C **[1]**
  b) B **[1]**; because all the tests were negative apart from with iodine solution. **[1]**
  c) A control is when the *independent* variable is not applied, so you can tell if this variable is having the effect. **[1]** A suitable control would be (distilled/pure) *water*. **[1]**
4 Three of:
  • both insoluble carbohydrates and proteins are chains of smaller molecules
  • both insoluble carbohydrates and proteins contain the elements carbon, oxygen and hydrogen
  • insoluble carbohydrates are made of glucose/sugars but proteins are made of amino acids
  • insoluble carbohydrates never contain nitrogen/sulfur atoms but proteins do **[3]**
5 a) Solution Z **[1]**
  b) Solution X **[1]**
6 a) ethanol **[1]**
  b) milky (emulsion) **[1]**
7 a) double helix **[1]**
  b) bonds **[1]**; between pairs of bases/A-T and C-G **[1]**

Page 23: Enzymes and how they work

1 C **[1]**
2 C **[1]**
3 a) substrate **[1]**
  b) Three of the following:
    • substrate sticks/binds/fits into active site
    • substrate-enzyme complex (formed)
    • change in shape of enzyme
    • bonds made/broken in substrate/molecule
    • products no longer fit in the active site **[3]**
4 a) reactions are too slow (to support life/without enzymes) **[1]**
  b) Any two named reactions that occur in organisms (for example, aerobic respiration, photosynthesis, digestion, starch production) **[2]**
5 active site **[1]**; only fits correctly-shaped/complementary substrates/molecules **[1]**
6 a) turns blue-black **[1]**
  b) ii) • three correct calculations (excluding value for 80 °C)
    • three further correct calculations (excluding value for 80 °C)
    • all values given to two significant figures **[3]**

Temperature (°C)	Rate of reaction (g/s)
20	0.028
30	0.045
40	0.083
50	0.063
60	0.033
70	0.017
80	0.000

  c) line graph with the following features:
    • four points plotted accurately with small, neat crosses
    • three further points plotted accurately with small, neat crosses
    • divisions on the scales evenly spaced
    • axes are labelled with units given
    • points linked with straight lines or a curve of best fit **[5]**
    Additionally, students should try to:
    • fills as much of the paper as possible
    • draw in axis lines
    • write in numbers on the scales
    • write a title
    • plot points and draw lines in (sharp) pencil
  d) answer between 40 °C–45 °C **[1]**
  e) i) denatured **[1]**
    ii) (enzyme) shape is changed permanently **[1]**
  f) • more collisions/greater frequency of collisions
    • more energy in each collision **[2]**
7 a) starch synthase **[1]**
  b) • increase rate of reaction **[1]**
    and two of:
    • greater frequency of collisions/more collisions
    • more energy in each collision
    • greater frequency of effective collisions/more effective collisions **[2]**

Page 26-29: Section 6 Revise Questions

Page 27: Photosynthesis

1 any two from: starch (use energy store), cellulose (cell walls), sucrose (transported in phloem) and nectar (attracts insects for pollination)
2 chlorophyll
3 There would be no starch at A and B but there would be starch at point C.
4 **S** light intensity, carbon dioxide concentration and temperature

Page 29: Leaf Structure

1 Most photosynthesis takes place in the palisade mesophyll layer.
  Palisade cells in this layer are packed closely together and contain large numbers of chloroplasts to absorb as much energy from light (energy transferred by light) as possible for photosynthesis.

2 The spongy mesophyll layer contains cells with a large surface area to enable the exchange of carbon dioxide and oxygen. Air spaces between the cells allows these gases to enter and leave the cell easily.
3 Stomata are pores in the leaf surrounded by guard cells. During daylight when photosynthesis is taking place the guard cells keep the stomata open to allow carbon dioxide needed for photosynthesis to enter the cell and for the oxygen produced to leave. At night when photosynthesis stops the guard cells close stomata to preserve water in the leaf.
4 Plants have large leaves to increase the amount of energy from light (energy transferred from light) for photosynthesis. Having thin leaves means that carbon dioxide for photosynthesis, and oxygen released from it diffuse over small distances. Having a large surface area inside leaves means that the cells that need carbon dioxide for photosynthesis receive as much as possible and the oxygen produced can be rapidly removed.

Pages 30-35: Section 7 Revise Questions

Page 31: Diet and the digestive system

1 lack of vitamin C causes scurvy. Lack of vitamin D causes rickets.
2 a) calcium and iron
    i) Calcium is needed for strong bones and teeth and for blood clotting. Iron is needed to make haemoglobin in red blood cells.
    ii) calcium: milk/eggs. Iron: red meat leafy green vegetables/liver/kidneys
3 fibre helps food move through the alimentary canal preventing constipation and protecting against bowel cancer
4 Teeth break up food, saliva moistens food into a bolus (for ease of swallowing), salivary glands secrete a digestive enzyme which begins starch digestion.
5 Food broken down during digestion and water is absorbed by from the small intestine into the blood

Page 33: Enzymes and digestion

1 to check whether the pH changed (due to the experiment)
2 **S** Boiled trypsin was a control which showed that any digestion of the protein had been due to trypsin and no other factor. Boiled trypsin would be denatured and would not break down any proteins.
3 **S** small intestine
4 37 °C is the optimal temperature for enzymes to work in the human body so this amylase would break down more starch at this temperature than the others. At the lowest temperature the reaction would be slow because the molecules would not have enough energy to move and collide. At the highest temperature the reaction would be slow because the enzyme would be denatured.
5 **S** Protease acts in the stomach, which has a low pH. Protease will work best at pH 4.

Page 35: Physical digestion and absorption

1 The pulp cavity is a soft tissue containing nerves and blood vessels.
2 The muscular walls of the stomach expand and contract to churn food into chyme which breaks it down into particles with a larger surface area for digestive enzymes to act upon
3 the small intestine (duodenum and ileum).
4. **S** Villi increases the surface area for the absorption of nutrients. The surface area is increased further by microvilli on the outer epithelial membrane of each villus which provides an additional surface area for absorption
5 **S** Capillaries in the villi enable nutrients to be rapidly absorbed into the blood stream. The lacteal is part of the lymphatic system which transports fat and oil molecules

Pages 36-39: Section 8 Revise Questions

Page 37: Tissues for transport in plants

1 transport of water and dissolved mineral ions, support to plant structures
2 transport of sucrose and amino acids
3 vascular bundles, leaf veins
4 Root hairs are fine protrusions extending into the soil. They have an increased surface area for the absorption of water and minerals from the soil.
5 Xylem is made of dead cells with walls thickened by lignin, which offers support to stems and leaves. Xylem cells have no end walls, forming a continuous tube which enables water and minerals to travel directly from the roots to the rest of the plant.

Page 39: Transpiration and translocation

1 Transpiration is the process of water loss from the leaves of a plant.
2 **(1)** When the temperature is low and there is no wind the rate of transpiration will be low. This is because the water particles have less energy at low temperatures so do not diffuse as quickly; and if water particles are not removed by the wind from around the leaf there is a shallower concentration gradient between the inside and outside of the leaf.
    (2) When the temperature is higher and there is wind the rate of transpiration will be higher. This is because the water particles have more energy to diffuse and there is a concentration gradient for water particles between the inside and outside of the leaf.
3 **S** water moves upwards as a single column of water from the roots into xylem tissue as a result of transpiration 'pull'. This is caused by the difference in water potential between the two tissues and the attractive forces between water molecules.
4 **S** Translocation is the movement of amino acids and sucrose in phloem.
5 **S** Sinks include tubers which store glucose as starch and fruits/leaves/stems which store amino acids. Sources include places such as leaves and flowers where starch is converted into glucose and used for respiration/growth.

Pages 40-43: Section 9 Revise Questions

Page 41: Circulatory systems and hearts

1 i) A base line reading at rest means that the increases in pulse rate during the experiment can be related to the exercise rather than any other factor.
   ii) The heart rate increases with exercise in order to increase the amount of oxygen in the muscles and allow increased respiration. As the exercise becomes more intense the heart rate will increase further.
   iii) **S** One minute is 60 seconds, so $\frac{60}{15} = 4$. If 25 beats were recorded over 15 seconds the number of beats is $4 \times 25 = 100$ beats per minute.
   iv) **S** Pulse rates increased when the intensity of the exercise increased. This is because more glucose and oxygen was needed for increased respiration by the muscle tissues.
2. The chambers of the heart are made of thick muscle to withstand the pressure of blood inside the chambers when they are full. The heart muscles elasticity means heart muscles can expand and contract to pump blood to the lungs or the rest of the body.
3 A hole in the septum would cause deoxygenated blood to mix with oxygenated blood. Less oxygenated blood would reach the body's tissues and there would be less oxygen available for respiration in cells. The affects on health might include
    • fatigue due to reduced oxygen delivery to the tissues
    • breathlessness, because the breathing rate increases the drive more oxygen into the body
4 Having a double circulation is an advantage because blood can reach the lungs at low pressure which prevents damage to lung capillaries. Another advantage is that blood can be pumped faster to and from the lungs rapidly to provide the tissues with oxygen at a faster rate.

Page 43: Blood vessels and blood

1 Arteries have thick walls and a narrow lumen. Veins have valves, a thinner wall and wider lumen than arteries.
2 Any four from: amino acids, carbon dioxide (or carbonic acid), fatty acids, glucose, hormones, ions, oxygen, urea, water.
3 **S** Artery walls are thick to withstand high blood pressure and have elastic recoil to maintain blood pressure throughout the body.
    Veins have thinner walls, transport blood at lower pressure and have valves to stop blood flowing in the wrong direction (backflow).
    Capillaries have a narrow lumen and walls that are one cell thick. This allows the rapid exchange of substances between the blood and the body tissues.
4 Phagocytes and lymphocytes
5 **S** Soluble fibrinogen is converted into insoluble fibrin by an enzyme released by platelets in the blood plasma.

Pages 44-47: Section 10 Revise Questions

Page 45: Diseases

1 A (micro)organism that causes disease.
2 Transfer of blood/named method of transfer, for example, wound/syringe/medical procedure
    Transfer of other bodily fluids, e.g. semen by sexual contact
3 Forms a barrier (to pathogens)
    Anti-bacterial enzymes/lysozyme in sweat
4 Phagocyte
    Lymphocyte

Page 47: Immunity

1 A protein produced by the body that will bind to antigens on the surface of pathogen or foreign cells and either destroy pathogen OR mark a pathogen/microorganism for phagocytosis
2 In active immunity, antibodies are produced by the body
    In passive immunity, antibodies are acquired from another individual/preparations containing antibody
3 Memory cells remain in the blood after the infection (has been dealt with)
    Can quickly (divide/differentiate into lymphocytes/plasma cells and) produce large quantities of (specific) antibodies if exposed to the microorganism/pathogen again.
4 Antibodies are transferred (from mother to baby) in milk
    The baby will have some immunity before its own immune system develops fully.

Pages 48-65: Section 6-10 Practice Questions

Page 48: Photosynthesis

1 D [1]
2 a) (Starch)   (nectar)
       amino acids   (cellulose)
       protein   (sucrose)   (glucose)   [5]
   b) i) glucose [1], oxygen [1]
      ii) chlorophyll [1] in chloroplasts [1]
                                    [Total: 9]
3 **S** $6 CO_2 + 6H_2O \longrightarrow C_6H_{12}O_6 + 6O_2$
    Answer circled shown plus 1 mark each part of the equation: $6 CO_2$ [1] $6 H_2O$ [1] $C_6H_{12}O_6$ [1] and $6H_2O$ [1]   **[Total: 5]**
4 I would change the **temperature** of the water and measure the **number of gas bubbles**.
                                    [Total: 2]
5 **S** a) Photosynthesis needs energy from light. [1]
           The rate of photosynthesis increases with increasing light intensity [1] until another factor limits the rate of reaction. [1]
       b) light [1], temperature [1], carbon dioxide [1]   **[Total: 6]**

Page 49: Leaf structure

1 a) Any one from: guard cell, (lower/upper) epidermis, palisade mesophyll layer (accept palisade layer), spongy mesophyll layer, stoma (or stomata), waxy cuticle (accept waxy layer)   [1]
   b) Palisade cells have lots of chloroplasts [1] and need to absorb as much light as possible [1].   **[Total: 3]**

2 a) Large air spaces between cells enable carbon dioxide to diffuse easily into cells for photosynthesis and oxygen from photosynthesis to be released. **[1]** The cells have a large surface area to volume ratio for efficient gaseous exchange. **[1]**

b) The waxy cuticle prevents moisture loss from the top of the leaf. **[1]**

c) Stomata are open during the day to allow for gaseous exchange for photosynthesis **[1]** and close at night when photosynthesis stops to retain moisture in the leaf. **[1]**

d) Transparency **[1]** enables sunlight to pass directly to the cells beneath for efficient photosynthesis **[1]**.   **[Total: 7]**

3 a) deep roots: allows the plant to access to **water [1]** and **minerals [1]**

b) Long spiky leaves with a thick waxy coating rather than flat thin leaves: **prevent water loss [1]**

c) Yucca plants close their stomata during the day when it is hot and open them at night for carbon dioxide to enter, which is stored for photosynthesis during daylight.
Stomata close during the day to: **prevent water loss [1] during hot temperatures [1]**   **[Total: 5]**

Page 50: Diet and the digestive system

1 a)

Balanced diet	food and drink high in fat and sugar should make up half all food eaten
	Fruit and vegetables and startchy foods should both be eaten equal amounts
	water is not needed.
	must supply essential nutrients
	does not include grains
	should include fibre

[3]

b) Vitamin C **[1]** Vitamin D **[1]**
      [Total: 5]

2 a) i) food is broken down into small pieces by chewing **[1]** and moistened by saliva (creating a bolus) **[1]**

ii) salivary glands **[1]**

iii) Chewing breaks the food down into small pieces **[1]** increasing the surface area for digestive enzymes to work **[1]**.

b) i) Food is broken down into a liquid **[1]**, protein is digested by digestive enzymes **[1]** (accept food is digested).

ii) it is absorbed (into the bloodstream) **[1]**

iii) The fluid needs to be alkaline to provide an optimal pH for digestive enzymes in the small intestine to work OR food has come from the stomach, which is acidic, so needs to be neutralised **[1]**.   **[Total: 9]**

3 a)

| Fats and oils | One from: oily fish, meat, nuts, avocados, milk products **[1]** |
| Protein | One from: red meat, liver, kidney, egg, fish, legumes, nuts, seeds **[1]** |

Starch (carbohydrate)	One from: bread, pasta, yams **[1]**
Calcium	One from: milk, eggs, dried fruit, leafy green vegetables **[1]**
Iron	One from: red meat, kidney, liver, green leafy vegetables, legumes **[1]**

[5]

b) Describe absorption and assimilation
Absorption is the process where nutrients from food are taken up into the **bloodstream**. **[1]**
Assimilation incorporates nutrients into cells where they are used in various functions. **[1]**   **[Total: 7]**

4 a) i) stores /makes glycogen **[1]**, produces bile **[1]**

ii) stores bile **[1]**   **[Total: 3]**

5 a) Vitamin C **[1]**

b) iron **[1]**

c) Vitamin D **[1]**   **[Total: 3]**

Page 52: Enzymes and digestion

1

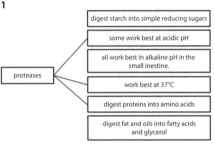

proteases
- digest starch into simple reducing sugars
- some work best at acidic pH
- all work best in alkaline pH in the small intestine.
- work best at 37°C
- digest proteins into amino acids
- digest fat and oils into fatty acids and glycerol

[Total: 3]

2 a) Lipase is produced in the pancreas **[1]** and acts in the small intestine **[1]**

b) Lipase breaks down fats and oils **[1]** into fatty acids and glycerol **[1]**
      [Total: 4]

3 I would change the **temperature [1]** of the water bath and use the stopwatch to record the **time [1]** when the iodine tests showed that there was no **starch [1]** present in the tubes.
I would write down the number of the tube where there was **the fastest [1]** reaction with iodine and the temperature of the solution in that tube. This would tell me the **optimum [1]** temperature for amylase in the investigation
      [Total: 5]

4 S A.   **[Total: 1]**

5 S **a)** proteases **[1]**

b) stomach **[1]** small intestine **[1]**

c) amino acids **[1]**
      [Total: 4]

Page 54: Physical digestion and absorption

1 a) i) nerves **[1]** provide sensation to the tooth **[1]**. Blood vessels **[1]** supply the tooth with blood **[1]**

ii) To protect the dentine **[1]** and provide a surface to grind up/cut up food **[1]**

b) i) The greater the amount of sugar eaten **[1]**, the greater the number of decayed teeth **[1]**.

ii) 4. **[2]**   **[Total: 9]**

2 a) (water) protein starch (nutrients) enzymes   **[2]**

b) Three of: Provides a large surface area for absorption **[1]** more surface for nutrients to diffuse across **[1]**; Increases the time food spends in the intestine **[1]**; Gives more time for digested food to be completely absorbed into the bloodstream **[1]**
      [Total: 5]

3 C   **[Total: 1]**

4 S Bile emulsifies large **fat [1]** droplets producing smaller **fat [1]** droplets which **increases [1]** the surface area for lipase enzymes to digest fats and oils. This makes the rate of fat digestion much **faster/ quicker/efficient**. **[1]**   **[Total: 4]**

5. S **a)** any two from: lacteal , blood capillaries , outer thin cell layer containing microvilli. **[2]**

b) network of capillaries which means nutrients quickly enter the blood **[1]** villi have thin walls which reduces the distance for diffusion of nutrients **[1]**. Increased surface area for absorption is provided by microvilli **[1]**
      [Total: 5]

Page 56: Tissues for transport in plants

1 B. **[1]**

2 C. Xylem contains dead xylem vessels which transport water and minerals.

3 S The baobab trunk has more numerous and **wider [1]** xylem vessels. This adaptation means that xylem can function as a **water [1]** store under drought conditions which trees in wetter climates do **not [1]** need.
      [Total: 4]

5 S Root hairs are thin and protrude into the soil **[1]**. Their shape creates a large surface area for absorption of water and mineral ions **[1]**.   **[Total: 2]**

Page 58: Transpiration and translocation

1 a) Transpiration **[1]**

b) Water passes from the xylem in the vascular bundles **[1]** through the palisade layer to the spongy mesophyll layer. Water evaporates from the surfaces of the mesophyll cells into the air spaces **[1]** and then diffuses through the stomata as water vapour, leaving the leaf **[1]**
      [Total: 4]

2 I would time how many seconds it took for the air bubble in the potometer to move 5 cm. The bubble moves as water is taken up and lost from for the leaf by **transpiration [1]**.
I would vary the conditions so that the leaves were in warm and windy conditions and **repeat [1]** the investigation with **cold [1]** conditions with **no [1]** wind.
I would keep the amount of **light [1]** and the **plant [1]** the same to make the investigation a **fair [1]** test.   **[Total: 7]**

3 S Transpiration pull produces a column of water **[1]** which is 'pulled' up xylem tissue from the roots **[1]** to vascular bundles in the leaf **[1]**. Transpiration pull is caused by a difference in the water potential between the roots and the leaves **[1]** and the attractive forces between water molecules **[1]**. The difference in water potential is caused by loss of water by osmosis **[1]** from spongy mesophyll cells **[1]**.   **[Total: 7]**

4 [S] Wilting occurs when plants do not have enough water **[1]** and the rate of transpiration is greater than water uptake **[1]**. This causes the water pressure in the plant's cells to reduce **[1]**, making them soft. The reduced support **[1]** for the plant stems and leaves causes drooping.

[Total: 4]

5 [S] B **[1]**

Page 59: Circulatory systems and hearts

1 **a)** (septum) separates oxygenated from deoxygenated blood **[1]**

b) The left ventricle muscles are thick because they need to pump blood at high pressure **[1]** across long distances throughout the body **[1]**. In contrast, the right ventricle only needs to pump blood to the lungs (short distance). **[1]**

[Total: 4]

2 Valves in the heart are located between the **atria [1]** and the **ventricles [1]**. When the valves **close [1]** they prevent blood flowing in the **wrong [1]** direction. **[Total: 4]**

3 [S] **a)** The 'double circulatory system' in mammals describes how blood flows through the heart twice **[1]**. Blood in the circulation travels from the heart to the lungs and back to the heart **[1]**. The blood passes through the heart again before being pumped to the rest of the body **[1]**

b) In fish, the single circulatory system is not able to pump blood a high pressure so oxygen delivery to tissues is slow **[1]** compared to double circulatory systems in mammals where oxygen delivery is faster **[1]** due to the heart receiving the blood from the lungs and pumping it to the body at high pressure **[1]**.

[Total: 6]

4 [S] **a)** $4.5 - 0.5 = 4.0$ **[1]** [Allow slight deviation from numbers, e.g. (4.3-4.7) – (0.4-0.7) as long as calculation is correct.]

b) Blockage to the coronary arteries reduces the amount of oxygenated blood reaching the heart muscle **[1]**. The heart muscle needs oxygen and glucose for respiration **[1]** and can't pump effectively if these are reduced **[1]**.

c) i) Blood would flow backwards into the atrium from the ventricle **[1]**. The ventricle muscle would have to work harder to deliver the blood to the lungs **[1]**.

ii) Blood would flow back into the ventricle **[1]**.

[Total: 7]

Page 61: Blood vessels and blood

1 White blood cells are involved in phagocytosis **[1]** and antibody production **[1]**. Platelets are involved in blood clotting **[1]** **[Total: 3]**

2 **a)** i) The red blood cells do not have a visible nucleus **[1]**.

ii) [S] Lymphocytes have a large active nucleus/no nucleus needed to make antibodies **[1]**. Red blood cells have a very small nucleus to create space in the cell for haemoglobin **[1]**.

[Total: 3]

3 [S] soluble, plasma, insoluble, red

[Total: 4]

4 **a)** The number of red blood cells increased. **[1]**

b) between days 30 and 38 **[1]** **[1]**

c) Red blood cell numbers increased because they contain haemoglobin **[1]**. Haemoglobin carries oxygen **[1]** so having more red blood cells ensures oxygen to the tissues is maintained. **[1]**

[Total: 5]

Page 63: Diseases

1 D **[Total: 1]**

2 **a)** reduces or prevents the spread of pathogens that cause food poisoning **[1]**

b) Any two from:
Not washing hands correctly **[1]**
by keeping uncooked food – which may contain pathogens – and uncooked food together **[1]**
by organisms such as flies **[1]**
by using dirty kitchen utensils or chopping boards. **[1]**

[2]

c) Any three from:
Clean water supply **[1]**
(Good) personal hygiene **[1]**
Waste disposal **[1]**
Sewage treatment **[1]**

[3]
[Total: 6]

3 [S] **a)** Any one of:
Sewage/poor sanitation **[1]**
Natural disaster/earthquake/flood **[1]**

[1]

b) As a result of the **toxin [1]** produced by the bacterium, **chloride [1]** ions are secreted into the small intestine. The cells of the small intestine have partially **permeable [1]** membranes.
Water [1] molecules will move from a region of higher **water potential [1]** to a region of lower **water potential [1]**. There will therefore be a **net [1]** movement of **water molecules [1]** into the small intestine by **osmosis [1]**. The faeces will be very watery. **[9]**

c) Antibiotics **[1]**
(Antibiotics) used to treat bacterial diseases/diseases caused by bacteria **[1]**

[2]
[Total: 12]

4 **C** Hydrochloric acid **[1]**
[Total: 1]

Page 64: Immunity

1 [S] A **[Total: 1]**

2 **a)** Rabies is caused by a virus/is a viral disease. **[1]**
Antibiotics will only kill bacteria. **[1]**

[2]

b) May/would take too long for antibodies to be produced **[1]**
Person may have died before immune response/immunity (develops) **[1]**

[2]

c) 4.3/4.5/5 (cm^3)

[3]

Working:
The dose required = $20 \times 64 = 1280$ units **[1]**
Calculation of volume required **[1]**
the volume of HRIG required = $\frac{1280}{300}$ cm^3 = 4.27 cm^3
Idea of rounding up so that adequate dose is given **[1]**

[Total: 7]

3 Any two from:
(Vaccinated people), if exposed to the pathogen, will just have a mild infection or not become infected. **[1]**
If a large proportion of a population is vaccinated against a disease, it is difficult for someone to become infected. **[1]**
Cases of the infection will disappear/the disease may become eradicated. **[1]**

[Total: 2]

4 [S] **a)** Before vaccination, the concentration of antibodies against cholera is **0/zero [1]**.
Following vaccination, the concentration increases **slowly [1]**, reaches a **(small) peak [1]**, then falls to **near zero/zero [1]**.
After exposure to the cholera pathogen, the antibody concentration **increases/rises [1] rapidly [1]** and to a **higher [1]** concentration than following vaccination.
After reaching a peak, the antibody concentration then falls **slowly [1]**. **[8]**

[S] **b)** Any two from:
Mutation of bacteria/idea that vaccine is no longer effective **[1]**
Idea that memory cells do not live forever/do not last for a person's life **[1]**
Accept: idea that antibody levels fall **[1]**

[2]
[Total: 10]

Pages 66-67: Section 11 Revise Questions

Page 67: Gas exchange

1 Short distance required for (efficient) diffusion of gases/oxygen and carbon dioxide.
Or answers related to thickness of walls:
(The wall of each) alveolus is one cell thick.
(The wall of a) capillary is one cell thick.

2 [S] The diaphragm contracts/flattens.
The external intercostal muscles contract.
The volume of the thorax is increased.
Air pressure in the thorax is decreased.
The air pressure in the lungs is lower than in the air
Air is inspired/breathed in.

Pages 68-69: Section 12 Revise Questions

Page 69: Aerobic and anaerobic respiration

1. Three from:
for protein synthesis
growth
cell division
active transport
maintaining a constant body temperature

2. glucose + oxygen → carbon dioxide + water

3. [S] $C_6H_{12}O_6 \rightarrow 2C_2H_5OH + 2CO_2$

4. [S] Transported to liver.
Removed by (aerobic) respiration.

Pages 70-71: Section 13 Revise Questions

Page 71: Getting rid of metabolic wastes

1. The getting rid of waste products of metabolism and substances in excess of requirements.

2. carbon dioxide
urea

3. [S] Any two from: water, urea, ions

4. [S] Assimilation of proteins
Receives amino acids from digestion (in blood)
Synthesises proteins
Deamination/removes the nitrogen-containing part of the molecules of excess amino acids
To produce urea

Pages 72-79: Section 14 Revise Questions

Page 73: The nervous system
1. Central nervous system/CNS
Peripheral nervous system/PNS
2. The nerve impulse is electrical, so the myelin sheath insulates/protects neurones from other electrical impulses OR Myelin sheath speeds up the transmission of impulses..
3. receptor → sensory neurone → relay neurone → motor neurone → effector
4. [S] The gap between two nerve endings
The axon/nerve ending of the first/presynaptic neurone has vesicles
Containing neurotransmitter molecules
The next/postsynaptic neurone has receptor proteins.

Page 75: Sense organs
1. (An organ) with groups of receptor cells that respond to certain stimuli/light, sound, touch, temperature, chemicals.
2. retina.
3. [S] Thin/less convex.
4. [S] **a)** Rods are responsible for vision in dim light
Rods are concentrated away from visual axis of eye where light rays will be focused.
b) Cones are responsible for colour vision
There are no cones at the periphery of the eye/retina.

Page 77: Hormones and homeostasis
1. A chemical substance produced by an endocrine gland that is transported in the blood/plasma and affects the activity of the target organ(s).
2. Increases breathing rate
3. [S] Diagram to include the following:
blood glucose concentration rises following a meal
insulin released by the pancreas
insulin increases the uptake of glucose into the liver and the conversion of glucose to glycogen
blood glucose levels fall back to the set point value
blood glucose levels fall below the set point value
glucagon released
glucagon increases the conversion of glycogen to glucose in the liver
blood sugar levels rise back to the set point value.
4. Vasodilation
Increased diameter of arterioles (supplying skin)
Shunt vessels closed
Blood flow through skin surface capillaries increased
More heat lost (from skin surface) to the environment
Sweating increased
As water evaporates
More heat lost (from skin surface) to the environment

Page 79: Tropic responses
1. Gravitropism/geotropism
2. [S] Auxin produced in the growing tip
Diffuses down stem
Where it causes cell elongation
If illumination from one side:
auxin redistributed to the shaded side (of the shoot)
So shoot curves towards the light.

Page 80-81: Section 15 Revise Questions

Page 81: Drugs and medicines
1. substance that affects chemical reactions in the body
2. used if the infection is caused by bacteria, the antibiotic kills the bacteria or slows their growth
3. [S] taking the whole course of antibiotics will ensure all bacteria have been killed. any bacteria that have not been killed can mutate and lead to a population of bacteria that are resistant to the antibiotic

Page 82-95: Section 11-15 Practice Questions

Page 82: Gas exchange
1 **a)** D [1]
b G [1]
c) B [1] **[Total: 3]**
2. **a)** limewater
b) One of: wear eye protection/wash hands immediately if any splashes onto skin [1]
c) A [1] because the limewater has gone cloudy indicating the presence of carbon dioxide [1] **[Total: 4]**
3 **a)** Idea that not possible to measure (the areas) accurately, or words to that effect OR idea that different people will have different sized lungs and can't account for everyone. [1]
b) 70 per cent [2]
$\frac{49}{70} \times 100 = 70$
c) Any **three** from:
Large surface area [1]
Thin surfaces/distances for diffusion [1]
Good blood supply [1]
Good ventilation (by air) [1]
[3]
[Total: 6]
4 [S] **a)** External intercostal muscles relax [1]
Diaphragm relaxes/becomes dome-shaped [1]
This decreases the volume of the thorax [1]
Pressure is increased [1]
(Pressure in the thorax is now greater than in the air so) air leaves the breathing system/lungs [1]
During forced breathing/exercise, the internal intercostal muscles contract [1]
[6]
b) Sketch shows:
the ribs (and vertebral column) [1]
external intercostal muscles pointing forwards [1]
internal intercostal muscles pointing backwards [1]
clarity of sketch/labels/quality of annotation [1]
[4]
[Total: 16]

Page 84: Aerobic and anaerobic respiration
1 Energy is required to transport substances against a concentration gradient. **[Total: 1]**
2 **a)** Idea of:
protecting them from potassium hydroxide/exposure to potassium hydroxide would kill them/prevent them from respiring. [1]
b) Increasing the surface area over which carbon dioxide can be absorbed [1]
So that all/increasing the amount of carbon dioxide absorbed [1]
[2]
c) 108 mm/hr **[3]**
Distance moved = 72 mm [1]
(This is the distance moved in 40 minutes)
distance moved in one hour $= 72 \times \frac{60}{40}$ [1]
Units [1]
d) 85 or 84.8 or 84.834 mm^3/hr. **[4]**
Recall of formula for area of circle/πr^2 [1]
Recall value of pi/3.14 or 3.142 [1]
Substitution into formula [1]
$108 \times 3.14 \times 0.5 \times 0.5$ **[Total: 10]**
3 **Three** from:
Both processes release energy from food/nutrients [1]
Aerobic respiration releases more energy/anaerobic respiration produces less energy [1]
The products of aerobic respiration are carbon dioxide and water [1]
The product of anaerobic respiration is lactic acid [1] Aerobic occurs with oxygen, anaerobic occurs without [1]
(Similarity required for full marks.) **[3]**
[Total: 3]

Page 85: Getting rid of metabolic wastes
1 Urea is excreted by the kidneys in urine [1]
[Total: 1]
2 [S] **a)** protein [1]
glucose [1]
[2]
b) 67 **[2]**
$\frac{20.00}{0.30}$ [1]
c) **i)** Molecules too large [1]
to pass through membranes of capillaries in glomerulus [1]
[2]
ii) Reabsorbed [1]
Along nephron/(proximal) kidney tubule [1]
[2]
d) 172.8 dm^3 μm^2 **[2]**
Working out but incorrect answer:
rate per day = 120 × 60 × 24 = 172,800 cm^3/day [1]
Division by 1000 [1]
[Total: 10]

Page 86: The nervous system
1 Coordination of body functions/systems [1]
Regulation of body functions [1]
[Total: 2]
2 **a)** **i)** C [1]
ii) A [1]
iii) B [1]
[3]
b) muscle [1]
c) Motor neurone [1]
Two from:
Position of cell body/cell body at one end of neurone [1]

Long axon **[1]**
Terminates/ends in muscle **[1]**

[3]
[Total: 7]

3 **Five** from:
The nerve impulse arrives at the end of the first/presynaptic neurone **[1]**
(The arrival of the nerve impuls**e)** stimulates the release of neurotransmitter molecules **[1]**
From/stored in vesicles **[1]**
The neurotransmitter molecules <u>diffuse</u> across the synaptic gap **[1]**
Bind to (protein) receptors on the next/post synaptic neurone **[1]**
Generate a nerve impulse in the next/postsynaptic neurone **[1]**

[Total: 5]

4 **a)** **Eight** from:
Hot object/stimulus detected **[1]**
By receptors **[1]**
Nerve impulses travel along sensory neurone(s) **[1]**
To spinal cord **[1]**
Connect with/impulses transmitted to relay neurone(s) **[1]**
By synapses **[1]**
(Trigger) impulses in motor neurone(s) **[1]**
Received by effector/cause biceps (muscle) to contract **[1]**
Hand removed from (hot object) **[1]**

[8]

b) **i)** 40 m/s **[2]**
Use of equation **[1]**

$$speed = \frac{distance}{time}$$
$$speed = \frac{0.8}{0.02}$$

ii) 45 mm **[4]**
Rearrangement of the equation from i)/states the equation
Distance = speed × time **[1]**
Conversion of 1.5 milliseconds to seconds
0.0015 s **[1]**
Calculation: distance = 30 × 0.0015 = 0.0045 m **[1]**
Conversion to mm
0.0045 m = 0.0045 × 1000 = 45 mm **[1]**

[Total: 14]

Page 88: Sense organs

1 **a)** light; sound; touch; temperature; chemicals **[2]**
Four, three or two correct = 1 mark.

[Total: 2]

2 **a)** **i)** Retina **[1]**
ii) Cornea **[1]**

[2]

b) **i)** H and G **[1]**
ii) C **[1]**

[2]
[Total: 4]

3 **S** As the person walks along the dark street, their pupil is **dilated [1]** because the **(outer) radial [1]** muscles in the iris of their eyes are **contracted [1]**.
As the person looks into the brightly-lit shop window, their pupils **constrict [1]**. This is because the **(inner) circular [1]** muscles in the iris of their eyes **contract [1]**.

The muscles in the iris work as **antagonistic [1]** pairs.

[7]
[Total: 7]

4 **a)** Key points on sketch:
(From distant object) light rays (reaching the eye) are nearly parallel **[1]**
Only slight refraction (of light rays) needed **[1]**
Thin convex lens **[1]**
Light rays brought into focus (on retin**a)** **[1]**

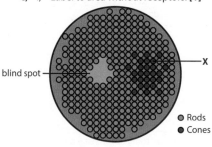

light rays are brought into focus on the retina [1]
light rays reaching the eye are nearly parallel [1]
only slight refraction of light rays is needed [1]
thin convex lens [1]

[4]

b) **Five** from:
Ciliary muscle relaxes **[1]**
Suspensory ligaments pulled tight/taut **[1]**
Lens (in capsule) pulled tight **[1]**
Lens becomes less convex/thinner **[1]**
Because only slight refraction of light rays needed **[1]**
To focus light rays onto retina **[1]**

[5]
[Total: 9]

5 **a)** **i)** 0 **[1]**
ii) 1.4×10^5 **[2]**
Answer in incorrect version of standard form, for example, 14×10^4 = 1 mark
Correct answer but not in standard form = 1 mark

[3]

b) 12 ±1 to 18 ±1 **[2]**
°/degrees **[1]**

[3]

c) **i)** Label to area without receptors. **[1]**

blind spot

X

○ Rods
● Cones

ii) fovea **[1]**
cones concentrated there. **[1]**

[3]
[Total: 9]

Page 90: Hormones and homeostasis

1 The nervous system and endocrine system are both involved in the human body's coordination and response.
The nervous system uses **electrical [1]** impulses to communicate. The endocrine system uses **chemical [1]** substances, secreted into the **blood [1]**.
The responses of the nervous system are **rapid [1]** while those of the endocrine system are **slower [1]** and usually last for a **longer [1]** period of time. **[Total: 6]**

2 Pancreas **[1]**

3 C **[1]** **[Total: 1]**

4 **S** **Eight** from:
Vasoconstriction **[1]**
Shunt vessel open **[1]**
Blood diverted away from surface capillaries **[1]**
Less energy/heat lost to the environment **[1]**
Contraction of hair erector/erector pili muscles **[1]**
Layer of still air trapped that insulates **[1]**
Shivering **[1]**
Involuntary contraction of muscles **[1]**
(no work done) so heat released by respiration warms body **[1]**

[8]
[Total: 8]

5 **a)** To ensure that the patient's blood glucose concentration was low **[1]**
To ensure that the patient's blood glucose concentration was stable **[1]**

[2]

b) 60 minutes/1 hour **[1]**

c) 12.5 mmol/Any sensible number between 12.1-12.5 mmol/dm3 **[1]**
dm^3 **[1]**

[2]

d) **Six** marks from:
The concentration of glucose was 5 $mmol/dm^3$ at the start **[1]**
After drinking the glucose solution the (blood glucose) concentration increased rapidly over 30 minutes/to 90 minutes **[1]**
To a concentration of 9.5 $mmol/dm^3$ **[1]**
because the glucose had been absorbed from the gut into the patient's blood **[1]**
There was (then) a slower rise between 90 and 105 minutes **[1]**
to a concentration of 9.75 ± 0.1mmol/dm^3 **[1]**
because the patient secreted insulin **[1]**
which lowers blood glucose concentration **[1]**
The patient's blood glucose concentration returned to normal/5 $mmol/dm^3$ after 195 minutes **[1]**
because the insulin (that was secreted) encouraged the uptake of glucose into the liver/body's cells **[1]**

[6]

e) **i)** Patient B
One from:
The patient's starting blood glucose concentration was high/12.4 mmol/dm^3 at the start/time 0 **[1]**
It had not returned to normal after 210 minutes/by the end of data collection **[1]**

[3]
[Total: 12]

Page 92: Tropic responses

1 Root will (continue to) grow horizontally **[1]**
Klinostat eliminates effects of gravity **[1]**

[2]
[Total: 2]

2. C **[1]** **[Total: 1]**

3 a) axes labelled with units **[1]**
suitable linear scale and data occupies at least half the grid in both directions **[1]**
eight points plotted accurately ± half a small square **[1]**
suitable line of best fit drawn. **[1]**
Example graph:

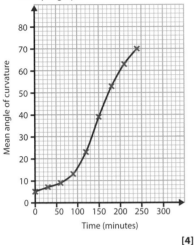

Mean angle of curvature (y-axis, 0 to 80); Time (minutes) (x-axis, 0 to 300)

[4]

b) initial delay/lag **[1]**
(then) increase **[1]**
curvature less/graph levels off with increased time **[1]**

[3]

c) First phase:
Idea that it takes time for perception of stimulus/auxin synthesis/auxin redistribution/water absorption by cells/alternative sensible answer **[1]**
Second phase:
Approaching maximum response as cells elongating/elongated **[1]**
Third phase:
Maximum response achieved/idea of optimum orientation/any sensible answer **[1]**

[3]
[Total: 10]

4

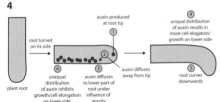

Sketch shows:
Auxin produced at root tip **[1]**
Auxin diffuses to lower part of root **[1]**
Under influence of gravity **[1]**
Auxin inhibits root growth **[1]**
More cell elongation/growth on upper surface **[1]**
Root curves downwards **[1]**

[6]
[Total: 6]

5 **S a)** Produced in the shoot tip **[1]**
Diffuse away from shoot tip **[1]**
Able to diffuse through gelatine block **[1]**
Produce cell elongation/growth further back **[1]**

[4]

b) Four from:
Auxin produced in (shoot) tip **[1]**
Illumination leads to redistribution of auxin/towards shaded side **[1]**

But mica prevents movement down shaded side **[1]**
No response on lighted side **[1]**
So no response/growth **[1]**

[4]
[Total: 8]

Page 94: Drugs and medicines

1 A **[Total: 1]**

2 a) (slows down growth of bacteria) until the person's immune system controls/destroys/suitable alternative them **[1]**

[1]

b) **Two** from:
when (the infection is) caused by a virus. **[1]**
if the infection is mild/suitable alternative answer. **[1]**
antibiotic chosen not the most effective against the bacterium causing the infection **[1]**

[2]
[Total: 3]

3 a) i) The Netherlands **[1]**
ii) France **[1]**

[2]

b) 8 ± 0.5 (per cent) **[1]**

c) As the daily dose of penicillin (per 1000 inhabitants) increases **[1]** the percentage of resistant pneumonia bacteria increases **[1]**
Looking at the pattern in the data, the percentage of resistant pneumonia bacteria for particular doses of penicillin is higher than would be/might be expected in Spain/Hungary **[1]**

[3]

d) i) France **[1]**
ii) **One** from:
Effectiveness of antibiotic reduced **[1]**
Eventually, (antibiotic) no longer effective against (any) bacteria **[1]**

[2]

e) **S** **Four** from:
Rapid reproductive rate (of bacteria) **[1]**
Mutation/genetic variation in bacteria **[1]**
Exposure to antibiotic leads to struggle for existence/survival/applies selection pressure **[1]**
Some bacteria better able to survive (antibiotic) than others **[1]**
These pass on resistance to offspring **[1]**
Resistance spreads through population (of bacteria) **[1]**
Spreads quickly owing to rapid reproductive rate **[1]**
Allow one mark for natural selection alone.

[4]
[Total: 12]

Pages 96–101: Section 16 Revise Questions

Page 97: Reproduction in plants

1 a) (Process where) one parent produces (genetically identical) offspring
b) **S** Advantage: only one parent is needed OR large numbers of identical offspring OR produced very quickly OR offspring suited to conditions in which they find themselves
Disadvantage: no genetic variation in the population OR population only survives in one type of habitat

2 Fertilisation
3 Any three from: light, small, smooth or made in large amounts

Page 99: Reproduction in humans

1 a) produce sperm; **b)** produce eggs; **c)** carries eggs from ovary to the uterus and is where fertilisation happens.
2 a) A – amniotic sac; B – placenta; C – amniotic fluid.
b) A – contains and holds amniotic fluid; C – protects fetus OR keep temperature stable
3 Oxygen and nutrients diffuse in from mother excretory products/carbon dioxide diffuse out to the mother

Page 101: Sex hormones and sexually transmitted infections

1 a) testes
b) any two from: Voice deepens; facial OR body OR underarm OR pubic hair grows; testes start producing sperm; increased muscle development; reproductive organs grow and develop; growth spurt to adult size.
2 Egg is released from the ovary.
3 Needles might have another person's blood on them/ body fluids are exchanged.

Pages 102–106: Section 17 Revise Questions

Page 103: Chromosomes, genes and proteins

1 A gene is a length of DNA that codes for a protein; an allele is an alternative form of a gene.
2 There are a pair of sex chromosomes; the chromosomes are XX and XY. Offspring inherit an X chromosome from the mother and either X or Y from the father.
3 **S** Different sequences of amino acids make protein molecules with different shapes.
4 **S** mRNA copies one strand of DNA; mRNA moves out of nucleus.
5 **S** 23 pairs OR 46 chromosomes

Page 105: Mitosis and meiosis

1 **S** Nuclear division; produces two genetically identical cells
2 **S** Any two from growth; repairing tissues; replacing worn out cells; asexual reproduction.
3 **S** Unspecialised cells that divide by mitosis to produce cells that can become specialised for specific functions.
4 **S** A reduction division; where the chromosome number is halved OR from diploid to haploid; this results in genetically different cells.
5 **S** Gametes.

Page 107: Monohybrid inheritance

1 a) Only expressed when no dominant allele is present in the genotype;
b) Observable features of an organism;
c) Two identical alleles for a feature are present
2 a) Tall OR T
b)

		Male parent alleles	
		T	t
Female parent alleles	T	TT	Tt
	t	tT	tt

c) 3 tall : 1 small

3 **S** All alleles present contribute to the phenotype equally.

Page 109: Variation and adaptation
1 Genes; the environment.
2 **S** Meiosis; random mating; random fertilisation; changes in the base sequence of DNA/mutation.
3 A genetic change; that forms new alleles.
4 Inherited features of an organism; that increase its chances of survival.

Pages 108-111: Section 18 Revise Questions

Page 111: Selection
1 Populations become more suited to their environment over many generations
2 Individuals with desirable characteristics; are bred together; over generations to give more individuals with the selected features
3 **S** Natural selection is slow /happens over many generations ; artificial selection is much faster in a shorter time.

Pages 112-123: Section 16-18 Practice Questions

Page 112: Reproduction in plants
1 **a)** asexual
  b) Another organism that reproduces sexually is potato/onion/banana [1]. It does this by producing tubers/ producing bulbs/producing offshoots from the base of the plant [1]. **[2]**
  c) For asexual, only one parent needed; sexual needs two parents. Asexual offspring are identical to parent; sexual offspring are different to parents/show variation **[2]**
  d) **S** Any **two** from: large numbers of plants, produced very quickly, all plants suited to the conditions, farmers know that product features produced by the plant are desirable **[2]**
  e) **S** Variation [1] means that some offspring may survive if conditions change adversely. [1] **[2]**
                                      [Total: 9]
2 **a)** Fertilisation is the **fusion** [1] of the **nuclei** [1] of the **gametes** [1]. **[3]**
    (a) **S** Zygote **[1]**
    (b) **S** Each gamete [1] is haploid [1].
                                      [Total: 6]
3 **a)** B anther; D stamen; E stigma; F style; H ovule; I carpel **[3]**
  b) B produce pollen grains; E pollen lands here; H female gamete **[3]**
  c) **S** Pollen grain and ovule **[1]**
  d) **S** Zygote **[1]**
  e) Transfer of pollen grains from an anther to a stigma **[1]**
  f) **S** Cross-pollination mixes **genetic information** from two **gamete**s. This means that there is **variation** in the offspring which is a survival **advantage**. **[2]**
  g) Any **two** from: Large amounts of small, smooth, lightweight pollen **[1]** Large feathery stigma often outside flower to catch pollen **[1]** Many, large, anthers often outside flower for easy dispersal **[1]** **[2]**
  h) In the ovary/ovule **[1]**
                                      [Total: 14]

4 **a)** independent variable named as temperature **[1]** dependent variable named as time to germinate. **[1]** At least two controlled variables named from: amount of light; amount of water; number of seeds in dish; amount of oxygen; seeds equally spread from each other/separated by the same distance; look at all test dishes at the same time for example, every day **[2]** Add more water if needed. **[1]** Count the number of germinated seeds present every day. **[1]** **[6]**
  b) I think that the **warmer** [1] the temperature the seeds are in, the **faster** [1] they will germinate. This is because **the enzyme-controlled reactions will happen faster** [1]. **[3]**
                                      [Total: 9]

Page 114: Reproduction in humans
1 **a)** A – oviduct [1]; B – ovary [1]; C – cervix [1]; D – vagina [1].
  b) i) uterus **[1]**
     ii) ovary **[1]**
     iii) oviduct **[1]**
  c) fusion of sperm and egg **[1]**
  d) embryo is a ball of cells fetus has formed organs. **[1]**
                                      [Total: 9]
2 **a)**

Part		Function
Testes		Carry sperm from testes
Scrotum		Transfer sperm into vagina
Sperm ducts		Produce sperm
Urethra		Carry sperm to vagina
Penis		Keep testes cooler than body temperature

  b) i) they both have a nucleus/they are both haploid/both contain half the genetic information of a body cell. **[1]**
     ii) Any **two** from: they have a flagellum for movement; they are much smaller; they are made in much larger numbers; they have many mitochondria; they have an acrosome with enzymes. **[1]** mark for each difference. **[2]**
                                      [Total: 7]
3 **a)** A – placenta [1]; B – umbilical cord [1]
  b) **S** Dissolved nutrients; oxygen **[1]**
  c) Diffuse from uterus wall [1] into the placenta [1]. **[2]**
                                      [Total: 5]

Page 115: Sex hormones and STIs
1 **a)** Hips get wide [1]; breasts develop [1]; ovaries produce eggs [1].
  b) i) Day 1 [1]; ii) around Day 14 [1].
  c) thickens (around Day 6-28) [1]; breaks down/is shed (Day 1- around 5) [1].
  d) testosterone [1]
                                      [Total: 8]
2 **S** **a)**

Hormone		Function
		Uterus lining breaks down
FSH		Maintains uterus lining
LH		Causes release of egg
Progesterone		Causes egg to develop

                                      [3]

  b) They fall/drop/decrease. **[1]**
                                      [Total: 4]
3 **a)** virus **[1]**
  b) HIV causes the infection [1]; AIDS is caused by the virus attacking the immune system [1].
  c) Spread is caused by any two from: unprotected sex. sharing used needles to inject drugs/ exchange of bodily fluids. during pregnancy/breastfeeding [2] Prevented by any two from: protected sex/using a condom. not sharing needles/take other precautions not to exchange bodily fluids. only having sex with partners who do not have HIV. Taking antivirals [2]
                                      [Total: 7]

Page 116: Chromosomes genes and proteins
1 **a)** i) chromosome [1]; ii) double helix [1]; iii) gene [1]; (iv) alleles [1]
  b) DNA has **two** [1] strands twisted into a **double helix** [1]. The strands are connected by pairs of **bases** [1].
  c) Strand 2: T T G A C C [1]
                                      [Total: 8]
2 **a)** i) XX [1]; ii) one X replaced by Y/XY [1]; (aiii) X chromosome comes from mother and either an X or Y comes from father [1].
  b) i) 46 OR 23 pairs [1]
     ii) When haploid [1] gametes fuse [1], a diploid nucleus forms [1] in the zygote [1]
                                      [Total: 8]
3 **a)** Any **six** points from:
    • A single-strand copy of DNA is made in the nucleus
    • Called mRNA
    • mRNA moves out of nucleus into cytoplasm
    • To the ribosome
    • As the mRNA moves through the ribosome amino acids are assembled
    • To match the sequence of bases in the mRNA
    • To form a specific protein **[6]**
  b) Any **two** from:
    • produce enzymes which control chemical reactions
    • carrier molecules control the movement of substances across cell membranes /in active transport
    • receptors for neurotransmitters in the synapses/control how impulses pass along neurones **[2]**
  c) ensures that each new cell has an identical copy of the DNA/genetic information. **[1]**
                                      [Total: 9]
4 Any **three** from:
    • different parts of the plant/specialised cells have different functions
    • genes code for proteins
    • specific proteins needed in different cells
    • some genes are not needed in some cells
                                      [Total: 3]
5 **a)** DNA, chromosome, nucleus
  b) B/DNA
  c) 28 per cent **[Total: 3]**

Page 117: Mitosis and meiosis

1 **S** a)

Statement	Type of cell division described by the statement
Genetically identical cells produced	mitosis
How cells for growth are produced	mitosis
How gametes are made	meiosis
How genetic information is copied	mitosis
How the zygote divides to grow	mitosis
Every division produces four daughter cells	meiosis

2 correct answers **[1]**; 4 correct answers **[2]**; all correct **[3]**

b) mitosis **[1]**

c) i) undifferentiated cells **[1]**
ii) produce (daughter) cells that become specialised /can perform a certain function **[1]**

[Total: 6]

2 **S** a) Equal number in all gametes **[1]** come in pairs, one set from mother and one set from father **[1]**.

b) i) 4 **[1]**
ii) **a)** 28 **[1]**; **b)** 45 **[1]**; **c)** 36 **[1]**

[Total: 6]

Page 118: Monohybrid inheritance

1 a) Features/characteristics/appearance **[1]**

b) i) different forms of a gene **[1]**
ii) A – 6; B – 4 **[1]**

c) **S** Cross the unknown parent with a homozygous recessive/short plant (tt) **[1]**
If no short plants produced, it means the parent was homozygous (TT). **[1]**
If short plants are produced, it means the parent was heterozygous (Tt). **[1]**

d)

Male parent alleles

Female parent alleles		T	t
	T	TT	Tt
	t	Tt	tt

Correct parental alleles **[1]**
Correct offspring genotypes **[1]**
75 per cent chance of tall/25 per cent short **[1]**

[Total: 9]

2 a) Leopard 1 is Heterozygous **[1]**
Leopard 2 homozygous recessive **[1]**

b) Leopard 5 is black **[1]**; leopard 8 is spotted **[1]**

c) 1:1 **[1]**

d) i) pure bred **[1]**; ii) bb **[1]**; black **[1]**

[Total: 8]

3 a) **S** Caused by recessive allele **[1]** on X chromosome **[1]**. Males only have one copy of the allele **[1]** as the Y chromosome has no equivalent allele **[1]**.

[4]

b)

Male parent alleles

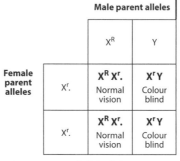

Female parent alleles		X^R	Y
	X^r.	$X^R X^r$. Normal vision	$X^r Y$ Colour blind
	X^r.	$X^R X^r$. Normal vision	$X^r Y$ Colour blind

Correct parental alleles **[1]**
Correct offspring genotypes **[1]**
Probability: 1:1 OR all girls normal vision: all boys colour blind **[1]**

[Total: 7]

Page 120: Variation and adaptation

1. a) The differences between individuals of the same species. **[1]**

b) Discontinuous: any **one** from colour, shape. **[1]** Continuous: any one from: length, circumference **[1]**

c) some members of the species are more likely to survive **[1]** if conditions change **[1]**

d) i)

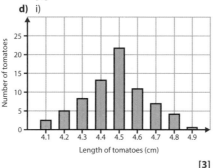

[3]

ii) 4.1 – 4.9cm **[1]**
iii) 4.4 + 4.5 + 4.8 + 4.1 + 4.7 OR 22.5 **[1]**
/5 **[1]**
= 4.5cm **[1]**

[3]

[Total: 12]

2. a) It is an **inherited** **[1]** feature that helps an organism to **survive** **[1]** and reproduce **[1]** in its **environment** **[1]**. **[4]**

b) it camouflages them/predators cannot see them **[1]** against green leaves (on the trees) **[1]**

[2]

[Total: 6]

3 Explanation must be linked to the correct feature. Any **three** from:
• leaf is curled **[1]** to trap air inside **[1]**
• thick waxy cuticle **[1]** to prevent water loss/ evaporation/transpiration **[1]**
• no stomata on the upper surface **[1]** to prevent water loss/evaporation/ transpiration **[1]**
• stomata in pits on the underside of the leaf **[1]** to retain moist air and reduce water loss/evaporation/transpiration **[1]**
• hairs on the lower surface **[1]** reduce air movement **[1]**

[Total: 6]

4. a) DNA mutation **[1]**

b) discontinuous **[1]**

c) When there is pollution, the light moths are no longer **camouflaged** **[1]** on the dark trees so they are **eaten** **[1]** by birds and could not **survive/reproduce** **[1]**. The dark moths were **camouflaged** **[1]**

so they **survived/reproduced** **[1]** and could pass on their **genes/alleles** **[1]** to their offspring.

[6]

[Total: 8]

Page 122: Selection

1 a) choose or select cows that produce the most milk **[1]**
Choose bull from a high milk yield cow **[1]**
Only let these cows reproduce **[1]**
Select offspring producing the most milk **[1]**
Keep repeating the process of selection and breeding **[1]**
Until the herd is all high milk yield **[1]** **[6]**

b) no thorns **[1]**; large flowers **[1]**; scented flowers **[1]**

[3]

[Total: 9]

2 a) Xerophytes **[1]**

b) To find water: **No more than four marks from**:
• Deep roots **[1]** to find water **[1]**;
• Extensive root system **[1]** to absorb water quickly after rain before it evaporates **[1]**;
• High salt concentration inside cells **[1]** to increase osmosis **[1]**;
• To preserve absorbed water: **No more than four marks from**:
• Thickened leaves/stems **[1]** to store water **[1]**
• Small, needle-shaped leaves **[1]** reduces surface of leaf for evaporation **[1]**
• Leaf rolled /stomata inside **[1]** reduces transpiration **[1]**
• Inner leaf surface covered in hairs **[1]** keeps air moist and reduces transpiration **[1]**
• Thick waxy cuticle **[1]** reduces transpiration/evaporation **[1]**
• shiny cuticle **[1]** reflects heat/lowers temperature **[1]**

c) adaptation **[1]**

[Total: 8]

3 **S** Any **three** from:
• mutation occurs/there is a change in DNA/ in the gene in the bacteria causing the infection **[1]**
• when antibiotic is taken only the resistant bacteria survive /non-resistant bacteria are killed **[1]**
• resistant bacteria reproduce and pass on the gene/allele **[1]**
• The more times the antibiotic is taken the greater the chance of this happening. **[1]**

[Total: 3]

4 a) **S** Populations become more suited to their environment **[1]**; over many generations **[1]**; due to natural selection **[1]**.

[3]

b) Any **three** adaptations with the correct explanation from:
• streamlined body **[1]** to reduce drag when swimming **[1]**
• wings shaped flippers **[1]** to help them swim very fast underwater **[1]**
• stay upright **[1]** to reduce heat loss compared to when lying down **[1]**
• rock back on to their heels and use stiff tail feathers for support (which have no blood supply) and so do not lose heat **[1]**
• dark back feathers **[1]** absorb heat from the sun **[1]**.

[6]

[Total: 9]

ANSWERS

Pages 124-129: Section 19 Revise Questions

Page 125: Energy flow, food chains and food webs

1. a) stickleback, water boatman
   b) water flea, mayfly larva
2. D → B → C → A
3. **S** one of: (heat from) respiration, wastes/faeces/urine
4. pyramid of stacked bars; grass at bottom; bars labelled; bars get shorter further up the pyramid

Page 127: Carbon cycle and nitrogen cycle

1. Two of: proteins/amino acids, carbohydrates/sugars, fats/oils/lipids
2. a) photosynthesis
   b) respiration
3. combustion/burning produces carbon dioxide
   increases carbon dioxide concentration in the air
4. **S** Flow chart showing:
   • urea
   • decomposition of urea into ammonium ions
   • action of nitrifying bacteria to change ammonium ions into nitrite ions
   • action of nitrifying bacteria to change nitrite ions into nitrate ions
   • absorption of nitrate ions by grass
5. **S** denitrifying (bacteria)

Page 129: Populations

1. • predators eat prey
   • prey population decreases
2. **S** • waste/ethanol poisons the yeast
   • food supply/glucose is exhausted

Pages 130-133: Section 20 Revise Questions

Page 131: Factors affecting biodiversity

1. a) One of: land for housing/farming, extracting natural resources/stone/oil/wood
   b) deforestation
   c) • reduces biodiversity
      • because organisms/species no longer have enough resources/food/shelter to survive
2. Two of:
   • fertilisers add/replace mineral ions
   • help plant growth

   • herbicides kill weeds/plant pests
   • reduce competition for the crop plants

   • insecticides kill insects
   • reduce amount of crop lost/improve quality of crop

   • antibiotics to treat animal diseases
   • use less energy fighting infections and improves livestock health

Page 133: Pollution and conservation

1. a) methane, carbon dioxide
   b) • (methane from) oil exploration/(rice) paddy fields/livestock
      • (carbon dioxide from) burning fossil fuels
2. **S** a) • limits the catch
      • to ensure that no more are taken than can be replaced/reproduce
   b) nets with large mesh

Pages 134-137: Section 21 Revise Questions

Page 135: Biotechnology

1. glucose → carbon dioxide + ethanol
2. • break down stains (from foods/blood/plants)
   • at low temperatures
3. • removes/digests pectin
   • pectin holds apple cells/tissue together/strengthens cell walls
4. **S** One of:
   • reproduce very quickly
   • make complex molecules
   • easy to genetically modify.

Page 137: Genetic modification

1. Genetically modified organism
2. to produce a useful (human) protein/produce insulin
3. **S** a) joining DNA/sticky ends
   b) cutting DNA
4. **S** recombinant plasmid
5. **S** One of:
   • contains gene(s) for insect resistance
   • so less crop eaten by insects
   OR
   • contains gene(s) for better growth
   • more product produced

Pages 138-145: Section 19-21 Practice Questions

Page 138: Energy flow, food chains and food webs

1. a) producer [1]
   b) i) orca [1]
      ii) **One** of: cod, orca [1]
   c) leopard seal, orca, elephant seal [1]
   d) energy transfer [1]
   e) **Two** of:
      • fewer leopard seals; they have less (cod) to eat
      • more zooplankton; (fewer cod means that) less are eaten/more phytoplankton to eat
      • more phytoplankton; (fewer cod means that) less are eaten
      • more squid; more zooplankton to eat [2 for each correct pair to a maximum of 4]
      [4]
   f) phytoplankton → zooplankton → squid → elephant seal → orca [1]
   g) pyramid of bars that get shorter and shorter as you go up the pyramid [1]
      • phytoplankton at bottom AND/OR bars correctly labelled [1]
   h) **S** • fewer organisms as you go up the pyramid
      • less energy at each trophic level
      • because energy is lost by heat from respiration/in waste/in urine/in faeces [3]
   i) **S** the mass of tiny organisms (such as phytoplankton, at any one time) is small
      [Total: 15]
2. A [1]
3. • trapped by photosynthesis
   • stored as 'chemical energy'/energy stored in substances in plant (biomass)
   • plants eaten by herbivores and plant biomass used to make animal biomass (but energy remains stored). [3]
4. More energy is available from the corn/energy is lost when transferred from corn to chicken. [1]

Page 139: Carbon cycle and nitrogen cycle

1. a) • decrease (concentration of carbon dioxide)
      • used for photosynthesis [2]
   b) eaten by zooplankton, which are eaten by squid, which are eaten by elephant seals [1] OR similar answers which shows molecules moving through the food web
   c) decomposition [1]
   d) i) **One** of: fossil fuels/petrol/diesel/oil/coal/natural gas/plastics [1]
      ii) any problem linked to the answer in i) for example:
         • burning fossil fuels
         • causes global warming/climate change
         OR
         • microplastics
         • damage bodies of organisms
         OR
         • oil spills
         • kill birds/sea creatures
         [Total: 8]
   e) absorb nitrates (from seawater) [1]
2. D [1]
3. i) B; ii) A; iii) D; (iv) B [4]
4. a) proteins
   b) nitrogen-fixation
   c) ammonium
   d) nitrate
   e) deamination [5]
5. • denitrifying bacteria
   • convert nitrates to nitrogen (gas) [2]

Page 140: Populations

1. a) • (elephant seal population) decreases
      • because orcas are predators of elephant seals [2]
   b) competition for food (supply)/zooplankton [1]
   c) space/territory [1]
   d) • cod population falls
      • because the disease kills the fish/the fish are less healthy and do not reproduce
      • squid population falls
      • because leopard seals have to eat more squid [4]
   e) **One** of:
      • increased light (intensity)
      • causes population increase
      • because phytoplankton photosynthesise (to make their food)
      OR
      • increased temperature
      • causes population increase
      • because phytoplankton enzymes work faster [3]
      [Total: 10]
2. A [1]
3. a) Number in sample = 20
      Study area = $15 \times 10 = 150 \, m^2$
      Sample area = $0.5 \times 15 = 7.5 \, m^2$
      [1]
      estimated population = number in sample
      $\times \dfrac{\text{study area } (m^2)}{\text{sample area } (m^2)}$
      estimated population = $20 \times \dfrac{150}{7.5}$
      estimated population size = 400
      [2]
   b) quadrat [1]

c) to avoid bias/to avoid influence by the experimenter [1]

d) • takes more time
• result is more accurate
• (400 dandelions in 150 m^2 is 400/150 =) 2.7 dandelions per m^2/3 dandelions per m^2
• a more accurate answer is unlikely to more than double the estimate (for dandelions per m^2)
• not worth doing [5]

[Total: 9]

4 a) i) stationary (phase) [1]
ii) glucose [1]

b) **One** of:
• glucose has run out
• without food the yeast die
OR
• ethanol/wastes
• poison/kill the yeast [2]

[Total: 3]

Page 141: Factors affecting biodiversity

1 A [1]

2 a) Y [1]

b) • kills insects
• less of the useful product eaten (by insects)/lack of damage makes plants healthier [2]

c) 40 per cent increase [1]

d) • kills other/non-target insects
• which reduces biodiversity/affects food chain/affects food webs/reduces food supply for wild organisms [2]

[Total: 6]

3 Any **three** from:
• pollution caused by animal wastes
• (animals are close together, so) diseases spread easily (including to wild animals)
• pollution caused by chemicals used to control diseases
• animals produce a lot of carbon dioxide/methane (which contributes to climate change) [3]

4 • lack of tree roots plant roots (to hold soil)
• soil washed away
• lack of soil to hold water back means more flooding [3]

5 • burning of trees produces carbon dioxide
• removal of trees reduces photosynthesis/reduces removal of carbon dioxide [2]

Page 142: Pollution and conservation

1 B [1]

2 a) If too much carbon dioxide is released it can cause warming in the atmosphere. [1]

b) Increased carbon dioxide levels cause global warming. [1] Warming causes melting of sea ice and rises in sea levels. [1] Rising sea levels could have caused loss of habitat for the melomys leading to extinction. [1]

3 a) hunted by humans/for food OR habitat destruction (by humans) [1]

b) **Three** of:
• increases (biodiversity)
• changes food webs
• increases competition
• seeds of tree spread further (due to being eaten by the tortoises)
• tortoises may restore balance in the ecosystem (before humans) [3]

c) **One** of:
• education (to stop local people destroying its habitat/killing it)
• setting up a protected area/nature reserve/stopping people entering its habitat [1]

d) S • lack of genetic diversity
• for population to evolve/change in response to environmental change [2]

[Total: 7]

4 S **Five** of:
• nutrients in fertilisers/animal waste
• nutrients dissolve in water and wash into rivers
• eutrophication is high levels/concentrations of nutrients in water
• plants and algae grow rapidly
• large populations of plants and algae block light
• without light producers die
• bacteria/decomposers feed on dead organisms
• aerobic respiration of bacteria/decomposers uses up oxygen
• too little oxygen for other organisms/fish to survive. [5]

Page 143: Biotechnology

1 C [1]

2 • (anaerobic) respiration produces carbon dioxide (gas)
• bubbles of gas make dough rise [2]

3 biotechnology is the use of any biological process to make a useful product [1]

4 a) lack of blue-black colour/colourless [1]

b) 14 mm [1]

c) to get a more accurate value/estimate/to get a value closer to the true value [1]

d) • Z
• there was no zone of digestion (only the width of the well)
• because there was no enzyme [3]

e) i) • X
• gave the largest zone of digestion on milk (which contains casein, a protein) [2]

ii) • high temperature denatures the enzyme/shape of enzyme is changed
• substrate will no longer fit the active site (well) [2]

[Total: 10]

5 a) • control
• to check that the pectinase has the expected effect [2]

b) • pectin strengthens cell walls/sticks cells together
• (without pectin) cells fall apart more easily/release their contents
• pectinase digests pectin
• more pectinase, the quicker the pectin is removed and the more juice is produced [4]

c) 40 per cent (increase) [1]

d) **Two** of: volume of pectinase solution, mass/volume of apple pulp, time left, temperature, length of time of filtering [2]

[Total: 9]

6 a) • to stop other microorganisms growing/to sterilise it/to kill microorganisms
• stop competition with other microorganisms and the mold/stop other microorganisms from producing unwanted substances [2]

b) • respiration produces heat/increase temperature
• if contents get too hot, enzymes do not work as effectively/need to keep temperature at optimum for enzymes [2]

c) • ensure even distribution (of contents/temperature/pH)
• so all microorganisms have the best conditions (not just some) [2]

d) • removes lactose
• for people who cannot digest it/are allergic to it/have an intolerance to it [2]

e) mycoprotein [1]

[Total: 9]

Page 145: Genetic modification

1 C [1]

2 • both enzymes
• restriction enzymes cuts DNA but DNA ligase joins DNA [2]

3 B [1]

4 **Two** of:
• insect resistance
• herbicide resistance
• increased yield
• resistance to cold/heat
• production of certain nutrient/substance (useful for humans)
• disease resistance [2]

5 **One** of:
• GM crops not permitted in that area
• GM seed costs too much
• farmer is worried about foreign genes getting into wild plants
• farmer cannot afford chemicals needed to grow the GM crops [1]

6 An advantage and explanation:
• toxin kills pests/insects
• crop is less damaged/increased yield/needs fewer chemicals
A disadvantage and explanation:
• pollination/fertilisation with wild plants
• wild plants produce the toxin
• GM crops are expensive
• farmers cannot afford the seeds [4]

7 a) **Two** of:
• cheaper
• can be used by people who do not use pork products
• takes up less room to make
• purer product/less likely to be contaminated (for example, with other substances made by pigs, viruses)
• no ethical concerns in growing bacteria compared with pigs [2]

b) **Six** of these points in order:
• cut gene out of human DNA
• cut plasmid from bacteria
• using restriction enzymes (which leave sticky ends)
• insert (cut) gene into (cut) plasmid from bacteria
• using DNA ligase
• to produce recombinant plasmid
• (recombinant) plasmid inserted into bacteria
• bacteria multiply
• cause multiplication of (recombinant) plasmids
• insulin gene is expressed [6]

[Total: 6]

ANSWERS

Pages 146-156: Mixed Exam-Style Questions

1 B [1]
2 C [1]
3 A [1]
4 D [1]
5 C [1]
6 A [1]
7 D [1]
8 D [1]
9 A [1]
10 A [1]
11 A [1]
12 B [1]
13 C [1]
14 A [1]
15 **S** A [1]
16 **S** B [1]
17 **S** C [1]
18 **S** C [1]
19 **S** B [1]
20 **S** C [1]
21 **S** B [1]
22 **S** B [1]
23 **S** A [1]
24 **S** B [1]
25 **S** C [1]

26 **a)** fat(s)/oil(s) [1]
cheese/eggs/fish/liver/milk/other correct answer [1]
to make haemoglobin/to make red blood cells [1]
[3]

b) A [1]
D [1]
[2]

c) smaller [1]
physical [1]
surface area [1]
chemical [1]
[4]

d) i) peripheral nerves [1]
sensory neurones [1]
[2]

ii) *for:* antibiotics kill bacteria [1]
against: bacteria could be resistant (to antibiotics)
OR *idea that* could promote development of resistant bacteria [1]
[2]

27 **a)** biodiversity – the number of different species that live in an area
community – all the populations of different species in an ecosystem
ecosystem – a community of organisms and their environment
population – a group of organisms of the same species living in the same area at the same time
one correct link = 1 mark
two correct links = 2 marks
three or four correct links = 3 marks [3]

b) **Two** of increased land for building/farming [1]
extraction of wood [1] extraction of other named resource
[2]

c) i) *any two from:*
reduced biodiversity [1]
loss of soil [1]
flooding [1]
increase of carbon dioxide in atmosphere [1]
[2]

ii) *idea that* species bred in captivity to increase numbers so some can be released into their natural environment [1]

iii) *idea that* testosterone causes development of secondary sexual characteristics, e.g. sperm production [1]

d) *idea that* less biomass/fewer producers means less light energy absorbed/less photosynthesis [1]
idea that fewer consumers means less chemical energy passed along food chains/through food webs [1]
[2]

28 **a) i)** (add) iodine solution [1]

(brown colour changes to) blue-black [1]
[2]

ii) (add) Benedict's solution [1]
heat [1]
(blue colour changes to) red/yellow/orange/green [1]
[3]

b) i) starch broken down/digested to glucose [1]
by enzymes/in chemical digestion [1]
glucose absorbed/passes into blood [1]
[3]

ii) used in respiration [1]
insulin decreases blood glucose concentration/insulin converts glucose to glycogen [1]
[2]

iii) **S** blood glucose concentration returns to its original value/set point/maintains constant internal environment [1]
idea that a change in one direction/increase leads to a change in the opposite direction/decrease [1]
[2]

29 **a)** to improve crop yield/increase crop production [1]

b) root hairs/root hair cells **allow** 'root' [1]

c) to make amino acids [1]
(which are needed) to make proteins [1]
[2]

d) decomposition/decay/rotting [1]
(by action of) decomposers/microorganisms [1]
[2]

e) **S** *idea that* active transport is the movement of particles/ions from a region of lower concentration to an area of higher concentration OR active transport is movement up/against a concentration gradient [1]
idea that mineral ions are (usually) found in the soil/environment in lower concentrations than inside the plant [1]
[2]

f) **S** excess fertilisers/nitrates/mineral ions [1]
leach/run off/flow into water/streams/rivers [1]
increased growth of algae/plants/producers [1]
increased death/decomposition of algae/plants/producers [1]
increased aerobic respiration by decomposers [1]
reduction in dissolved oxygen [1]
[6]

30 **a)** (lens,) C [1], focuses light on to the retina [1]
optic nerve [1], (D,) carries impulses to the brain [1]
retina [1], E [1], (contains light receptors)
[6]

b) i) an automatic action [1]
in response to a stimulus [1]
[2]

ii) lets more light into the eye [1]
so able to see (even though the light is dim) [1]
[2]

iii) **S** circular muscles contract [1]
radial muscles relax [1]
[2]

c) i) phototropism
allow 'positive phototropism' but **reject** 'negative phototropism' [1]

ii) **S** auxin is made in the shoot tip [1]
auxin diffuses from the tip down the shoot [1]
auxin becomes more concentrated on the shaded side [1]
auxin stimulates cell elongation (on the shaded side) [1]
[4]

31 **S a) i)** 60 (µm) [1]

ii) *any three pairs from:*
idea that have a finger-like shape [1]
(that) provides large surface area (for absorption) [1]
OR
microvilli (on surface) [1]
to increase surface area (for absorption) [1]
OR
contain capillaries [1]
to absorb sugars/amino acids [1]
OR
contain lacteals [1]
to absorb fatty acids/glycerol [1]
OR
thin wall(s) [1]
short distance for (digested) nutrients to diffuse to capillaries/lacteals [1]
[6]

b) i) A: hepatic artery [1]
B: hepatic portal vein [1]
C: hepatic vein(s) [1]
[3]

ii) *any one from:*
excess glucose is converted to glycogen/stored in the liver [1]
assimilation of amino acids/amino acids converted to proteins (in liver) [1]
deamination/excess amino acids are converted to urea (in liver) [1]
[1]

c) i) *idea that* blood passes through heart twice on each complete circuit of the body [1]

ii) thick muscular/elastic wall [1]
to prevent artery bursting/to recoil/to maintain pressure [1]
[2]

Pages 157-165: Practice Paper 1 (1 mark each)

Question	Answer
1	B
2	B
3	C
4	B
5	B
6	A
7	A
8	B
9	C
10	A
11	D
12	C
13	D
14	B
15	C
16	B
17	B
18	B
19	D
20	B
21	C
22	B
23	D
24	A
25	D
26	D
27	A
28	C
29	A
30	A
31	A
32	B
33	B
34	A
35	D
36	C
37	D
38	B
39	D
40	A

[Total: 40]

Pages166-175: Practice Paper 2 (1 mark each)

Question	Answer
1	B
2	D
3	B
4	B
5	C
6	C
7	D
8	B
9	A
10	B
11	B
12	D
13	C
14	C
15	A
16	B
17	A
18	D
19	B
20	B
21	B
22	B
23	B
24	D
25	D
26	A
27	B
28	C
29	D
30	C
31	C
32	D
33	C
34	D
35	C
36	C
37	B
38	C
39	C
40	B

[Total: 40]

Pages 176-183: Practice Paper 3

1 a) (energy for) photosynthesis/to make carbohydrates [1]
   b) chloroplast(s) [1]
   c) (to make) chlorophyll [1]
   d) i) leaf/leaves [1]
       allow stomata
      ii) diffusion [1]
   e) *any two bullet points from:*
      • chloroplasts [1] have chlorophyll to absorb light [1]
      • (waxy) cuticle [1] prevents water loss [1]
      • guard cells [1] open and close stomata [1]
      • stomata [1] allow gas exchange/control water loss [1]
      • epidermis [1] is transparent/allows light to enter leaf [1]
      • palisade mesophyll/tightly packed column cells [1] *idea that* more efficient light absorption [1]
      • spongy mesophyll [1] to absorb light [1] OR air spaces [1] allow diffusion of gases [1]
      • vascular bundles/xylem and phloem [1] to transport substances OR xylem transports water/mineral ions OR phloem transports sugars/sucrose/amino acids [1]
      [4]
      [Total: 9]

2 a) production of genetically identical offspring [1]
      from one parent [1]
      [2]
   b) fusion of the nuclei of two gametes [1]
      production of offspring that are genetically different from each other [1]
      [2]
   c) i) fertilisation [1]
      ii) ovule [1]
   d) food store [1]
      jelly coat that changes at fertilisation (to prevent entry of more sperm) [1]
      [2]

allow nucleus containing genes/chromosomes/genetic material [1]
   e) *number:* many more sperm than eggs [1]
      size: egg is much larger than sperm [1]
      [2]
   f) *any two from:*
      chloroplast(s) [1]
      cell wall(s) [1]
      (large) vacuole(s) [1]
      [2]
      [Total: 12]

3 a) breakdown of food into smaller pieces [1]
      with no chemical change to the food molecules [1]
      [2]
   b) *incisors:* cut [1]
      canines: tear/hold [1]
      molars: chew/grind [1]
      [3]
   c) i) Biuret (test) [1]
      ii) blue to violet/purple/lilac [1]
   d) i) B/C/D [1]
      ii) D [1]
   e) as temperature increases, (the rate of) enzyme activity increases [1]
      enzyme activity peaks at the enzyme's optimum temperature [1]
      as temperature continues to increase (above the optimum temperature), (the rate of) enzyme activity decreases [1]
      (because) above the optimum temperature, the enzyme's active site changes shape/is denatured [1]
      [4]
      [Total: 13]

4 a)

organism   description

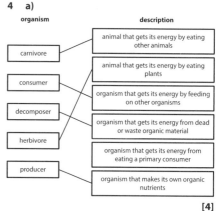

      [4]
   b) *any one from:*
      grass → grasshopper → bird → fox [2]
      grain → grasshopper → bird → fox [2]
      [2]
   c)
   vultures
   cheetahs
   giraffes
   trees
      [2]
   d) *any one from:*
      measuring (dry) mass may be difficult for (very) large organisms [1]
      measuring dry mass is difficult/will kill organisms [1]
      counting population size(s) may be difficult [1]
      organisms may be in other food chains/more than one trophic level [1]
      [1]

e) i) *any two from:*
climate change [1]
habitat destruction [1]
hunting [1]
pollution [1]
decrease in available food [1]
[2]

ii) *any one from:*
monitoring/protecting habitats [1]
education [1]
captive breeding programmes [1]
[1]
[Total: 12]

5 **a)** *any two bullet points from:*
• sandy coloured fur [1] *idea that* acts as camouflage [1]
• thinner/less fur [1] prevents overheating/(helps) maintain body temperature [1]
• large(r) ears/(more) pointed face [1] *idea that* increases surface area (to volume ratio) to help/increase heat loss [1]
[4]

b) continuous [1]
c) fur/hair [1]
d) *Vulpes* [1]
e) *idea that* variation in coat colour in (original) population [1]
idea that individuals with a white(r) coat were more likely to survive/reproduce [1]
idea that individuals with a white(r) coat were more likely to reproduce/pass on alleles to next generation [1]
[3]
[Total: 10]

6 **a)**
A trachea/windpipe [1]
B diaphragm [1]
C bronchus [1]
D rib [1]
E intercostal muscle [1]
[5]

b) *any three from:*
more oxygen [1]
less carbon dioxide [1]
dryer/less water vapour [1]
cooler [1]
[3]

c) *any two from:*
large surface area [1]
thin surface [1]
good blood supply [1]
good ventilation (with air) [1]
[2]

d) *any four in total from:*
similarities:
max two from:
both processes release energy [1]
both processes use glucose [1]
differences:
max three from:
aerobic respiration uses oxygen but anaerobic respiration does not use oxygen [1]
aerobic respiration produces carbon dioxide and water but anaerobic respiration produces lactic acid [1]
aerobic respiration releases (much) more energy per glucose molecule than anaerobic respiration OR reverse argument [1]

idea that most energy is released by aerobic respiration but anaerobic respiration occurs in muscles during vigorous exercise [1]
[4]
[Total: 14]

7 **a)**

genetic term	meaning
genotype	having two different alleles of a particular gene
homozygous	having two identical alleles of a particular gene
phenotype	observable features of an organism
	the alleles present

[3]

b)

		purple flowers	
		F	f
white flowers	f	Ff	ff
	f	Ff	ff

(phenotypic ratio) 1 (white) : 1 (purple)
[3]

c) i) genetic change
[1]

ii) ionising radiation [1]
(some) chemicals [1]
[2]

iii) it increases [1]
[Total: 10]

Pages 184-197: Practice Paper 4

1 **a)**

function of part of flower	name of part of flower	letter on Fig. 1.1
produces pollen grains	anther	A
contains the ovule	ovary	F
protects the flower while in bud	sepal(s)	E

[3]

b) i) the transfer of pollen (grains) to the stigma/female part of a flower [1]
ii) *any three from:*
anthers/stamens inside flower in insect AND hang down/outside flower in wind [1]
filament/stamens more rigid in insect AND on long flexible filament in wind [1]
style is upright/long in insect AND hangs down outside flower in wind [1]
stigma (usually) inside flower and smaller in insect AND *idea that* stigma is feathery/has large surface area in wind [1]
petals are brightly-coloured/have nectar/may have scent in insect AND petals/bracts are small and inconspicuous/absent in wind [1]
[3]

c) *advantage:*
any one from:
greater (genetic) variation in offspring [1]
offspring (therefore) better able to respond to environmental changes [1]
disadvantage:
any one from:
reliance on pollinator/method of pollination [1]
reliance on pollen from/presence of other plants [1]
[2]

d) i) neonicotinoids/ insecticides reduced percentage that laid eggs AND percentage alive after four weeks [1]
quantification:
any one from:
percentage that laid eggs reduced from 89 % to 55 % [1]
percentage still alive (after four weeks) reduced from 79 % to 52 % [1]
[2]

ii) *any three from:*
impulse stimulates release of neurotransmitter molecules [1]
from vesicles [1]
neurotransmitter molecules diffuse/move across synaptic gap [1]
(neurotransmitter molecules) bind to receptor proteins (on postsynaptic neurone) [1]
impulse stimulated in next/postsynaptic neurone [1]
[3]
[Total: 14]

2 **a)** *any three from:*
skin [1]
hairs in nose [1]
mucus (in respiratory system/digestive system/reproductive system) [1]
acid in stomach [1]
white blood cells [1]
immune system/antibodies [1]
[3]

b) *any three from:*
weakened/attenuated pathogen/microorganism introduced into body [1]
by injection/through mouth/nose [1]
antigens of pathogen [1]
stimulate immune response/cause lymphocytes to produce antibodies [1]
memory cells remain after pathogen killed [1]
[3]

c) i) 1940 to 2020/81 years/80-year time period [1]
ii) 780 000 [1]
iii) *any two from:*
introduction of vaccination (in 1968) reduced numbers (slowly)/numbers quantified [1]
idea of anomalous data/rise in 1970/fell in year prior to introduction [1]
after introduction of MMR numbers (of cases) reduced to below 10 000 from 1990/1991 [1]
[2]

d) *any two from:*
(amino acids) used to build/assembled into proteins [1]
(amino acids) used to assemble protein coat (of viruses) [1]

(amino acids) used to synthesise enzymes (for named biosynthesis, e.g. replication of genetic material/RNA/DNA or protein synthesis) **[1]**

[2]
[Total: 12]

3 a) $6CO_2 + 6H_2O \rightarrow C_6H_{12}O_6 + 6O_2$ **[2]** one mark for reactants; one mark for products.

b) i) B

ii) *any one from:*
sucrose **[1]**
amino acids **[1]**
reject: mineral ions/ions

c) i) *any four from:*
(as CO_2 concentration increased) increase in rate of photosynthesis in species A across the concentration range **[1]**
(as CO_2 concentration increased) increase in rate of photosynthesis in species B to about 1100 ppm **[1]** then no further increase as concentration of CO_2 increased **[1]**
(as CO_2 concentration increased) increase in rate of photosynthesis in species C until about 950 ppm **[1]** then decrease **[1]**
[4]

ii) *any two from:*
(below about 1100 ppm) rate of photosynthesis proportional to CO_2 concentration **[1]**
(below about 1100 ppm) CO_2 concentration is the limiting factor **[1]**
(from about 1100 ppm) some other factor/named factor becomes limiting **[1]**
[2]

d) *any five from:*
increased growth of producers/algae **[1]**
only uppermost layers photosynthesise **[1]**
(increased) death of producers **[1]**
(increased) decomposition of producers after death **[1]**
increased aerobic respiration of decomposers **[1]**
reduction in dissolved oxygen in water **[1]**
death of aquatic life/named aquatic life **[1]**
[5]
[Total: 15]

4 a) *Leontopithecus* **[1]**

b) *any three from:*
reduced biodiversity (leading to unbalanced ecosystems) **[1]**
soil erosion leading to flooding **[1]**
reduced photosynthesis/burning of waste leading to increase in the concentration of carbon dioxide/CO_2 in the atmosphere/leading to an enhanced greenhouse effect and global warming/climate change **[1]**
[3]

c) i) *any two from:*
not introducing disease/undesirable genetic traits into wild populations **[1]**
(captive-bred animals are) not susceptible to disease from wild populations **[1]**
idea that behaviour (from captive

breeding) would not prevent survival **[1]**
ensure that factors leading to reduction in numbers no longer applicable **[1]**
[2]

ii) 153 ± 2 **[1]**

iii) 1995 **[1]**

iv) 95% **[2]**
calculation of the total number $= 18 + 340 = 358$ **[1]**
calculation of percentage **[1]**
$\frac{340}{358} \times 100 = 95\%$

d) i) marmosets/*Callithrix* AND Goeldi's monkey/*Callimico* **[1]**
idea that most recent branch from ancestors (in tree) **[1]**
[2]

ii) *DNA:*
sequences of bases of DNA **[1]**
compared **[1]**
OR
protein:
sequence of amino acids of protein **[1]**
compared **[1]**
[2]
[Total: 14]

5 a) i) *E. coli:*
any one from:
faster/quantified production rate **[1]**
smaller final mass of cells justified by acceptable reason, e.g. processing/disposal **[1]**
S. cerevisiae:
higher/quantified concentration of insulin in medium **[1]**
larger final mass of cells justified by acceptable reason, e.g. use for next fermentation **[1]**
[2]

ii) *any six from:*
between 0 and 5/6 hours, lag phase **[1]** in which bacteria are starting to reproduce **[1]**
(followed by) exponential/log phase **[1]** specified time period, e.g. six to 16 hours **[1]**
rapid population increase/doubling/specified doubling rate **[1]**
stationary phase **[1]** specified time period, 16 to 19 hours **[1]**
reproductive rate = death rate **[1]** as nutrients run out/wastes build up **[1]**
[6]

b) i) heat generated by respiration will raise temperature **[1]**

ii) *any one from:*
monitor pH **[1]**
monitor oxygen concentration **[1]**
monitor concentration of waste products **[1]**
[2]

c) i) *a total of four from, with at least one from each stage:*
stage 1:
gene for insulin production cut from (human) DNA/chromosome **[1]**
using restriction enzyme **[1]**
(often) forming sticky ends **[1]**

stage 2:
cut made in (*E. coli*/bacterial) plasmid using same restriction enzyme **[1]**
stage 3:
gene (for insulin production) inserted into plasmid **[1]**
using (DNA) ligase **[1]**
sticky ends make it easier for DNA to be inserted **[1]**
[4]

ii) plasmid (re)inserted into bacterium/*E. coli* **[1]**
[1]
[Total: 15]

6 a) i) *any three from:*
radial muscles **[1]**
(radial muscles) contract **[1]**
circular muscles **[1]**
(circular muscles) relax **[1]**
pupil dilates **[1]**
[3]

ii) *any one from:*
idea that light gathered by three/several rods used to fire/generate nerve impulses in (connecting) neurone **[1]**
idea that one rod might not be sufficient to fire/generate impulse in (connecting) neurone, but several could **[1]**
[1]

b) i) 1 X^BX^b **[1]**
2   X^BY **[1]**
[2]

ii) *any one from:*
(person/mother) 1 has colour vision but 7 is colour blind/ (person/mother) 8 has colour vision but 11 is colour blind **[1]**
so person(s)/mother(s) 1/8 must be heterozygous/carriers **[1]**
or idea that the allele cannot be dominant:
if (the allele) were dominant, the daughter, 13, of person/father 7, would be colour blind **[2]**
[2]

iii) females have two X chromosomes (and males one) **[1]**
so probability of a female having two recessive/defective chromosomes (far) less likely (than a male having one) **[1]**
[2]
[Total: 10]

Pages 198–205: Practice Paper 6

1 a) time after exercise **[1]**

b) *any two from*
type of exercise **[1]**
intensity of exercise **[1]**
duration of exercise **[1]**
[2]

c) table drawn with 3 columns with line separating headings from data **[1]**
headings with correct units: minutes **and** beats/minute **[1]** Do **not** award a mark for beats/15 seconds
correct recording of data **[1]**
[3]

example table:

Time after exercise/minutes	Pulse rate/(beats per minute)	
	Student A	Student B
0	112	156
1	100	160
2	96	156
3	80	148
4	68	132
5	64	96

d) i) *lines/layers:* single clear lines to show layers and no shading **[1]**
 size: equal to/larger than micrograph, original **[1]**
 detail 1: three layers and lumen shown **[1]**
 detail 2: layers/lumen in (approximately) correct proportions **[1]**

           [4]

 ii) length of PQ = 29 ± 1 mm **[1]**
 calculation (1)
  width $= \dfrac{29}{40} = 0.725$ mm
 0.73 mm (to two significant figures) **[1]**
 allow error carried forward (ecf) from incorrect measurement of PQ:
 allow 0.70 based on measurement of 28 mm
 allow 0.75 based on measurement of 30 mm

           [3]

e) i) 0.8 s **[1]**
 ii) 75
 working out:
 convert 1 minute to seconds (1)
 calculation (1)
  heart rate $= \dfrac{60}{0.8} = 75$

           [2]

f) i) easy to measure/just requires stopwatch/stopclock/mobile phone/ alternative sensible answer **[1]**
 ii) *any one from:*
 (ECG) measured electronically/gives accurate measurement **[1]**
 manual measurement is multiplied by 4 so increases error **[1]**
 pulse can be difficult to find **[1]**

           [1]
          [Total: 18]

2 a) beginning 7 mm
 after 30 minutes 61 mm
 Allow answers of 5 mm and 59 mm, but the two measurements must be taken from the same part of each bubble. **[1]**
b) 54 (mm) **[1]**
c) *axes labelled with units:*
 time and minutes **and** distance moved by bubble and mm **[1]**
 scale and size:
 linear scale with both scales occupying at least half the grid in both directions **[1]**
 plots:
 7 values plotted accurately ± ½ small square **[1]**
 line of best fit is appropriate **[1]**

example graph:

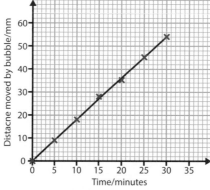

           [4]

d) linear relationship/distance moved by bubble proportional to time **[1]**
 over duration of experiment/30 minutes **[1]**

           [2]

e) *any one from:*
 same species of plant **[1]**
 same size/number of leaves/surface area of leaves of leafy shoot **[1]**
 ignore mass (as shoots of identical mass will have different surface areas of leaves)

           [1]

f) *independent variable*
 at least two different light intensities **[1]**
 control variables/variables that are kept constant **[1]**
 any one from:
 same plant (shoot) – for replicates **[1]**
 same physical conditions/temperature/ humidity (in laboratory) **[1]**
 dependent variable
 any one from:
 measure distance travelled by bubble (using ruler) and resolution of measurements/to nearest millimetre **[1]**
 time intervals at which measurements taken and duration of experiment identical or specified **[1]**
 detail of new method
 any one from:
 appropriate method for varying light intensity, for example, set up lamp at different distances **[1]**
 use same light source – for replicates **[1]**
 use LEDs to prevent heating of plant/ shoot/apparatus **[1]**
 detail of given method
 any one from:
 filling of potometer **and** cutting of shoot under water/in sink **[1]**
 drawing bubble into capillary tube **[1]**
 reset the position of the bubble after a set of measurements **[1]**
 additional
 any one from:
 relevant safety precaution, for example, care when connecting glassware, handling of plant (general hygiene/ allergies/possible toxicity/any reasonable suggestion) **[1]**
 two or more replicates **[1]**

           [6]

g) Idea that a very small proportion/ some water taken up is not transpired/ used for plant's metabolism/used for photosynthesis/(additional) water produced by respiration. **[1]**
h) i) 13 **[1]**
 ii) 104 stomata
  Accept 103.50 stomata / 103 stomata
  Correct answer = 3 marks
  Three or more decimal places in correct answer = 2 marks
  Allow answer based on an incorrect count.
  recall of formula for area of a circle/ πr^2 **[1]**
  calculation of area **[1]**
  area $= 3.14 \times 0.2 \times 0.2 = 0.1256$ mm^2
  calculation of number of stomata per mm^2 **[1]**

  13 stomata in
  0.1256 m^2 $= \dfrac{13}{0.1256}$
  $= 103.50$ stomata/mm^2

 iii) *any two from*
  (fields of view included in counts) must be sufficient in number/ increase the number of repeats **[1]**
  (fields of view included in counts) must have sufficient stomata **[1]**
  (fields of view included in counts) should be random **[1]**
  idea of avoiding counts that are unrepresentative of stomatal distribution **[1]**
  idea of avoiding counts from poorly-prepared areas of slide **[1]**
  idea of reviewing/discounting if there is a reason anomalous results/ outliers **[1]**
  sampling from different leaves (of same plant) **[1]**
  sampling from leaves of different individuals (of same) plant species **[1]**

           [2]
          [Total: 22]

A

absorption movement of a substance into part of an organism, for example the movement of digested food molecules from the intestines into the blood 12, 35

accommodation how the lens of the eye changes so that light from objects at different distances is focused onto the retina 75

acrosome a 'bag' of enzymes at the front of a sperm cell that makes it possible for the sperm nucleus to enter the egg cell 98

active The opposite of passive, needing energy from respiration 11

active immunity defence against a pathogen by antibody production in the body; gained after an infection by a pathogen or by vaccination; memory cells are produced 47

active site the space in an enzyme into which the substrate molecule fits 16, 17

active transport the movement of particles through a cell membrane from a region of lower concentration to a region of higher concentration (i.e. against a concentration gradient), using energy from respiration 11, 71

adaptation the process, resulting from natural selection, by which populations become more suited to their environment over many generations 110

adaptive feature an inherited feature that helps an organism to survive and reproduce in its environment 109

adenine a chemical compound that is used to make one of the building blocks of DNA and RNA 102

adrenal gland endocrine gland that secretes the hormone adrenaline 76

adrenaline the hormone secreted by the adrenal glands that prepares the body for action 76

aerobic respiration the chemical reactions in cells that use oxygen to break down nutrient molecules (e.g. glucose) to release energy; produces carbon dioxide and water 69

AIDS acquired immunodefciency syndrome, caused by the human immunodefciency virus (HIV) 101

alimentary canal the tubular part of the digestive system, from mouth to anus 31

alleles an alternative form of a gene, producing one form of the characteristic that the gene codes for 102

alveoli (singular alveolus) tiny air sacs in the lungs where gases diffuse between the air in the lungs and the blood 66

amino acid the basic unit of a protein. amniotic fluid Fluid surrounding the developing fetus in the uterus 14, 26, 32

amniotic fluid fluid surrounding the developing fetus in the uterus 99

amniotic sac the tough membrane surrounding the developing fetus and amniotic fluid in the mother's uterus 99

amphibian one of the main groups of vertebrates 6

amylase an enzyme that breaks down starch to the simple reducing sugar maltose 16, 32, 134

anaerobic respiration the chemical reactions in cells that break down nutrient molecules (e.g. glucose) to release energy without using oxygen (also called *fermentation*); in animal cells produces lactic acid; in plant cells and yeast produces alcohol (ethanol) and carbon dioxide 69

animal one of the five kingdoms of living organisms 70

antagonistic action in which one muscle or set of muscles opposes another muscle or set of muscles 74

anther part of the stamen (the male part of the flower) that produces pollen. 97

antibiotic resistance resistant bacteria resistance in bacteria to the effect of an antibiotic that normally kills them 110

antibiotics drugs used to kill bacteria but which do not kill viruses 80

antibodies proteins that bind to antigens, leading to direct destruction of pathogens or marking of pathogens for destruction by phagocytes; specific antibodies have complementary shapes which fit specific antigens 45, 46

antigens chemicals on the surface of cells, including pathogens, that have specific shapes 46

antiviral drug a drug used to treat infections caused by viruses 101

anus opening at the end of the large intestine through which faeces are egested 31

aorta the largest artery, which receives blood from the left ventricle of the heart 40

arachnid one of the main groups of arthropods 7

arteriole small blood vessel that connects an artery to a capillary 77

artery blood vessel that carries blood away from the heart 40

arthropods one of the main groups of invertebrates 7

artificial insemination (AI) artifcially placing sperm from a male into the uterus of a female 177

artificial selection see *selective breeding*

asexual reproduction process resulting in the production of genetically identical offspring from one parent; production of young without fertilisation. 96

assimilation the uptake and use of nutrients by cells 31

atrioventricular valve heart valve between the atrium and ventricle 40

atrium (plural atria) one of two chambers of the heart that receives blood from veins and pumps it into the ventricles 40

auxin a plant chemical that controls growth of roots and shoots 79

axon a portion of a nerve cell (neuron) that carries nerve impulses away from the cell body 72

B

bacteria one of the main groups of prokaryotes (singular *bacterium*) 110, 127

balanced diet the intake of food that supplies all the protein, fat, carbohydrate, vitamins and minerals that the body needs in the right amounts 30

bases a subunit of DNA, of which there are four: A, C, G, T. The sequence of bases determines the sequence of amino acids used to make a specific protein 7

Benedict's solution solution that changes colour in the presence of reducing sugars; used to test for their presence in a food sample 22

bias a flaw in the study design or the method of collecting or interpreting information 129

biconcave a shape in which the middle is pressed inwards, making a red blood cell thinner in the middle than at the edges 43

bile liquid produced by the liver and stored in the gall bladder, which is highly alkaline and emulsifes fats and oils 35

binomial system a system of naming organisms using a genus and species name to identify a particular species 7

biodiversity the number of different species that live in an area 130

biofuel a fuel made from plants or animals 134

biological catalyst a catalyst of metabolic reactions inside living organisms; an enzyme 16, 134

biological factors any physical, chemical, genetic, or neurological condition associated with psychological disturbances 128

biological molecules a chemical compound found in living organisms 14

biomass the mass of living organisms. biotechnology The use of organisms to make products 124, 125

biotechnology the use of organisms to make products 134

birds one of the main groups of vertebrates 6

biuret solution a blue-coloured reagent used in biochemistry to test for the presence of proteins in a sample 15

bladder the organ of the excretory system that stores urine from the kidneys until it is released to the environment 31, 70

blind spot point in the eye on the retina where the optic nerve attaches, where there are no light-sensitive cells 74

blood capillaries the smallest type of blood vessel 35

blood clotting an important process that prevents excessive bleeding when a blood vessel is injured 43

blood vessel a tube through which the blood circulates in the body 34

bolus food that has been chewed and mixed in the mouth with saliva 31

bonds a force of attraction between atoms or ions 14

bone mineralized skeletal tissue 34

bronchus (plural bronchi) the division of the trachea as it joins to the lungs 66

C

calcium A mineral needed for healthy teeth, bones, and other body tissues 31

cancer a disease caused by uncontrolled division of cells 101, 108

canines a tooth with a pointed shape, behind the incisors in the mouth, which holds food while other teeth bite and chew 34

capillary smallest blood vessel, found within every tissue, which exchanges substances with the cells 66

carbohydrate a molecule, such as starch or glycogen, made up of simple sugars 14, 26, 30

root part of a vascular plant normally underground. Its primary functions are anchorage of the plant, absorption of water and dissolved minerals and conduction of these to the stem, and storage of reserve foods — 36-38

root hair cell a cell in the epidermis of roots that has a long extension of cytoplasm, where uptake of substances from soil water occurs — 9, 37

roughage see *fibre* — 30

S

sample any type of biological material derived from a living organism that can be studied and analyzed in a laboratory — 129

salivary glands glands in the mouth that produce saliva to aid digestion of food — 31, 32

saprotrophic nutrition the digestion of dead food material outside the body, as in fungi — 6

scrotum sac supporting the testes — 98

secondary consumer largely carnivores that feed on the primary consumers or herbivores — 124

seed bank a large collection of many different species of seed stored for use in the future — 133

selective breeding (also called artificial selectiom) the breeding together of individual organisms that have desirable features; carried out over many generations to improve crop plants and domesticated animals — 96, 111

self-pollination the transfer of pollen grains from the anther of a flower to the stigma of the same flower or a different flower on the same plant — 97

semilunar valve valve in the heart where an artery leaves a ventricle — 40

sense organ an organ that responds to a stimulus by causing an electrical impulse in a sensory neurone — 74

sensitivity the ability to detect and respond to changes in the internal or external environment — 6

sensory neurone a nerve cell that carries electrical impulses from a receptor to the central nervous system — 72, 73

septum wall dividing the left and right sides of the heart — 40

set point the value around which the normal range fluctuates, e.g. internal body temperature or blood glucose concentration — 76

sex chromosome a chromosome that affects the sex of the individual; for humans, the X and Y chromosomes — 102

sex-linked characteristic a feature in which the gene responsible is located on a sex chromosome; this makes the characteristic more common in one sex than the other — 106

sexual reproduction process involving the fusion (joining) of the nuclei of two gametes to form a zygote and the production of offspring that are genetically different from each other — 96

sexually transmitted infection (STI) an infection that is transmitted through sexual contact — 101

simple reducing sugar a basic sugar unit (e.g. glucose) that can join together with other sugar units to make large carbohydrates such as starch and glycogen — 32

single circulatory system like with fish, the blood is pumped by the heart to the gills then to the rest of the body before returning to the heart — 41

sink the parts of plants that use or store sucrose or amino acids — 39

slide a thin piece of glass used to hold objects which are examined under a microscope

small intestine part of the alimentary canal, made up of the duodenum and ileum, where nutrients are absorbed — 31, 32, 35

solute a substance that can dissolve in a liquid (the solvent) — 12

solvent a liquid that a substance (the solute) is able to dissolve in — 12

sources the parts of plants that release sucrose or amino acids — 39

specialised cell when a cell develops special features that help it work in a particular way — 8, 104

species a group of organisms that can reproduce to produce fertile offspring — 7, 44

specimen a sample of something, like a specimen of blood or body tissue — 9

sperm male reproductive cell, or gamete, in anisogamous forms of sexual reproduction — 96

sperm cell male gamete (sex cell) in animals — 8

sperm duct tube that carries sperm from a testis to the urethra in the penis — 98

spirometer an apparatus for measuring the volume of air inspired and expired by the lungs — 67

spongy mesophyll the layer of cells in the lower part of the leaf in which there are many air spaces, so increasing the internal surface area to volume ratio — 38

stain a discoloration — 134

stamen the male reproductive structure in flowers, made up of the anther and flament — 97

starch a complex carbohydrate made from many glucose units — 14, 26, 32

stem cell unspecialised cell that divides by mitosis to produce daughter cells that can become specialised for specific functions — 104

sticky ends short stretches of unpaired bases at the ends of DNA cut by some kinds of restriction enzymes — 136

stigma the female reproductive structure in flowers to which pollen grains attach in pollination — 97

stimulus a change in the internal or external environment that produces a response by an organism — 78

stomach part of the alimentary canal where acid and protease enzymes are secreted — 32, 34

stomata (singular stoma) tiny holes in the surface of a leaf (mostly the lower epidermis), which allow gases to diffuse into and out of the leaf — 38

stems the plant axis that bears buds and shoots with leaves and, at its basal end, roots — 36

sterilised a process that destroys or eliminates all forms of microbial life and is carried out in health-care facilities by physical or chemical methods — 135

sterility the freedom from the presence of viable microorganisms — 109

strengthening cells cells that give added support to plant leaves and stems — 36

style the female reproductive structure that supports the stigma in a flower — 97

substrate a molecule that fts into the active site of an enzyme molecule at the start of a reaction — 16, 32

sucrose common sugar produced by plants — 14, 26, 36, 39

sugars all carbohydrates of the general formula — 14, 32

surface area the total area that the surface of an object occupies — 10

survival of the fittest organisms best adjusted to their environment are the most successful in surviving and reproducing — 110

suspensory ligaments ligaments in the eye, attached at one end to the lens; under the control of the ciliary muscles, they control the shape of the lens — 74

sustainable resource a resource that is produced as rapidly as it is removed from the environment so that it does not run out (also known as a *renewable resource*) — 133

synapse the junction between two neurons — 73

synaptic gap the small space between two neurones within a synapse — 73

T

target organ an organ that is affected by a hormone — 76

teeth used for catching and masticating food, for defense, and for other specialized purposes — 31, 34

temperature a measure of how hot or cold something is — 39

tension a 'pull', such as the pull created by the forces of attraction between water molecules in xylem — 38

tertiary consumer animals that consume other animals to obtain nutrition from them — 124

test cross a cross made between an individual with the dominant phenotype and an individual with a homozygous recessive genotype to identify if the individual with the dominant phenotype has a heterozygous or homozygous genotype — 107

testis (plural testes) the site of sperm production; secretes the male sexual hormone testosterone — 98

testosterone the male sexual hormone that is secreted by the testes — 76, 100

thorax the chest, containing the heart and lungs — 67

thymine a chemical compound that is used to make one of the building blocks of DNA — 102

tissue a group of similar specialised cells that work together to carry out a particular function — 9

William Collins' dream of knowledge for all began with the publication of his first book in 1819.
A self-educated mill worker, he not only enriched millions of lives, but also founded a flourishing publishing house. Today, staying true to this spirit, Collins books are packed with inspiration, innovation and practical expertise.
They place you at the centre of a world of possibility and give you exactly what you need to explore it.

Collins. Freedom to teach.

Published by Collins
An imprint of HarperCollins*Publishers*
The News Building, 1 London Bridge Street, London, SE1 9GF, UK

HarperCollins*Publishers*
Macken House, 39/40 Mayor Street Upper, Dublin 1, D01 C9W8, Ireland

Browse the complete Collins catalogue at
collins.co.uk

© HarperCollins*Publishers* Limited 2024

10 9 8 7 6 5 4 3 2 1

ISBN 978-0-00-867089-4

British Library Cataloguing-in-Publication Data
A catalogue record for this publication is available from the British Library.

Authors: **Mark Levesley, John Beeby, Amanda Graham, Anne Pilling, Mike Smith**
Publisher: **Elaine Higgleton**
Product manager: **Jennifer Hall**
Editors: **Susan Lyons, Andrew Lowe**
Proofreaders and answer checkers: **Clodagh Burke, Arlo Porter, Judith Head**
Cover designer: **Gordon MacGilp**
Cover artwork: **Maria Herbert-Liew**
Internal designer and illustrator: **PDQ Media**
Typesetter: **PDQ Media**
Production controller: **Lyndsey Rogers**
Printed in India by Multivista Global Pvt. Ltd.

MIX
Paper | Supporting responsible forestry
FSC™ C007454

This book contains FSC™ certified paper and other controlled sources to ensure responsible forest management.

For more information visit: www.harpercollins.co.uk/green

Cambridge International Education material in this publication is reproduced under licence and remains the intellectual property of Cambridge University Press & Assessment.

This text has not been through the endorsement process for the Cambridge Pathway. Any references or materials related to answers, grades, papers or examinations are based on the opinion of the author(s). The Cambridge International Education syllabus or curriculum framework associated assessment guidance material and specimen papers should always be referred to for definitive guidance.

Acknowledgements
With thanks to the following teachers who provided feedback during the development stages: Shalini Reddy, Manthan International School; Gauri Tendulkar, JBCN International School.

The publishers gratefully acknowledge the permission granted to reproduce the copyright material in this book. Every effort has been made to trace copyright holders and to obtain their permission for the use of copyright material. The publishers will gladly receive any information enabling them to rectify any error or omission at the first opportunity.

Photographs
P 18 Peter Hermes Furian/Shutterstock, p 37 shubin42/Shutterstock, p 47(t) Mongkolchon Akesin/shutterstock, p 47(b) RioPatuca/Shutterstock, p 57 shubin42/Shutterstock, p 61 Jarun Ontakrai/Shutterstock; p 62 MattL_Images/Shutterstock, p 78(l) Artography/Shutterstock, p 78(r) Anest/Shutterstock, p 96(l) Oksix/Shutterstock, p 96(r) epsylon_lyrae/Shutterstock, p 98(t) ONYXprj /Shutterstock, p 102(t) Designua /Shutterstock, p 102(b) A Step BioMed/ Shutterstock, p 104 Designua /Shutterstock, p 106 Nandalal Sarkar /Shutterstock, p 108 Peter Hermes Furian /Shutterstock, p 114 Sonias drawings /Shutterstock, p 109(l) Aunt Spray / Shutterstock, p 109(r) Chris Button /Shutterstock, p 115 Hannet /Shutterstock, p 116 Designua /Shutterstock, p 117 Designua / Shutterstock, p 119(r) Eric Isselee/Shutterstock; p 119(l) Eric Isselee/Shutterstock; p 120 MaraZe/Shutterstock, p 121(t) Dennis Laughlin /Shutterstock, p 121(c) Dr. Norbert Lange / Shutterstock, p 121(b) Aldona Griskeviciene /Shutterstock, p 122(t) Olzas /Shutterstock, p 123(t) Brian Lasenby /Shutterstock, p 123(bl) Mel Horton /Shutterstock, p 123(br) TETSU Snowdrop/ Shutterstock, p 130 Holger Kleine /Shutterstock, p 131 Lucian Coman/Shutterstock, p 146 Eric Isselee/Shutterstock, p 157(lb) K.K.T Madhusanka /Shutterstock, p 157(rb) Achiichiii/ Shutterstock, p 157(rt) Oleksandr Drypsiak/Shutterstock, p 159 metsi/Shutterstock, p 164 (t) Pepermpron /Shutterstock, p 165, BearFotos /Shutterstock, p 166 PetlinDmitry/Shutterstock, p 164(b) Pepermpron/Shutterstock, p 176, Paulose NK / Shutterstock, p 179 Christos Georghiou /Shutterstock, p 180 (t) BlueRingMedia /Shutterstock,p 180(b) BlueRingMedia/ Shutterstock p 181(l) Jon Petur/Shutterstock, p 181(r) Artush/ Shutterstock, p 182 Pikovit /Shutterstock, p 189, Edwin Butter/ Shutterstock, p 198 tawanroong/Shutterstock

NOTES